THE
JOURNEY
FROM EDEN

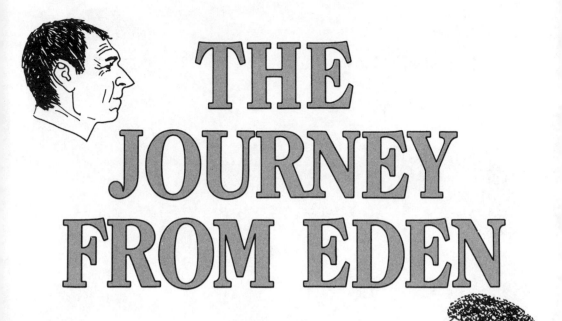

THE JOURNEY FROM EDEN

BRIAN M. FAGAN

The Peopling of Our World

With 96 illustrations

THAMES AND HUDSON

For Shelly Lowenkopf

Contents

PART ONE

IN SEARCH OF EVE

"And God said 'let us create man in our image, after our likeness: and let them have dominion over the fish of the sea, and over the cattle, and over all the earth, and over every creeping thing that creepeth upon the earth . . .'"

Genesis I:26

"And the rib, which the Lord God had taken from man, made he a woman, and brought her unto the man . . ."

Genesis II:22

CHAPTER ONE

A Question of Questions

"And Adam called his wife's name Eve; because she was the mother of all living people . . ." The scientists have called her Eve, but reluctantly, for the name evokes all manner of false images. The Biblical Eve was beguiled by a subtle serpent within little more than a week of Creation. She tempted Adam and passed into history as a weak-willed figure. Renaissance artists painted a milk-skinned beauty with voluptuous curves, caught in the act of plucking perfect apples from a paradisal tree. The image has changed little over the centuries . . . Meek, long-haired, invariably naked, Eve, the primeval woman, inhabits a lush, warm Garden of Eden where the fruit is always ripe and the grass always green.

The scientists know nothing for certain about their Eve, but they speculate that she was a dark-haired, well-muscled and black-skinned woman who roamed the African savanna some 200,000 years ago. She was a member of a small hunting and gathering band, strong enough to carry heavy loads of fruits and nuts, and to tear apart animal flesh with her hands. She was not the only woman on earth, not the most attractive, or even the one with the most children. But she was the most fruitful, if one measures fruitfulness by success in propagating a certain set of genes. Eve's genes are in every living human being. All five billion of us are blood relatives. One scientist gives a rough estimate: she is our 10,000th-great-grandmother. The geneticists who identified the African Eve do not, of course, claim they have found the first woman, but something quite different – a common ancestor for all of present-day humanity.

The search for our ancestors has been a long one. It really began with the discovery of a primitive-looking skull in Germany in 1856. This strange cranium from the Neander Valley caused a storm of controversy. Some anatomists dismissed it as the remains of a pathological idiot. Others thought it was the skull of a Cossack. Then, in his book *Man's Place in Nature* (1863), the great British biologist Thomas Huxley, "Darwin's Bulldog," compared the cranium with those of non-human primates and our own species, *Homo sapiens*. He proclaimed that the skull was indeed that of a primitive human being, an ancestor of modern humans. And he posed the "question of questions for mankind . . . the ascertainment of the place which man occupies in nature." The same question has preoccupied science to this day.

Huxley also made another prophetic statement: "Evolution will extend by long epochs the most liberal estimate that has yet been made of the Antiquity of Man." How right he was! Perhaps Huxley was thinking in terms of tens of thousands of years. Today, we know that the most primitive tool-using humans emerged in East Africa at least 2.5 million years ago, and we gaze back over an evolutionary landscape far more complex than anything the Victorians imagined.

The Leakeys and Olduvai Gorge, Donald Johanson and Hadar – the names of these anthropologists and their East African sites have become universally famous, thanks to the discovery in recent decades of early human fossils several million years old. These and other spectacular early finds have told us much about our remotest ancestors. These fossils have received the lion's share of worldwide publicity, while the search for the ancestry of our more recent direct forebears has gone on in much greater obscurity. There is something romantic about very remote prehistory, about the notion of primitive human beings hunting and foraging over the African savanna millions of years ago. In fact, scientific reality is more prosaic, for we now know that the earliest humans were far more ape-like in their behavior than was once suspected. Many experts now believe that perhaps the most important development in prehistory was the first appearance of anatomically modern people, *Homo sapiens sapiens*, human beings with vastly enhanced intellectual powers. These new researches encompass many fundamental questions – questions that we explore in *The Journey from Eden*.

The controversies surrounding the origins of *Homo sapiens sapiens* are fully as contentious as those over early human evolution. Did anatomically modern people initially evolve in one area or many? If in one place, how, when, and why did they replace earlier human populations? Were these biological changes associated with revolutionary changes in human behavior? How reliable is the evidence – whether from fossils, archaeology, or genetics?

The controversies over what has sometimes been called the "Human Revolution" divide paleoanthropologists into two broad camps. On the one hand, there are those who argue that our immediate ancestors evolved just in Africa, then radiated out from there to all other parts of the world. On the other hand, there are those who believe that, although the very earliest tool-using humans evolved in Africa, anatomically modern people developed independently in several different regions of the world – Africa, Asia, Europe – more or less simultaneously. In the pages that follow we examine the evidence for each hypothesis, and attempt to reconstruct a scenario for the evolution of modern humans.

Homo sapiens sapiens has been the most successful of all human forms, far surpassing its predecessors. Our anatomically modern ancestors were fully as intelligent and adaptable as we are, capable of mastering even the most savage environments on earth. *The Journey from Eden* sets out to answer another fundamental question: how did modern humans colonize the world, including entire continents where no earlier human hunters had ever trod? What biological and technological innovations made it possible for *Homo sapiens sapiens* to be the first to adapt to the full diversity of the world's environments, from tropical rainforests to arctic tundra?

The Journey from Eden travels down many little-known byways of the prehistoric world, describing archaeological discoveries from every corner of the globe. We track antelope hunters on the African savanna and reindeer hunters in Europe. We study stone blade-makers in the Near East and the pioneers of a unique bamboo technology in Southeast Asia. And we puzzle over the first settlement of Australia and the Americas. But before our journey begins we need to look briefly at who these people were – who we are – that hold center stage in this story; and we need to consider against what environmental backcloth these momentous events took place.

The Clever Person

Homo sapiens sapiens – this is the clever person, the wise person, an animal capable of subtlety, of manipulation, of self-understanding. What is it exactly that separates us from other animals, what are the faculties that give us the arrogance to call ourselves wise above all other creatures?

The most striking differences between ourselves and other living species lie in our ability to design and make tools, in our articulate speech and self-awareness, in our intellectual and creative skills, and in what one might loosely call our "psyche."

Chimpanzees, our closest living non-human relatives, make tools, but the sticks they fashion to extract grubs from anthills are a far cry from the bewildering multiplicity of artifacts we can fabricate. Toolmaking, the manufacture of implements to carry out a wide range of tasks rather than merely one limited goal, is a uniquely human ability. The very first artifacts were the simplest of sticks, stone flakes, and choppers. But these rudimentary implements were the ultimate ancestors of the intricate computers and machine tools of today. Did anatomically modern people have special skills in toolmaking that gave them an innate advantage over earlier human forms? The evidence from stone artifacts over hundreds of thousands of years makes up an important part of our story.

Human beings share many characteristics that serve to shape individual behavior, and perhaps the most important of all is fluent speech. We communicate, we tell stories, we pass on knowledge and ideas all through the medium of language – and when for whatever reason we are deprived of speech, "struck dumb," we feel in many ways outside society. Vocal communication exists in all non-human primates, but this is not genuine speech. When and how, then, did human beings first acquire the ability to speak in a fully articulate manner? Surprisingly, as we shall see, some scientists think they have the answer.

Consciousness, cognition, self-awareness, foresight, and the ability to express oneself and one's emotions: these are direct consequences of fluent speech. They can be linked with another attribute of the fully-fledged human psyche: the capacity for symbolic and spiritual thought, concerned not only with subsistence and technology, but with defining the boundaries of existence, and the relationship between the individual, the group, and the universe. In all societies, such themes find expression in art and in religion. When did the human capacity for symbolic creativity and belief in an afterlife evolve? The Stone Age cave paintings of western Europe are world-famous. Bison and wild horses prance on the walls of Lascaux in southern France and Altamira in northern Spain. Painted and engraved symbols appear too in Australian, Tasmanian, and southern African rockshelters. Did our artistic and spiritual gifts appear only with *Homo sapiens sapiens*, or do they characterize earlier humans as well?

Expert toolmaking, fluent speech, the full flowering of human creativity – these are some of the hallmarks of humanity. With these abilities humans eventually colonized the entire globe. It was a revolution that took place against a backdrop of constant and widespread climatic change – when the world was a very different place from what it is today.

The Great Ice Age

Today our individual experience of world climate comes from daily weather bulletins, or from news reports threatening that the ice sheets will melt in the next few years, thanks to humanly induced global warming. It is very difficult to adjust mentally from this global picture covering years or decades to a timescale measured in tens of thousands and even hundreds of thousands of years. But that is what we must do if we are to understand the worldwide climatic changes that above all else helped shape the human journey from Eden.

Contrary to popular belief, the Ice Age has not ended. Unless humanly created global warming reverses long-term climatic trends, we can expect a new glacial cycle several thousand years in the future. The verdict on global warming is still unclear, but we have a tendency to hail every short-term drought cycle or series of hotter-than-average summers as evidence of environmental catastrophe on the way. The scientists may be right to warn us of impending ecological armageddon, but the fact is that humans have always lived in, and adapted to, a world of immense climatic swings.

These fluctuations began as long as 35 million years ago (long before even the most primitive toolmakers), when the first ice sheets developed in Antarctica. About 3.2 million years ago, large ice sheets formed on the northern continents. Then, about 2.5 million years ago, glaciation intensified even more and the earth entered its present period of constantly fluctuating climate. Deep-sea core borings tell us that climatic fluctuations were relatively insignificant until about 900,000 years ago. They further intensified about 730,000 years ago, since when there have been at least eight glacial cycles separated by shorter interludes known as interglacials when climatic conditions were as warm as, if not warmer than, today.

The last warmer interlude before our own began about 128,000 years ago. The global warm-up was dramatic and, on an Ice Age timescale, short-lived. For about 10,000 years, global temperatures were as much as 1–3 degrees C (1.8–5.4 deg. F) warmer than today. Thick forest mantled a Europe only a short time before covered with treeless tundra. Much of the Sahara Desert was open grassland. Sea levels rose to at least 20 ft (6 m) above modern levels, drowning huge areas of Scandinavia and the Low Countries, and isolating Australia even more from Southeast Asia. Then a major cooling trend began, ushering in the last glaciation some 100,000–90,000 years ago.

This so-called Würm glaciation° eventually reached its cold climax about 20,000–18,000 years ago. The vast Scandinavian ice sheet straddled northern Europe and Eurasia, and its Alpine equivalent flowed out into the open plains of what is now Germany and France. Treeless steppe-tundra stretched from the Atlantic in the west as far east as the Ural Mountains and beyond. World sea levels fell more than 425 ft (130 m) below modern shorelines in places. Siberia was joined to Alaska, the Southeast Asian islands to the nearby mainland, and Australia and New Guinea formed the now-sunken continent scientists called Sahul.

After about 15,000 years ago, the ice sheets began to melt in earnest. The dramatic environmental changes associated with this warm-up (described in Chapter Sixteen) make the climatic changes predicted by doomsday-sayers for the next millennium look puny in comparison. Experts on Ice Age climate believe that our present interglacial peaked several thousand years ago, when deciduous forests in Europe and North America reached their northern limits. Mountain glaciers and snowfields have since grown in many areas, and tropical deserts have expanded during the past 5,000 years. Nevertheless it is still possible that humanly caused atmospheric warming could influence or even partially arrest this long-term trend towards increasing cold.

°The Great Ice Age is referred to by geologists as the Pleistocene. The term Würm comes from a river valley in the Alps, where Austrian geologists first identified deposits of the last glaciation in the late 19th century. There are numerous local terms for the Würm used throughout the world, among them the Weichsel in Scandinavia, Valdai and Sartan in the Soviet Union, and the Wisconsin in North America.

The immense climatic fluctuations of the Ice Age thus presented human beings with extraordinary challenges over tens of thousands of years. These challenges our ancestors rose to with great brilliance and elan, conquering environments that were harsher than any known today. In the chapters that follow, we explore the complex evolutionary developments that led to the appearance of modern humans, and tell the heroic story of their colonization of the earth.

CHAPTER TWO

Of Candelabras and Noah's Arks

It was the Harvard anthropologist William Howells who named them the Candelabra and Noah's Ark hypotheses. Scientists have long been divided into two camps when it comes to explaining the origins of modern humans. Those of the Candelabra persuasion argue that our most recent ancestors evolved independently and in parallel (like the branches of a candelabra) in different parts of the world – Africa, Asia, Europe. Adherents of the Noah's Ark school believe, in terms of Howells' image, that we were once more or less all in the same boat – that we evolved in Africa and radiated out from there to colonize the rest of the globe. The issues are huge. The story of how we evolved, of our very humanity, is at stake. No wonder that the arguments provoke fierce debate at academic conferences, where the strength of feeling in one camp or the other is not always fully matched by the weight of the scientific evidence presented.

In order even to understand what the arguments are about, let alone choose between one hypothesis or the other, we need to go back in time to the period of the first toolmakers, well over 2 million years before the appearance of modern humans. Here at any rate the scientists are united: our earliest forebears evolved in Africa.

The Earliest Humans

According to current scientific thinking, the human evolutionary line diverged from the African apes (chimpanzees and gorillas) between about 10 and 5 million years ago. The earliest well-documented hominids° come from Hadar in northern Ethiopia and date to between 3.75 and 3 million years ago. These primates walked upright almost as we do, as well as being nimble tree-climbers, but their brains were not much larger than those of apes. Paleoanthropologists Don Johanson and Tim White, based in Berkeley, California, believe that the Hadar hominids are an early form of *Australopithecus*, ape-like hominids first identified in South Africa as long ago as 1924.

° A hominid is a primate of the order Hominidae, which includes modern humans, earlier human subspecies, and their direct ancestors.

After 2.3 million years ago, the australopithecines were joined on the African savanna by a more advanced hominid with a larger brain, higher and rounder head, and less-protruding face. This was *Homo habilis*, so named by Louis Leakey after he and his wife Mary discovered the first specimen in 1960 in the fossil-rich lake beds at Olduvai Gorge in Tanzania. *Homo habilis* was the first representative of the genus *Homo*, to which all modern people belong.

Homo habilis means "handy person," for these hominids probably made the earliest stone tools ever fabricated by humans. Their makers had somewhat more curved hands than those of modern people, ideal for grasping, for climbing trees. But the thumbs were opposable, allowing both gripping and manipulation of fine objects, something essential for holding and flaking the edges of stones. *Homo habilis* struck sharp-edged flakes to use as knives for slitting skin and butchering animal carcasses, for cutting wood and soft plant matter. But the flakes were never the same size, never standardized tools.

Only a few sites used by *Homo habilis* have come under the excavator's trowel. Archaeologist Glynn Isaac and a team of graduate students from the University of California at Berkeley uncovered several such locations at Koobi Fora in East Turkana, Kenya, in the 1970s. The months of excavations were painstaking, laborious work. Isaac and his team laid out a square measuring grid over the site, then dissected it minutely with trowel and brush, recording the exact position of every stone artifact, every fractured bone, where it lay. One site lay in a dry stream bed, where a group of hominids found the carcass of a hippopotamus about 1.9 million years ago. They gathered round and removed the bone and meat from the dead animal with small stone flakes. At another site, the hominids camped in a shady, dry creek close to abundant stone supplies. Here Isaac and his colleagues found more than 2,100 animal bones, mainly from antelope, that had been cut with stone flakes and smashed with stone hammers. However, many of the limb bones had no ends, as if they had been bitten off by lions, hyenas, and other carnivores. These early humans probably only had the means to hunt and kill smaller game, waiting opportunistically to scavenge the larger kills of the carnivores as well as living off plant foods. Isaac believed that opportunism is an early hallmark of humankind, a restless process like biological mutation and natural selection.

Increased skills in opportunistic scavenging may have been one reason for the evolution of the larger brain of *Homo habilis*. But what else required more intelligence, more brain power? Almost certainly the need for more prolonged child care, and closer interactions with other people. Humans stand upright and have small pelvic openings, which means that infants have to be born when still very immature. Our children need prolonged maternal care to compensate for the relatively short gestation period in the womb. The brain of modern humans is ape-sized at birth, and relatively much smaller than that of an infant ape. Our brains grow very fast after birth, which obviates the necessity for an even more prolonged gestation period. This biological reality may have first manifested itself with the larger-brained *Homo habilis*, when the time an infant depended on its mother lengthened considerably, with major social consequences.

The increased complexity of social interactions is likely to have been a powerful force in the evolution of the human brain. For *Homo habilis*, the adoption of a broad-based diet with a food-sharing social group, perhaps a closely knit group of about 25 people from various families, would have increased the complexity and unpredictability of daily life. And the brilliant technological, artistic, and expressive skills of later humankind may well have been a consequence of the reality that our early ancestors had to be more and more socially adept.

Homo erectus

About 1.7–1.6 million years ago, East African mammals adapted to drier, more open grassland conditions. It was at about this time that a new form of human emerged in Africa, a hominid with a much larger brain, excellent vision, and limbs and hips fully adapted to an upright posture. Paleoanthropologists call this hominid *Homo erectus*, a human much taller than its diminutive predecessors, standing as much as 5 ft 6 in (1.67 m) high, with hands capable of precision-gripping and many kinds of toolmaking. The skull is more rounded than those of earlier hominids, but still had a sloping forehead and retreating brow ridges. *Homo erectus* was more numerous, more adaptable than *Homo habilis*, and, on present evidence, was a much longer-lived species. Archaeological sites now appear at higher, cooler elevations in southern, eastern, and northern Africa. *Homo erectus* may have been a skilled big-game hunter, capable of organizing quite elaborate hunting and foraging expeditions, and using multipurpose axes and cleaving tools.

Like all hunters and foragers, *Homo erectus* had probably learned to live with natural fires and was not afraid of them. In time, the new hominid may have made a habit of conserving fire, taking advantage of smoldering tree stumps ignited by lightning strikes and other natural causes to light dry brush. Then came the biggest step of all: the *making* of fire. Perhaps as early as 1.5 million years ago, *Homo erectus* may have learnt to create fire in East Africa and at Swartkrans in South Africa – scientists still debate the issue. Fire offers not only warmth, but protection against predators and an easy way of hunting game, even insects and rodents. The toxins from many common vegetable foods can be roasted or parched out in hot ashes, allowing people to use a wider range of foods in their diet.

Homo erectus was a much larger species than its predecessors, meaning that the newcomers needed larger quantities of food to satisfy higher

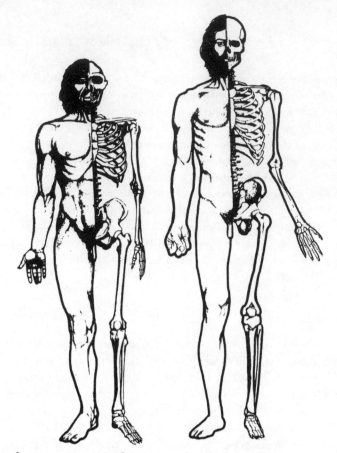

The modern human anatomy (right) compared with that of Homo erectus. *Note the hominid's flatter skull and pronounced brow ridges.*

metabolic rates. This meant they had to range over much larger hunting territories, perhaps moving into more open country, where trees were rarer. Conceivably, the bands now carried fire brands with them as a weapon that would enable them to operate safely away from trees, and to occupy dark caves where predators often lurked. It also enabled *Homo erectus* to settle in far cooler environments. It may be no coincidence that the earliest human settlement of Europe and Asia – temperate latitudes outside Africa – occurred after *Homo erectus* could make, as well as tame, fire.

Moving out of Africa

How did early human beings spread out of Africa? Was there a conscious population movement of hunting bands, who journeyed out of familiar territory in search of new lands? Or was the process more complex, the result of the interplay of ecological and climatic forces?

Biologist Elizabeth Vrba of the Transvaal Museum in Pretoria, South Africa, argues for the importance of a major fall in world temperatures around

900,000 years ago. A previous fall 2.5 million years ago coincided not only with the appearance of *Homo habilis*, but with the proliferation of new mammalian species, such as new species of antelope.

The last "pulse," as Vrba calls the plunge in global temperatures around 900,000 years ago, also appears to coincide with a wave of evolutionary activity among the antelope family. Deep-sea cores collected from the depths of the Atlantic and Pacific Oceans tell us that climatic fluctuations intensified after this event, especially after 730,000 years ago. Global climates were in transition from cold to warmer and vice versa for more than 75 percent of the past 720,000 years. There were long periods when the African savanna was periodically split into isolated regions, which were then reunited by changing climatic patterns. Even small shifts in rainfall patterns caused deserts to expand, or allowed the grasslands to establish themselves in formerly arid country.

If Vrba is right, *Homo erectus* populations had to adapt to these increasing rainfall and vegetational shifts after about 1 million years ago. They could do so by migrating with the changing vegetational zones, as many other mammals did, or they could adapt to new, less game-rich environments, changing their dietary emphasis as needed. Finally, they could move outside tropical latitudes altogether, into habitats that human beings had never occupied before. Hominids like *Homo erectus* were omnivores, and linked ecologically to other mammals. Thus, they behaved just like other mammals in their ecological community.

European paleontologists have long observed a major change in the mammalian population of Europe that took place about 900,000–700,000 years ago. Hippopotamuses, forest elephants, and other herbivores, and such tropical carnivores as lions, leopards, and hyenas appear in temperate latitudes at about this time. They migrated northward from Africa during a cycle of wetter climate when the Sahara Desert was capable of supporting animal life. *Homo erectus* may have moved out of the tropics at the same time. So the first human settlement of Europe and Asia may have coincided with a radiation of a major tropical mammalian community from Africa.

For all their ability to adapt to seasonal climates, and to a wide variety of temperate environments in central Europe, northern China, and the Near East, *Homo erectus* populations never penetrated extreme arctic or perigla-cial latitudes, nor did they cross the Bering Strait and settle in the Americas. Such settlement came much later, at the hands of *Homo sapiens*.

A Candelabra Model

The debate surrounding the origins of modern humans is remarkable for its volatility and for the rapid shifts of intellectual ground. Every new fossil discovery, every new date, can set off a fresh round of theorizing. There are but two points upon which everyone involved agrees. The first is that early humanity evolved in Africa and spread from there to other parts of the Old World after about 1 million years ago. The second is that *Homo erectus* played an important role in the ancestry of modern humans, being the species of the genus *Homo* that immediately preceded *Homo sapiens*.

Beyond that, the scientists disagree radically. Broadly, as we have seen, they fall into two camps – on the one hand, those who follow the Candelabra school of thought that envisages multiple origins for modern humans; and on the other, those who believe in a single origin, the Noah's Ark school.

The Candelabra model argues that *Homo erectus* populations, once having radiated out of Africa, evolved gradually and independently in different parts of the world into early, or archaic, *Homo sapiens*, then into anatomically modern humans, *Homo sapiens sapiens*. Modern humans thus emerged in many places, with today's living populations having very deep genetic roots, for they separated one from another at least 700,000 years ago, and probably earlier. This theory implies that one should be able to trace diagnostic anatomical features in human populations over very long periods, perhaps back to the time of *Homo erectus*. Milford Wolpoff of the University of Michigan, one of the main Candelabra model proponents, believes that there was indeed such regional continuity, as he calls it, and that it played an important role in the emergence of *Homo sapiens sapiens* in Asia. Others have argued that there is regional continuity in Europe, particularly as evidenced by the Neanderthals – *Homo sapiens neanderthalensis*. The Neanderthals appeared on the scene before 100,000 years ago, and are on the direct ancestral line to modern humans according to the regionalists.

However, other scholars have made studies in recent years, based on the now more than 300 Neanderthal specimens from Europe, Eurasia, and the Near East, that seem to show just how *different* Neanderthals were from modern people. Such scientists favor the Noah's Ark hypothesis – an African origin for all modern humans.

Noah's Ark

My mother prized our family tree, an enormous roll of dusty paper that lived in its own trunk in the attic. She would dig it out on winter evenings and trace our ancestry back through Victorian times, to landowning ancestors in 18th-century Yorkshire, and, ultimately, over to Ireland on my father's side back in the 12th century. His original ancestor came from "O'Reilly's country" in northern Ireland. Quite how genuine this magnificent piece of Victoriana was is difficult to say, but my mother was comforted by it. There is something equally comforting in the notion of a common ancestor for all of us, too, which is why, perhaps, such legends are a feature of origin myths the world over.

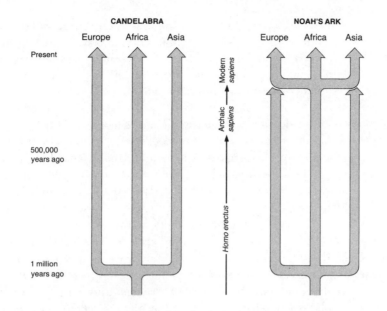

The two extreme views of the origins of modern humans. According to the Candelabra school, after the migration of Homo erectus *out of Africa around 1 million years ago, people evolved into modern humans independently in different parts of the world. Noah's Ark theorists, however, believe modern humans evolved first in Africa, migrating from there into other continents around 100,000 years ago and replacing earlier* Homo erectus *populations.*

The Noah's Ark hypothesis (or "Garden of Eden" theory according to taste) argues that fully modern humans (*Homo sapiens sapiens*) evolved relatively recently from a primeval African population, and spread from Africa into all corners of the world quite late in the Ice Age. The superficial biological differences between different "races" of *Homo sapiens*, such as skin color, hair form, build, and so on, then developed as adaptations to different environments. Under this theory, modern geographic populations have shallow genetic roots that are derived from species formation relatively recently.

The Candelabra theory enjoyed widespread popularity when most of the relevant fossil specimens came from Europe, the Near East, and Asia. Then *Homo erectus* and early *Homo sapiens* fossils were discovered in Africa in the 1970s, partially filling in a vast gap in the African story, from about 1.6 million to about 100,000 years ago. Some of these fragmentary human remains were anatomically modern, yet came from cave deposits dated to at least 100,000 years ago (see Chapter Five). Conventional wisdom and the Candelabra theory had it that modern humans had evolved from the Neanderthals or other archaic *Homo sapiens* populations in several regions only about 40,000 years ago. The new modern-looking fossils from eastern and southern Africa complicated the evolutionary picture, prompting Peter Andrews and Chris Stringer of the Natural History Museum in London to take a new look at the Noah's Ark hypothesis from the perspective of the technique called cladistics.

There are three major schools of classification used in the study of human evolution. The first is numerical taxonomy, which erects hierarchies on the basis of physical similarity. This tends to emphasize the results of evolution, of adaptations that develop and are successful. The second is cladistics, which studies only relatedness, and is not influenced by adaptation. The third one, evolutionary taxonomy, takes more of a middle ground and looks at both significant adaptations and relatedness. Andrews and Stringer carried out cladistic analyses on *Homo erectus* fossils from Africa, Asia, and Europe, redefining the species in a new way. Most of the features used to define *Homo erectus* are, they believe, primitive ones retained from earlier times. Since they appear on earlier hominids, they can hardly be used to define a new species. Once these features are removed, only a small number of derived characters remain, all of them found not on the African specimens, but on the *Homo erectus* populations from Southeast Asia and China. In short, proponents of cladistic analysis claim that the Asian *Homo erectus* populations are evolutionarily separate from those hominids in the same grade in Africa. Not only that, these scientists say that the Asian forms became extinct, and the African species of *Homo*, which should no longer be called *Homo erectus*, was the ancestor of early *Homo sapiens* and ultimately of anatomically modern humans (*Homo sapiens sapiens*) as well. On this basis, Andrews and Stringer argue for an African ancestry for modern humans and a subsequent migration to other parts of the world before 100,000 years ago.

This cladistic theory is still highly controversial, for there are many scientists, led by Milford Wolpoff of the Candelabra school, who argue that the anatomical differences between different groups of *Homo erectus* fossils are precisely those one would expect in isolated and widely dispersed populations.

Then, in the mid-1980s, the molecular biologists stepped into the arena, with results of genetic studies. Allan Wilson of the University of California and others suggested that *Homo sapiens sapiens* had evolved from an early *Homo sapiens* population in sub-Saharan Africa about 150,000 years ago.

The Candelabra and Noah's Ark models represent a polarity of theoretical positions. In the chapters that follow, we develop these two competing theories, reviewing both archaeological and biological evidence for the emergence and spread of modern humans.

CHAPTER THREE

The Genetic Detectives

Searching for our ancestors is like looking for a needle in a haystack. The chances of finding an early hominid are infinitesimally small, the equivalent in paleoanthropological terms of winning a lottery. Like other animals, our early predecessors abandoned the elderly or infirm to die on their own, left those killed in accidents or dead of natural causes where they fell to be eaten by carnivores or to rot away forgotten. It was not until about 100,000 years ago that human groups began to bury their dead, to contemplate the possibility of a life after death. Such deliberate burial practices shorten the archaeological odds slightly, but there remain few discoveries of fossil humans, making the task of the paleoanthropologist trying to fill in the gaps a frustrating one.

Quite apart from the difficulty of locating tiny bone fragments in weathered fossil beds, interpreting the finds is a difficult task. It is hard to know, by bone shape alone, whether a newly discovered fossil represents a familiar species or whether it is different enough to become a new species on its own. For all the drama of the research and the arguments over bones of contention, bone fragments cannot provide a complete picture of the ancestry of *Homo sapiens*. Fortunately, bones and artifacts are no longer the only clues to human evolution available to us. In recent years, biochemists have learned how to investigate the ancestry of *Homo sapiens* through living cells.

An air-conditioned biochemistry laboratory may not seem a glamorous work place. The quiet hum of cooling fans, subdued computer displays, and a gentle murmur of hard-working voices, can hardly compete with the excitement of uncovering a 1.6-million-year-old hominid skeleton in East Africa. The tools of the biochemist are powerful computers, tiny samples of body tissue, and sophisticated blenders, centrifuges, and microscopes – a far cry from the trowels, dental picks, and soft paintbrushes used at Olduvai Gorge and East Turkana. For all their unspectacular working conditions, the biochemists have stirred up a controversy over the origins of *Homo sapiens* that has given new meaning to the sparse fossil record – and identified a shadowy African common ancestor for all of modern humanity.

Genetic data are now taking pride of place in the study of our origins, simply because they are so plentiful and so easily comparable using modern scientific techniques. As paleontologist Stephen Jay Gould of Harvard University has pointed out, under the Noah's Ark theory we shared a common ancestry, and, therefore, a common genetic and morphological heritage. However, as *Homo sapiens sapiens* populations separated and diversified genetic differences accumulated. The greater these differences, the greater the time of separation. The family tree can be studied by measuring degrees of difference and dating the time of bifurcation using large numbers of genetic samples to blur minor, and often local variations. Only genes can supply the kind of rich and diverse data that can be used as an independent measure of distance between human groups.

The Molecular Time Clock

The controversy really began about 30 years ago, when scientists began to study our hereditary, or genetic, material for clues as to how life evolved. At first, they concentrated on the basics. How could minute changes in the fundamental units of inheritance (genes) carried on chromosomes in the cell nucleus lead to noticeable alterations in an animal's size, shape, and abilities? Eventually, it was discovered that genes consist of sequences of the molecule deoxyribonucleic acid (DNA) that provide recipes for making cellular proteins – the genetic code. Each DNA sequence consists of two, long paired chains of subunits called nucleotides in regularly repeating groups. A code of three consecutive nucleotide pairs (triplets) specify one amino acid in the protein chain. When DNA copies itself, some of the nucleotide sequences are accidentally altered, or mutated, which may also cause changes (mutations) in the protein they produce. Clearly, most evolutionary change begins with mutations in genetic molecules.

A turning point in this research came in 1962 when Linus Pauling and Emile Zuckerkandl at the California Institute of Technology were searching for reasons why some of our primate relatives never contract the human diseases malaria or sickle-cell anemia. Along the way, they discovered a property of proteins that would become the foundation of all later work in evolutionary biology. While studying the ways in which the primary blood protein, hemoglobin, differed from one primate species to another, they found a correlation between the degree to which the hemoglobin molecules of two species differ and the evolutionary distance separating them. For instance, the hemoglobin in two monkeys that shared a common ancestor 10 million years ago would be twice as different as the hemoglobin in species that had diverged only 5 million years ago. Could the same sort of correlation hold true for other proteins, they wondered? Could these proteins have changed at a constant rate over time, by accumulating a steady stream of accidental mutations? If it were possible to time the rate of change, a biologist could then count the number of amino acid differences in two samples of the same protein, each from a different animal, and pin down the date when the animals diverged from a common ancestor.

In the mid-1960s, two biologists at the Berkeley campus of the University of California, Vincent Sarich and Allan Wilson, concentrated their research on albumin, a protein that transmits nutrients through the bloodstream. They measured differences in the amino acid sequences of albumin from apes and Old World monkeys that were believed to have diverged 30 million years ago. Once they had established that albumin evolved at the rate of about one amino acid substitution every 1.25 million years, they were able to compare the protein in humans and African apes. To their astonishment, they found that the human family diverged from African apes as recently as 5 million years ago. This means that the Africans apes (chimpanzees and gorillas) are more closely related to human beings than to Asian apes (orang-utans), from whom they separated between 10 and 13 million years ago.

Sarich and Wilson caused a storm of controversy when they published their findings in 1967. Many paleoanthropologists, "stone and bone people," refused to accept their conclusions. Some dismissed Wilson's calculations as those of a lunatic. But the biochemists' findings were corroborated again and again, and came to enjoy widespread acceptance as laboratory technology took a quantum leap in the 1970s. New fossil discoveries from 15 million years ago also convinced Wilson's opponents that he was right, for these fossils were more ape-like than previous finds had suggested. The new technologies allowed geneticists to look beyond proteins, to examine the tiny and more intricate DNA molecules in the cell nuclei. Now they could identify genetic differences between species in much greater detail. They discovered enzymes in bacteria that destroy or "restrict" any foreign DNA that might invade a cell. These "restriction enzymes" achieve this by cleaving the DNA molecule in each place along the chain where they identify a particular sequence of subunits called restriction sites.

Wilson and his colleagues have now isolated more than 200 restriction enzymes, and have used them to "map" DNA molecules. They cut apart a DNA strand; then, in a process known as electrophoresis, they place the fragments in a synthetic gel, and pass an electric current through them. Each fragment carries an electrical charge, so the current causes them to line up in order of size, from the longest to the shortest. Since the lengths of the individual DNA segments have been determined by the pattern of restriction sites on the original strand, the result is a kind of "signature," a way of comparing the DNA signature of one animal with another. Electrophoresis has enabled geneticists not only to verify the general principles of the Sarich and Wilson timetable, but also to date the divergence dates of other mammals, such as horses and lions, from common ancestors.

Despite doubts expressed recently in some quarters about the global uniformity of the molecular clock, the Sarich and Wilson formula certainly seems to work, for example, in relation to the divergence of the African apes from the human family.

Mitochondrial DNA

In the late 1970s, biochemists began to concentrate on a separate set of DNA molecules found in structures called mitochondria, which lie outside the cell nuclei. A cell has two major components: the nucleus, which contains chromosomes bearing nuclear DNA, and the cytoplasm, a fluid matrix surrounding the nucleus, which contains a diversity of metabolically active organelles. One of them is the mitochondrion. Mitochondria are blob-shaped organelles that occur in all higher plants and animals, but not in single-celled organisms such as bacteria. Mitochondria are the cell's engines, for they metabolize food and water into energy. They may have evolved early in the history of life, before a billion years ago, when a new kind of bacterium somehow engulfed an older one. The two were joined in a symbiotic relationship, the internal organism metabolizing food for itself and for its captor and ultimately becoming the mitochondrion. This would explain why mitochondria have retained their own distinctive DNA over thousands of millennia. Mitochondrial DNA has only about 16,000 paired subunits of nucleotides (bases). It has the advantage of being much easier to analyze than nuclear DNA, which has several million.

Mitochondrial DNA has another advantage – it is inherited only from the mother. Some experts believe that this is because only the nucleus of the sperm makes its way into the egg during fertilization. As the egg contributes all the cytoplasm to a fertilized zygote, only the mother contributes mitochondrial DNA to the next generation. Thus, only the egg's mitochondrial DNA is reproduced in the offspring, and mitochondrial DNA is immune to change by sexual recombination of genes from each parent. This genetic recombination confuses the search for evidence of random mutations. But by studying mitochondrial DNA, the scientist can focus on the changes caused by mutations and by mutations alone.

The next stage was to calibrate a mitochondrial DNA "clock," by measuring the number of mutations that have taken place in the mitochondrial DNA of primates whose evolutionary divergence millions of years ago had been dated from fossil bones. The biochemists found that a mitochondrial DNA molecule mutates at a rate of about 2 or 4 percent every million years. This is 5–10 times faster than the rate of mutation in nuclear genetic material, partly because the external DNA in the mitochondrion is not as well protected from temperature changes, poisons, and other causes of mutation as the protein-coated DNA in the nucleus. Since mitochondrial DNA undergoes significant change every few hundred thousand years, the biochemists had the idea of using it as a gauge of short-term, rather than long-term, evolution, in particular, as a clock for measuring the time when modern humans diverged from a common ancestor.

The Mitochondrial Tree

In 1979, Rebecca Cann, then a graduate student under Allan Wilson at Berkeley, joined him and fellow biochemist Mark Stoneking in collecting mitochondrial DNA from the placentas of newborn children. The placentas contained the same genes as the children themselves, and were an easy way of obtaining large samples of body tissue. After 7 years, Cann and her colleagues had collected samples from 147 children, whose ancestors lived in five parts of the world: Africa, Asia, Europe, Australia, and New Guinea. The placentas were gathered and frozen, and the tissues analyzed in Wilson's Berkeley laboratory. First, the biochemists ground the tissues in powerful blenders, spun them in a centrifuge, then mixed them with a cell-breaking detergent that was dyed fluorescent before centrifuging them again. The resulting clear liquid contained pure DNA. Each DNA sample was cut into segments that could be compared with the DNA from other babies. They then spent months dividing the samples with restriction enzymes into more than 300 fragments. These in turn were arranged into distinctive patterns by starch-gel electrophoresis. Then a computer calculated the number of mutations that had occurred in each sample since it and the others evolved from a common ancestor. There were 133 distinct types of mitochondrial DNA in the sample. Some individuals had very similar sequences of bases, as if they had descended from a single woman within the past few centuries. In contrast, others were connected by a common female ancestor, who had lived tens of thousands of years ago.

Next, the computer constructed an "evolutionary tree," with the 133 mitochondrial DNA types at the ends of the tree's branches. It grouped those with the fewest differences in their base sequences in clusters of tiny branches. Each of these clusters is linked in turn to others at the points at which they diverged from common ancestors. The further back in time the common ancestor, the closer to the trunk the cluster lies. All but seven mitochondrial DNA types are on limbs that converge on a single branch. Descendants of people from the five geographical groups in the sample are mixed throughout this branch. A second major branch, much thinner than the first, contains the seven remaining mitochondrial DNA types, all of them of African descent. These seven are as different in their DNA composition from one another as are any of those on the more widely radiating, multiracial branch. Thus, our common ancestor is just as old as the common ancestor of the 126 on the larger branch. The base of the tree, the point at which the two branches split, is the position of the common mother – Eve. It was her children that diverged and spawned the two lines of descent.

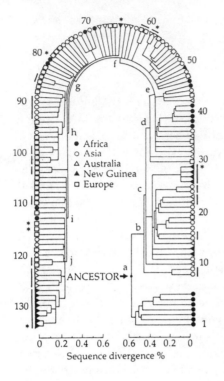

The evolutionary family tree for modern humans, constructed by measuring genetic divergence among living individuals whose ancestors came from Africa, Asia, Australia, New Guinea, and Europe. The tree has 133 different mitochondrial DNA types at the ends of its branches. There is a major split between African and non-African populations, with a common ancestor.

Rebecca Cann and her colleagues believe that Eve was an African. Their evolutionary tree shows that Africans can trace their ancestry to the base of the tree without running into any non-African ancestors. The descendants of the other areas have at least one African ancestor. Furthermore, the tree shows that the African-only branch contains more diverse types of mitochondrial DNA than any other geographic group. Thus, more evolutionary change has occurred among Africans than among members of any other group.

Why was this the case? Despite major climatic fluctuations in some parts of the world when humans were evolving, the climate in tropical and subtropical Africa did not change as much. There were significant rainfall shifts, but never changes sufficient to cause unusually high rates of evolution on the savanna. So, Cann and her colleagues believe that Africans accumulated the greatest number of mutations simply because their mitochondrial DNA is the earliest. Asians, on the other hand, have relatively homogeneous mitochondrial DNA, suggesting they are of more recent ancestry. "Eve, then . . . was an African and her descendants include both those who remained on her continent and others who struck out to populate the planet," wrote Cann in 1987.

How long ago did Eve live? Cann and her fellow biochemists point out that the rate of mitochondrial DNA evolution for a wide variety of vertebrates is a constant rate of 2–4 percent every million years. Using this divergence rate and a maximum divergence of 0.6 percent between the two main branches of their evolutionary tree, they calculated that the primeval Eve lived some time between 285,000 and 143,000 years ago, or, more simply, about 200,000 years ago. The biochemical team also calculated that the second split, which separated the *Homo sapiens* populations that stayed in Africa from those that moved out, took place somewhat later, with the ancestors of the non-Africans leaving the continent between 180,000 and 90,000 years ago. Allan Wilson recently refined his biochemical techniques to the point that he can obtain mitochondrial DNA samples from specimens as small as a human hair. This has enabled him to collect samples from !Kung San hunter-gatherers of the Kalahari Desert and other African groups who would never donate placentas for biochemical research. Wilson's new techniques cause him to refine his chronology for Eve in southern Africa to about 140,000 years ago. "We are all a derivative of one of the !Kung lineages," he said at an international genetic conference in San Diego, California, in 1989.

A team of geneticists headed by Douglas Wallace of Emory University in Atlanta agrees with Cann's time clock, but argues that the mitochondrial Eve lived not in Africa, but in Asia. Wallace's team collected blood from about 700 people on four continents, using somewhat different methods to chop up the DNA and arrange their types in a family tree. Their tree also goes back to a primeval woman living between 200,000 and 150,000 years ago. However, they argue that human races have distinctive forms of DNA and that the human DNA closest to that of apes occurs most commonly not in Africa but in Southeast Asia. Thus, they believe that early *Homo sapiens* emerged in that region. Wallace is quick to point out that his data can be interpreted in several ways, depending on what basic assumptions one makes, but criticizes the Berkeley researchers for taking samples from American blacks, whose ancestry could have been mixed with Europeans and American Indians. Both laboratory groups criticize the research methods of the other, but both agree that they have to gather more samples and refine their research methods before obtaining definitive answers.

Whatever their theories of genetic origin, both schools of thought agree that the mitochondrial Eve lived relatively recently, but the reliability of their chronologies are hard to assess. Mark Stoneking of the University of California and Rebecca Cann present a very cautious estimate, for they are aware that estimates of sequence divergence are subject to major sampling and other variances that are both difficult to calculate and perhaps of considerable size. "We can probably only state with certainty that the common ancestor was present at least 50,000 but less than 500,000 years ago," they write. This chronology can be narrowed only by further basic research, and with the aid of dated fossils. In the meantime, we have to rely on careful *estimates* for the dates of ancestral populations.

Milford Wolpoff and other Candelabra adherents have focused eagerly on this molecular clock. They challenge the time scale for calibrating rates of genetic mutation of mitochondrial DNA. They believe that Cann and others have overestimated the mutation rate. Geneticist Masatoshi Nei of the University of Texas worked independently and calculated a slower divergence rate of 0.71 percent every million years, between 2.8 and 5.6 times slower than the Cann rate of 2–4 percent. Wolpoff uses the Nei divergence rate to argue that what he calls "modern populations" diverged about 850,000 years ago.

The 850,000-year date agrees well with the Candelabra view of modern human origins – that human geographic variation dates to the initial spread of *Homo erectus* out of Africa. Stoneking, Cann, and others counter by saying that such a hypothesis makes it hard to explain the observed greater antiquity in the modern African gene pool. A battle royal over the methods of analysis used in mitochondrial and other genetic studies continues to rage in the academic literature, a battle not only between biochemists, but between anthropologists on both sides of the Candelabra/Noah's Ark issue.

Gene Frequencies and African Origins

The DNA research does not stand alone in supporting an African origin for *Homo sapiens sapiens*. Population geneticists and anthropologists have used data on the frequencies of genes in different populations to study human evolution for many years. Much of this research has focused on the measurement of genetic distance between populations using gene-frequency data from many locations. By using electrophoresis, geneticists have been able not only to study gene frequencies, but also to infer the magnitude of genetic variation within and between populations at the level of the codon. (Codons – triplets of nucleotides – are the "punctuation marks" in genetic codes.) This is possible because the genetic variation in proteins directly reflects any variation in DNA. Masatoshi Nei proposed a new measure of genetic distance that could be used to estimate the differences between the codon at a particular site on a chromosome. This measure showed that the genetic distances between Europeans, Africans, and eastern Asians are small when compared with the differences between the genetic complements of two randomly chosen individuals from within one racial group. However, although the genetic distances were small, they were of the magnitude that might be expected to occur when a pair of populations have been separated for 50,000–120,000 years.

These studies have enabled a number of scientists, among them Nei and Arun Roychoudhury of the University of Texas, to construct evolutionary trees for various human groups based on data from many locations. They

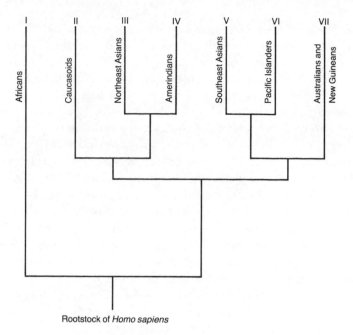

Cavalli-Sforza's tree, dividing modern humans into seven major groups.

calculate that Negroids (Africans) and Caucasoids (Europeans and Southwest Asians) diverged from one another about 113,000 years ago, Negroids from Mongoloids (East Asians) about 116,000 years ago, and Caucasoids diverged from Mongoloids about 41,000 years ago. On a worldwide basis, Negroids have a higher degree of genetic similarity to European populations than to Mongoloids. There are, then, genetic grounds for suspecting that Africans were the ancient *Homo sapiens sapiens* stock.

Luigi Luca Cavalli-Sforza of Stanford University and his Italian colleagues have recently compiled a "tree of 42 world populations" using the states and frequencies of genes in the different groups as revealed in amino acid sequences of enzymes and other proteins. Cavalli-Sforza's team sampled indigenous peoples that had had little or no mixing with outside groups. Inevitably, the geneticists had to pool their data from large geographical areas, so the values they obtained are average gene frequencies. When there was a possibility that this would mask genetic differences, they added linguistic data to differentiate such groups. In their reconstruction of human evolution, modern humans are divided into seven major groups. The first split in the family tree separates Africans from non-Africans, which may mark the initial migration of some *Homo sapiens sapiens* groups out of Africa. The next bifurcation separates two further major clusters, the Eurasians and the South Asians/Oceanians. The Northeurasian cluster, in turn, bifurcates into Caucasoids on the one hand and Northeast Asians and Amerindians on the other. The South Asian/Oceanians cluster splits into the mainland and island Southeast Asians proper and the Pacific islanders, and also the more distantly related New Guineans and Australians.

This simple and logical tree is little more than a hypothesis, which Cavalli-Sforza and his colleagues tested against archaeological data. If rates of evolutionary change are roughly similar for all groups, then the ratio between genetic distance and the age of separation should be pretty constant. The geneticists took estimates for the African–non-African split of 92,000 years ago, one of 40,000 years for the settlement of New Guinea and Australia, and 35,000 years for the separation of Caucasoids and Northeast Asians. Then they used Masatoshi Nei's measure of genetic distance and found that the gene/time ratios for these three events were consistent with the hypothesis that there were constant rates of change.

The Cavalli-Sforza research is elegant and devastatingly simple in its implications. Even if further investigations provide more precise information on when human groups split off and where they spread to, one still has a basic outline of that group's relationships with others. These relationships have not been erased by more recent, short-term adaptations, or by conquest, population movements, and other historical events. "We remain children of our past," wrote Harvard scientist Stephen Jay Gould in 1989, as he offered hope that one day the geneticists will provide a general portrait of our ancestry.

Did Eve Exist?

If one accepts the genetic theory of African origins for modern humans, was there actually an Eve, a woman of flesh and blood rather than just a genetic ancestor? In the sense that there was once a single person one could point to as the identifiable, single ancestor of *Homo sapiens*, the answer is no. Folklore and legend can point to single individuals who were the first, the originators of life, or, as in the case of Adam and Eve, the first sinners. The Eve of the Scriptures is one such person, said to have been the only woman alive in her time. She is a legendary, primeval female, a symbol of the beginnings of human existence. Scientific reality is very different, for genes are the products, not of a single individual, but of interacting populations of males and females. There may, indeed, once have been a single Eve, but we can never hope to identify her in person. Her identity is submerged in those of thousands of other archaic humans, who were living south of the Sahara around 200,000 years ago. The geneticists' Eve is, perforce, an anonymous individual, whose identity survives only as an elusive genetic signature. Eve may have been a representative of anatomically archaic *Homo sapiens* herself. All she contributed was her mitochondrial DNA to people who, perhaps many generations later, evolved into *Homo sapiens sapiens*.

1 **Primeval Eden** Eve tempts Adam in this conventionally lush 19th-century depiction of the Biblical Garden of Eden. But, for modern geneticists, the true Eden may have been the African savanna, where a dark-skinned Eve perhaps lived some 200,000 years ago.

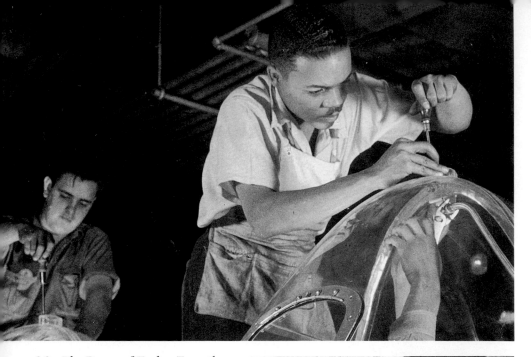

2,3 **The Power of Tools** From the Stone Age to the Machine Age, human hands have shaped our technological progress (*right*, an archaeologist recreates the ancient skill of flintknapping; *above*, workers on a production line). But were early humans as dextrous with their hands as anatomically modern *Homo sapiens sapiens*? Stone tools and the fossil record provide the answer.

4 **The Birth of Language** In addition to toolmaking, fully articulate speech is another uniquely human ability. Through speech we communicate with one another, we tell stories and pass on our collective wisdom to the next generation. A child can achieve the prodigious feat of learning a language (*right*) by the age of four or five. When did this special gift evolve? Were anatomically modern humans the first to "speak in tongues," or did their predecessors do so as well? Some scientists think they have the answer.

5,6 The Creative Imagination
Like toolmaking and speech, our capacity for art – the ability to imagine and represent structured worlds outside ourselves – sets us apart from other animals. An orang utan, when put before an easel (*below*), will enjoy producing a "painting" in quite an individual style. But this is a far cry from the human gift for accurate representation (*left*, a 14th-century French manuscript illumination). Archaeologists have been studying whether or not art is found among pre-modern human species.

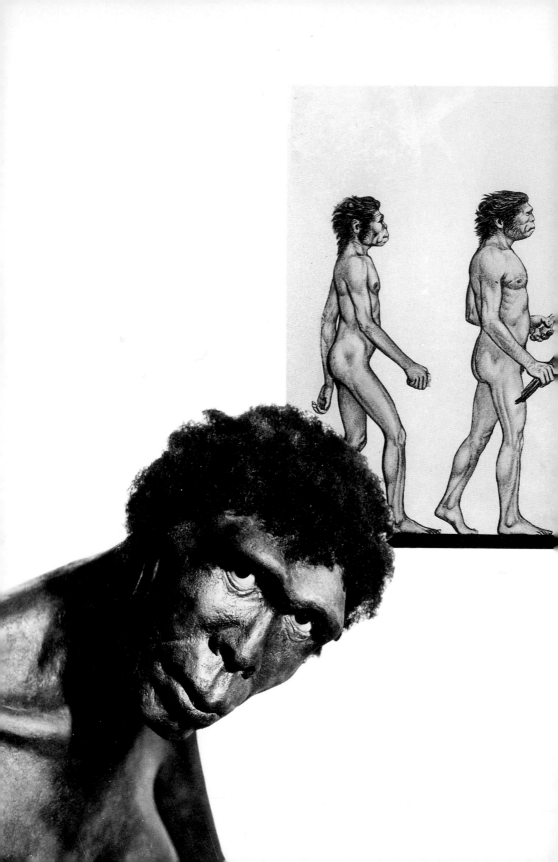

7,8   The Ancestral Line   Scientists agree that the earliest toolmakers – *Homo habilis* (*above left*) – evolved in Africa after 2.3 million years ago. Their taller, larger-brained successors – *Homo erectus* (*left* and *above, second from left*) – appeared on the savanna around 1.6 million years ago. Learning to tame and create fire, they were the first hominids to move out of Africa into the cooler, temperate climates of Europe and Asia. But where and how did *Homo erectus* evolve into modern humans (*above, last three figures*, the process simplified, with modern man on the right)? Proponents of the Candelabra school believe that the process involved independent evolution in many different parts of the world. Advocates of the Noah's Ark theory, however, maintain that modern humans emerged first in Africa, and then spread from there into other continents.

9–11 **The Savanna Homeland** Today's San hunter-gatherers are heirs to a tradition of mobile life stretching back hundreds of thousands of years. Early hunters would have been armed with spears rather than the bow invented in later prehistory (*left*), but the fundamental skills of the chase were the same: immense patience, an intimate knowledge of the prey's habits, and an ability to pursue a wounded animal for hours or even days before the final kill (*above left*). Women collectors, however (*above*), provided the most reliable supplies of food. Their detailed knowledge of a huge range of edible plants helped keep starvation at bay even during lean years.

12 **A View from the Cave**   The site of Klasies River Mouth, on South Africa's southeast coast, has yielded crucial evidence that anatomically modern people were living in this part of the world at least 100,000 years ago.

Stephen Jay Gould embraces the Cann mitochondrial tree with enthusiasm, the striking and simple topology of a tree with two major branches joined at the base. He points out that genetic detective work has yielded a fact of history that has stunning implications for human unity. They have demonstrated the underlying unity of all humankind, a contingent fact of history that we often forget. Despite our external differences of skin color, hair form, and size, all modern humans have a relatively recent, common ancestry in Africa. And if the geneticists are right, then we have a point of recent origin in history and a history of later spread.

Genetics, then, yield a tantalizing scenario for the origins of modern humans. They hint at the existence of interacting populations of archaic *Homo sapiens*, who flourished in sub-Saharan Africa some time after 200,000 years ago. The mitochondrial family tree hints, also, at a bifurcation of African and non-African *Homo sapiens* populations somewhat later, between 130,000 and 90,000 years ago. If the geneticists are correct, there *was* a movement of anatomically modern humans out of sub-Saharan Africa during this time period. But, as Rebecca Cann and other geneticists have pointed out repeatedly, it is archaeological and fossil evidence that must provide definitive proof of biological and cultural continuity between early *Homo sapiens* and *Homo sapiens sapiens* in sub-Saharan Africa. In the next two chapters, we try to flesh out the genetic scenario with fossil and cultural evidence, a detective story as intricate and fascinating as that put together by the geneticists.

CHAPTER FOUR

The Savanna Homeland

Both the biochemists and the paleoanthropologists agree that the savanna of sub-Saharan Africa was the cradle of earliest humankind. The same grasslands and woodlands, game-rich environments that were still a hunter's paradise in Victorian times, may also have been the homeland of *Homo sapiens sapiens*. What was special about the African savanna? What hunting and foraging skills were needed to survive here? And what kind of toolkit would one need to exploit its game animals of all sizes and many species of plants? The answers to these questions are important clues in the search for the origins of modern humans.

The African Savanna

Eastern and southern Africa are like an upturned soup dish. The flat, coastal plains that form the rims rise steeply to an interior plateau between 1,200 and 4,000 ft (365 and 1,220 m) above sea level. The highlands are the inverted bowl, the alleged homeland of primeval *Homo sapiens*, the general area where the putative Eve once dwelt around 200,000 years ago. The same mixed savanna and woodland plateau was also the cradle of early humanity some 2.5 million years ago. This is landscape on a grand scale, a landscape of rolling woodland, open plains, and occasional high mountain ranges. Earthquakes, crustal movements large and small, and ever-changing rainfall patterns have dissected and weathered the plateau into a varied jigsaw of local environments that extend from Ethiopia in the north deep into southern Africa thousands of miles away. The Great Rift Valley cuts through the plateau from north to south, petering out in Lakes Tanganyika and Malawi. The northern section, the Afar Rift of Ethiopia, dissects some of the hottest country on earth. Further south, it passes through highlands drained by the Nile, nurtures freshwater lakes, among them Lake Turkana in Kenya, where early hominids camped over 2 million years ago. South of Ethiopia and Somalia lies a vast region of undulating plains, great mountains, and plateaux that drain into the Indian Ocean on the eastern side and into the large lake basins of the far interior. This is mainly savanna country, where tropical woodlands and grasslands once supported a mammalian fauna even richer than today's. The plains extend far south, across what is now Zambia, Malawi, and parts of eastern Zaire and Angola, to the banks of the Zambezi River and beyond. South of the Limpopo, the "grey-green greasy Limpopo" of Rudyard Kipling's *Just So Stories*, the ubiquitous deciduous woodland gives way to more open country, to grassland plains that pass gradually into the desert landscape of the Kalahari, Namibia, and South Africa's Karroo.

At first glance, the savanna is a monotonous tapestry of evergreen trees, a monotony relieved by occasional badly drained grass clearings and seasonal watercourses. Look closer and you enter a fascinating, varied environment of subtle seasonal changes and great natural diversity. The rainy season clothes the bush in a rich, deep green, with lush grass fingering between the ubiquitous woodland. Timid small antelope called duiker and other woodland animals venture from the trees, grazing at the fringes of the forest. Vast herds of wildebeest and zebra range over open grassland plains, gathering near the ponds and seasonal waterholes where lions and other predators lie in wait. A myriad trees and plants burst into flower, yielding edible fruit and nuts for humans and animals alike.

I remember walking in search of Stone Age savanna camp sites along a small river in Zambia on a cool, winter evening, several years ago. The shadows were lengthening, a gentle greyness filling in under the trees. Wood smoke from nearby villages hung in the air. I stopped to sniff the air and enjoy the quiet of evening. Two small duiker slipped out of the trees and came to the water's edge, drinking warily from the fast-flowing river. For a moment I was transported back deep into Stone Age times, imagining hunters watching at this spot for game coming to drink in the evening cool. Then some children called out in the village and the spell was broken as the duiker ran quickly into the canopy of trees.

When the dry months come, the plateau dries up. The grass turns yellow, trees rustle with brittle leaves in the cool wind. Lightning strikes start huge brush fires that sweep across the tinder-dry woodland, filling the air with smoke and choking ash, driving animals large and small before them. The land is parched, burnt black, but only for a short while. Green shoots poke through the ash, black thunder clouds gather each hot afternoon. Antelope feed on the young shoots. The land is reborn, a game-rich landscape that has flourished south of the Sahara for millions of years.

Hunting the Savanna

The savanna is not an easy environment to exploit, especially if one does not have the benefit of modern firearms, or even a bow and arrow. The Victorian explorers who first traveled across the African interior left enduring portraits of "darkest Africa," a mysterious, game-rich land peopled by exotic tribes, a land ravaged by slave and ivory traders. Repeater-toting sportsmen, mineral prospectors, and farmers followed in their footsteps. Their writings gave the impression that vast herds of game were there for the shooting wherever one traveled. In fact, they were successful not only because they had powerful rifles, but because they employed local guides, who were expert trackers.

Those who depend on the natural environment for survival understand it better than anyone else. The Victorians' trackers used hunting and stalking methods that had been in use for thousands of years, since deep in Stone Age times. Wooden bows and poison-tipped arrows, sharp spears, carefully placed snares and traps, and, above all, an intimate knowledge of the habits of their prey and of the savanna itself – these were the weapons of the chase, as they had been since earliest times.

When anthropologist Stuart Marks of the University of Wisconsin spent a year studying elephant hunters in eastern Zambia in the 1960s, he found himself carried into a vanishing world, to a world where the hunters thought of themselves as predators like lions or hyenas. They would proclaim proudly: "I also belong to the chase." Their skill still depended on prehistoric expertise, on an intimate knowledge of a complicated patchwork of natural resources close to their homes. They knew the tell-tale signs of grazing elephants, what grasses impala preferred, the subtle, seasonal changes in fruit pods that were food for duiker for only a few weeks a year. These signs were far more effective weapons than the spears and inefficient muzzle-loading muskets in their hands – they enabled them to get close to the game.

Marks went out on the hunt, watching the hunter stalking kudu and other prey for hours, examining fresh droppings, testing the wind direction, studying the composition of the herd. The pursuer would move forward quietly, freeze when the herd looked up, then shift position again until he was close enough to fire. Seven out of ten times he missed, and the entire chase began again. And if a hit was scored, the animal almost never died outright. It could be hours, or even days, before the hunter could catch up with his quarry and kill it. In many cases, the wounded animal escaped or was killed and eaten by lions before the hunter arrived. What counted more than anything was not technology, but an intimate knowledge of the animals' habits and of the different environments in which they flourished. These environments, and the distributions of game and plant foods, varied greatly within a few miles. Scientists believe that this "mosaic effect," which concentrated resources in some areas and not in others, was a vital factor in the emergence of *Homo sapiens*.

Fundamental Hunting Skills

Homo erectus, the African ancestor of *Homo sapiens*, first appeared in Africa about 1.6 million years ago, also at a time when climatic conditions were drier than today. These humans were more expert hunters than their predecessors, but their expertise was a far cry from that of a present-day San hunter from the Kalahari Desert or one of Stuart Marks' Zambian friends. For tens of thousands of years, *Homo erectus* lived in tiny, scattered bands, occupying large, sparsely populated hunting territories. Judging from surviving limb bones, *Homo erectus* was fleet of foot, and quite capable of the sustained bursts of speed needed to run down small antelope and chase wounded animals. Their knowledge of the environment would have helped in preparing simple traps and snares along game trails, to catch guinea fowl and other walking birds. Expert stalking skills were, of course, vital. Otherwise, these early humans would never have been able to kill at all, armed as they were with just wooden spears, perhaps simple clubs, and stones.

This ancient hunting and foraging life persisted for more than a million years with only the smallest changes, reflected in a greater variety of stone tools. Perhaps the hunters learned how to hunt larger, more formidable animals like the buffalo and elephant, killing enmired animals or solitary beasts. They may also have used fire to drive game into traps and over cliffs, used their slowly evolving communication skills to cooperate with neighboring bands in the chase. As in modern hunter-gatherer societies, women were probably the collectors. Judging from modern foragers, the women knew of a very wide range of edible plants, but concentrated most of their efforts on a relatively small number of favorite foods. This conservative strategy paid off in scarce years, when the people simply fell back on a natural "cushion" of other edible species.

These, then, were the fundamental skills of hunting and gathering, the basic expertise needed by human beings to survive in the homeland of *Homo sapiens*. They were the ultimate survival skills that enabled *Homo sapiens sapiens* to develop the more sophisticated technologies and hunting methods that were to carry human beings to every corner of the world.

Technology

Homo erectus hunters probably relied on wooden spears and clubs in the chase, while hides and bark trays served as containers for carrying nuts and other foraged foods back to camp. But almost none of these perishable artifacts have survived from early prehistoric sites. It is stone artifacts and the debris from their manufacture that provide most of our knowledge of Stone Age technology. So simple were the technologies of *Homo erectus* and early *Homo sapiens* that the same fundamental stone toolmaking methods and artifacts were used from southern Africa to the Nile, from the Near East to western Europe, and in Asia. This enables us to generalize about the slow changes in stone-tool technology that are our signposts to worldwide cultural change in early prehistory.

Before about 300,000 years ago, Stone Age hunters everywhere used the simplest of techniques in stone toolmaking to fashion choppers, hand axes, scrapers and other simple, multipurpose artifacts. Any technological changes were mere refinements of methods that had been in use for millennia. In some areas, probably where exceptionally fine-grained rocks were to be found, the stoneworkers used two techniques to produce thin flakes of relatively predictable shape. With one technique, the toolmakers used a tortoise-shell-like core (the stone from which flakes are removed) with a flattened top to produce one or two largish flakes. This somewhat wasteful technique, often called "Levallois," after a site in the Paris suburb where it was first identified, required a great deal of fine-grained rock to produce a single flake. More commonly the stoneworkers used smaller "disc" cores, carefully shaped in such a way as to produce six or more flakes. Both the Levallois and disc core techniques are grouped under the general technological label of "Middle Paleolithic" or "Middle Stone Age," a technology that became established throughout Africa, Europe and Eurasia, and southern Asia after 200,000 years ago. Middle Stone Age technology and its associated techniques produced sharp-edged flakes that could be trimmed into a wide variety of smaller artifacts – triangular knives, scrapers, gouges, even crude borers for shaping wood, for butchery, and for processing skins, and simple chisels for grooving bone and wood. They also enabled the hunter to mount sharp-pointed stone points on wooden shafts. People may have mounted the occasional point on a wooden spear with resins and a fiber binding very early in prehistory, but the practice did not, apparently, become commonplace until much later, after about 100,000 years ago.

By 150,000 years ago, African Stone Age people began to develop toolkits adapted for different local conditions, for life in forests, on the open savanna, or near sea coasts. For example, heavier tools such as crude picks are common artifacts among societies that flourished in, or on the margins of, the rainforest. The people scattered over the more open landscape of the savanna had no need of such heavy tools. As time went on, especially after 100,000 years ago, they developed a lighter toolkit with many more scrapers and knives, also sharp-edged spear points, an effective weaponry for use against antelope of all sizes.

The toolkits used by Stone Age Africans after 100,000 years ago display considerable variety, and include occasional collections of much thinner and finer "blades" of far more standardized size and shape, struck from carefully prepared cores that were fashioned to produce considerable numbers of versatile artifact blanks. Such blades (fine, thin, and often parallel-sided blanks) often occur where local raw materials are of the finest quality, such as the fine quartzites of the Sahara and of coastal southeastern Africa. These technologies represent refinements made by human beings slowly becoming more adept at exploiting their savanna territories.

One of the basic hand axe types used by Stone Age hunters in much of the Old World before 200,000 years ago.

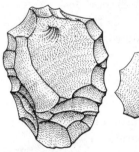

The Levallois (above) and disc-core (right) techniques that became established after 200,000 years ago. The somewhat wasteful Levallois method yielded a single flake from a specially prepared core. Disc cores might produce six or more flakes.

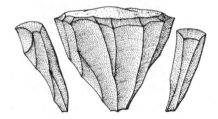

Blade technology – the first signs of which occur after 100,000 years ago – allowed flintknappers to produce numerous parallel-sided blanks (known as blades) from a carefully prepared core.

A Scenario for the Savanna

The development of lighter-weight, more varied stone-tool technologies may be a general barometer of slow cultural and even biological change on the African savanna after 200,000 years ago. They are part of a provocative scenario that puts the ways in which humans adapted to the savanna at the center of controversies about the origins of *Homo sapiens sapiens*.

There are compelling ecological reasons for believing that the savanna helped make Africa the cradle of *Homo sapiens sapiens*. As physical anthropologist and ecologist Robert Foley of the University of Cambridge argues, the impact of Ice Age climatic change may have been important. There were no ice sheets in Africa, but nevertheless highly significant environmental shifts profoundly affected animals and humans. During glacial periods, climatic conditions were cooler and drier, with much less rainforest and more savanna. Interglacials brought a brief reversal of the pattern, with more restricted woodland and grassland and more extensive rainforest. Foley observes that there was a close relationship between Ice Age climatic change and the formation of new species in Africa in fish, invertebrates, mammals, and primates. The guenon monkey group is instructive, for it diversified into at least 16 species occupying different local environments in Central Africa over the very period when *Homo sapiens* was evolving in sub-Saharan Africa. There was a close relationship between the fluctuations in forest and the formation of new species among these monkeys, for they were forest dwellers. Foley believes that exactly the same processes were at work among humans, with changes in distribution of open savanna playing the same role as forest for the monkeys.

Foley hypothesizes that early populations of *Homo sapiens* ranged over large territories, lived in relatively large groups with some kin-based social structure, and were highly selective in their eating habits, preferring meat and nutritious nuts and fruits. Judging from modern baboon behavior, such conditions are most likely to occur in patchy environments with high-quality, predictable foods – in precisely the kind of environments found on the African savanna. However, to exploit these environments to the full, *Homo sapiens* needed the adaptive ability to become a much more efficient hunter. Plant foods are usually relatively predictable, for they come into season at regular times of the year. Game animals, the major human prey on the savanna, are much less predictable, for they can change distribution rapidly. Even more important, they are far from easy to kill once located, especially if one has to kill them at close quarters. It may be that *Homo sapiens sapiens*, a more intelligent human, was able to maximize opportunities for a kill, through better planning, and, perhaps, through the development of stone projectile points that could be used to kill game from a greater distance. By better planning, with more efficient technology, and more carefully organized foraging activities, the new humans could increase the predictability of the savanna environment in which they and their forebears lived.

Foley believes that the evolution of modern humans resulted from a process of species formation in Africa during the approximate time frame suggested by the geneticists. At first, biological changes were relatively slow. Ultimately, important cultural and social changes took hold, resulting in the rapid dispersal of anatomically modern humans throughout the Old and the New Worlds.

The Foley scenario, combined with the genetic data, provides a general, if hypothetical, framework for the appearance of *Homo sapiens sapiens* in sub-Saharan Africa over 100,000 years ago. In Chapter Five, we attempt to clothe this scenario with African archaeological and fossil data.

CHAPTER FIVE

African Ancestors

The characteristics of the African Eve identified by the geneticists are entirely theoretical formulations, intelligent speculation based on mitochondrial genes and other genetic approaches. Rebecca Cann and others argue that *Homo sapiens sapiens* originated in sub-Saharan Africa, that the ancient populations in which anatomically modern people evolved once flourished on the savanna. But does this image have any grounding in paleontological reality? We now turn to some of the African fossil finds that straddle the critical period between about 300,000 and 50,000 years ago when proponents of the Noah's Ark hypothesis claim *Homo sapiens sapiens* evolved south of the Sahara.

Australopithecus, *Homo habilis*, and the many artifacts and fractured bones from Olduvai Gorge, East Turkana, and the South African caves, have established beyond all reasonable doubt that sub-Saharan Africa was the cradle of early humankind. However, the very scientists who unearthed *Australopithecus* and other early hominids believed until recently that Africa then became an evolutionary backwater, one of the last places settled by *Homo sapiens sapiens*.

One can hardly blame them for this assumption, for they had few fossil discoveries to go on. Most archaeological sites were little more than scatters of stone artifacts – and undated because radiocarbon and other scientific dating techniques did not exist at the time the sites were discovered. Above all, anthropologists' notions of African prehistory were colored by a remarkable fossil discovery made at Broken Hill Mine in what was then Northern Rhodesia in 1921.

Broken Hill Man

On the afternoon of 17 June 1921, miner Tom Zwigelaar and his men exposed a human skull in a subterranean cave in the Broken Hill (modern Kabwe) lead and zinc mine in what is now Zambia in central Africa. Zwigelaar picked up the skull and suspended it on a pole to encourage his workers to greater efforts. There it remained for a few days, a massive, heavy cranium that so

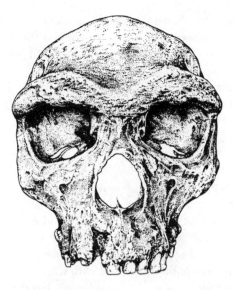

The skull found in 1921 at Broken Hill (Kabwe) in modern Zambia.

impressed the mine management that they took the trouble to send it to anatomist Arthur Woodward at the Natural History Museum in London.

At first glance, Woodward thought he was looking at a fossil gorilla, but he soon realized that it was a primitive-looking human being. The skull had massively developed brow ridges over the eye sockets, a flat and sloping forehead, and a marked constriction of the skull behind the brow. A strong ridge of bone lay at the back of the head, the place where very strong neck muscles were once attached. Woodward described the face as unusually large and elongated, with a wide palate and "blown-out" cheek bones. Weeks later, he received parts of a second individual, fragments of a more modern-looking face, a thigh bone, some limb pieces, also some fossil animal bones and some primitive-looking stone tools. The limb bones and thigh fragments were entirely modern.

Woodward compared the Kabwe remains to Neanderthals, who had lived in Europe from before 100,000 years ago to about 35,000 years ago. In fact, the Kabwe people differed from the Neanderthals in several important respects, especially in the position of the foramen magnum, the hole at the base of the skull where the head joins to the spinal column. These and other anatomical features led Arthur Woodward to create a new human species: *Homo rhodesiensis* or "Rhodesian man."

The newly discovered Kabwe skull had a strangely archaic appearance to European eyes, a massiveness that added to the impression of primitiveness. In an era when most scientists believed in racial superiority, and assumed that our species had originated in northern latitudes, it was hardly surprising that the primitive Kabwe fossils were taken as evidence for the late survival of archaic humans in southern Africa. They assumed that these archaic forms had evolved into *Homo sapiens sapiens* at a very late period in time indeed, perhaps as recently as 15,000 years ago.

These backwater theories persisted until the 1960s, not because of any inborn racism on the part of African archaeologists, but because there were almost no human fossils to work with.

Border Cave

As so often happens in archaeology, the evidence for very early *Homo sapiens* in Africa was discovered years before its true significance was realized. Border Cave lies high on the western flank of the Lebombo Mountains, just inside South Africa's frontier with Swaziland. The cave is about 100 ft (31 m) deep, with a 23-ft (7-m) high overhang at the entrance, accessible up a long slope, an ideal Stone Age habitation place with water nearby. In 1940, farmer William Horton dug for fertilizer in the soft cave deposits that spilled out of the entrance down a steep slope. He uncovered portions of a human skull and some limb bones in his diggings, and reported them to Professor Raymond Dart, the discoverer of *Australopithecus* in the 1920s. The human bones looked modern, but the stone implements were of Middle Stone Age form, quite different from those one might expect with *Homo sapiens sapiens*, a maker of blade tools. Dart was sufficiently intrigued to arrange for an excavation.

Three of Dart's colleagues excavated Border Cave in 1941 and 1942: geologist Basil Cooke, archaeologist Berry Malan, and physical anthropologist Lawrence Wells. They found more human remains – a 4- to 6-month-old infant buried in a shallow grave, more fragments of the original skull, and the jaw of a third individual, all of them apparently associated with Middle Stone Age occupation levels. The three young scholars described their finds in 1945, identifying the skeletal material as indeed being that of anatomically modern people. The Border Cave fossils were thought of as somewhat of an anomaly, perhaps modern bones that had been buried into earlier strata. It was not until 1970 that excavations resumed, this time in the hands of University of the Witwatersrand archaeologist Peter Beaumont.

By this time, excavation techniques were much more sophisticated than they had been a generation earlier. Beaumont called in American geologist Karl Butzer of the University of Chicago to examine the cave deposits. He could rely on local experts for the radiocarbon dating, and he arranged for zooarchaeologist Richard Klein, also Chicago-based, to study the animals hunted by the inhabitants. The new excavations confirmed that Border Cave had indeed been occupied by Middle Stone Age people. They had hunted an extinct form of horse and an extinct antelope, as well as animals living in the area today. The artifacts made by the Border Cave people were typical of Middle Stone Age toolkits elsewhere in southern Africa – disc and Levallois cores, and many flake tools. But there was a difference – a short period of occupation in the midst of Middle Stone Age levels where blades and blade knives with blunted backs were commonplace. There was no other conclusion: Border Cave had apparently been occupied by anatomically modern people long before 15,000 years ago, and blade tools were in use for at least part of this occupation.

The radiocarbon dates from the Border Cave excavation added to the puzzle. Unfortunately, none of the dating samples came from layers where human fossils were found, so Beaumont and Butzer used intricate correlations from deep-sea cores and climatic data from other archaeological sites to estimate the duration of occupation. They produced a date of at least 49,000 years for the Middle Stone Age levels, and estimated they were first accumulated as early as 115,000–90,000 years ago.

In 1972, Beaumont claimed that his excavations proved that southern Africa was no cultural backwater, but the cradle of modern humankind perhaps as early as 100,000 years ago. Most archaeologists took a wait-and-see attitude, as they had doubts about the dating of the cave. Three years later, German physical anthropologist René Protsch claimed not only that the Border Cave fossils were anatomically modern *Homo sapiens*, but that modern humans had spread rapidly into other continents from Africa about 40,000 years ago.

Most experts tended to discount a very early age for the Border Cave finds, as they were hard to date, and there were some doubts about exactly which levels the human bones had come from. However, even the doubters realized that even if the Border Cave bones were much later, dating to some time before 30,000 years ago, they were among the oldest *Homo sapiens sapiens* fossils in the world.

Klasies River Mouth Caves

Before Beaumont started work at Border Cave, it was clear that the only prospects for understanding what happened during the Middle Stone Age were to investigate an area where it was known that such populations had lived for long periods of time, and one where fossil animal and human bones might be well preserved. In the mid-1960s, University of Chicago anatomist Ronald Singer teamed up with British archaeologist John Wymer, an expert on Stone Age digs, to excavate some apparently undisturbed coastal caves near the mouth of the Klasies River on the southeastern Cape coast of South Africa.

This is a wild, rugged coastline with steep cliffs, giving way to a narrow coastal plain about 6 miles (9.5 km) wide. In prehistoric times, year-round rainfall, lush forests, plentiful water supplies, and ample grazing made this an exceptionally favorable area for hunters and foragers, with the additional bonus of shellfish and sea mammals from the ocean close by. Singer and Wymer selected a cave with a floor about 26 ft (7.9 m) above present sea level for their excavations, and labeled it Klasies River Mouth 1. Because of its proximity to the ocean, this wave-cut cave was an ideal location for studying the complex relationships between human occupation and Ice Age sea-level changes, reflected in geological evidence for raised, high sea-level beaches in the area.

Klasies River Mouth 1 (KRM 1) was excavated by John Wymer between 1966 and 1968. The site proved to be a complex of interconnected caves and rockshelters. Wymer probed 59 ft (17.9 m) of archaeological deposits and estimated that at least another 20 ft (6 m) had been eroded away by the ocean. This constant process of erosion complicated the excavations a great deal. Dissecting the site was an unusual challenge, but an important one, for fragments of human skulls, jaws, isolated teeth, and some broken limb bones lay scattered in the Klasies River deposits. These skeletal remains were those of anatomically modern people, all of them associated with Middle Stone Age artifacts.

The Wymer excavations gave a general impression of the site, but left many questions about the Middle Stone Age occupants unanswered. Since 1984, South African prehistorian Hilary Deacon of Stellenbosch University near Cape Town has been re-sampling the KRM 1 layers with meticulous care. He and his team slowly dig meter-squares following the natural layers of the cave deposits. This "microexcavation" technique enables Deacon to distinguish thin layers of sand that are devoid of artifacts from layers containing many tools and animal bones, accumulated during sporadic human visits to Klasies River. He plots the smallest of features, even individual hearths. Everything is sifted through fine mesh screens, some as fine as 2 mm. At the same time, the excavators collect plastic bags of sediment samples. Back in the laboratory, Deacon and his students break the soil samples down into coarse and fine fractions, so that they can study the soil layers. These tiny grains of sediment provide important clues about climatic conditions at the time they were deposited because many of them are rounded and weathered by the action of the strong winds that blew them into the caves.

After months of peering through high-powered microscopes, Deacon developed a much more complex history of the Klasies River occupation than the original excavators. He also solved the problem of dating in an ingenious way. He selected some of the seashells from the lowermost Middle Stone Age level and sent them to geophysicist Nick Shackleton of Cambridge University, well known for his dating of deep-sea sediments deposited during the last glaciation. Shackleton's oxygen-isotope technique gave a date of about 90,000 years ago or earlier for this level. The two anatomically modern human upper jaw fragments from the same level were estimated to date to a time bracket that extends from before 100,000 years ago to about 80,000 years ago.

There was then a break in human occupation. Then followed another period of regular human visitation, at a time when the sea level was close enough to the cave for the inhabitants to bring numerous seashells back home. The inhabitants relied heavily on shellfish, accumulating a midden as large and extensive as many accumulated by later, post-Ice Age people. This was a surprising discovery, for Middle Stone Age people elsewhere appear to have relied almost exclusively on game and vegetable foods. Again, Deacon relied on oxygen-isotope correlations from deep-sea cores to date this occupation to earlier than 80,000 years ago.

The last Middle Stone Age occupation at the Klasies River sites occurs during what Deacon calls the Upper Member. Traces of many hearths suggest that people used the caves a great deal. Shackleton's laboratory dated the occupation to about 70,000 years ago. It coincided with a period of world-wide lower sea levels between 80,000 and 60,000 years ago.

Hilary Deacon's meticulously detailed dissection of the Klasies River Mouth sites has placed the study of *Homo sapiens* in southern Africa on a much more secure footing. If Deacon's chronology is correct – and most of his colleagues believe it is – Middle Stone Age occupation at Klasies River began during the last interglacial (128,000–100,000 years ago) and continued into the last glaciation, to a time when the Indian Ocean was several miles from the cave complex. Klasies River was in use until at least 80,000 to 60,000 years ago, before being abandoned for the remainder of the last glaciation. Thus, anatomically modern *Homo sapiens sapiens* was flourishing in southern Africa at least 100,000 years ago, during the warm interglacial cycle before the last glaciation cooled world temperatures.

When John Wymer came to study the thousands of stone tools from Klasies River, he found himself dealing with a relatively homogeneous collection of implements and waste debris. Only one episode stood out as exceptional: a series of occupations from the Upper Member, dating to about 70,000 years ago. As at Border Cave, the stone implements from these layers contrast dramatically with those from earlier levels. These stoneworkers emphasized the production of small, thin flakes and flake-blades, which could then be worked into more specialized tools, or used as they were. Not only that, they relied more heavily on non-local rocks, choosing to bring in fine-grained rock of many types from as much as 12 miles (20 km) away. The flake-blades they manufactured were smaller than the earlier ones, less than 2 in (5 cm) long, and were probably struck off with punches. Many of them were snapped, perhaps for use as spear barbs. They turned some of these diminutive flake-blades into knives with blunted backs, some of them crescent or trapeze-shaped, even triangular forms. Once again, these were probably used as spear barbs. Small scrapers, gravers (cutting tools), and borers were also common.

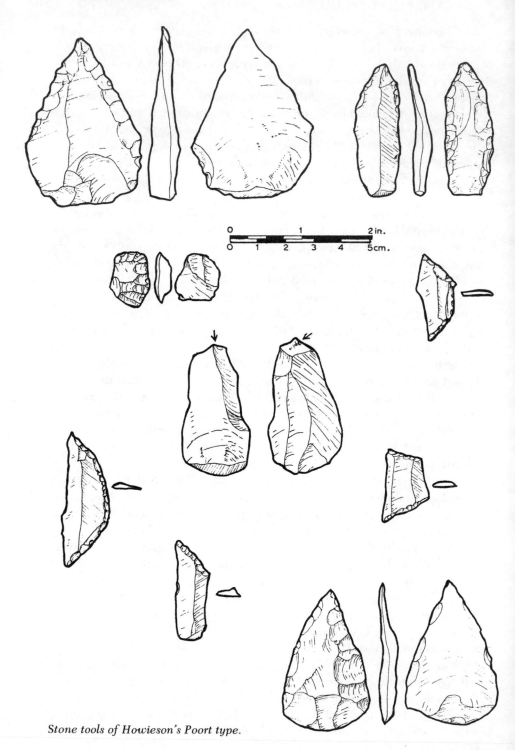

Stone tools of Howieson's Poort type.

The Howieson's Poort Mystery

Wymer and other experts were surprised by this diminutive toolkit and blade technology that suddenly appears, and equally suddenly vanishes. What happened at Klasies River around 70,000 years ago? Had new people settled in the cave, or had the existing, regular visitors simply adopted entirely new artifacts, and perhaps a new lifeway? Since *Homo sapiens sapiens* was associated with earlier Middle Stone Age levels, the new implements could not be attributed to the arrival of anatomically modern people. When Wymer looked around for similar toolkits, he found them not only at Border Cave to the north, but also in the collections excavated in the 1920s from another rockshelter named Howieson's Poort further south along the Cape coast.

Howieson's Poort had been excavated before radiocarbon dating, and, for a long time, local archaeologists assumed that the distinctive artifacts used there were made by late Ice Age people, which would have made them much later than the Klasies River blade technology. Now, thanks to the isotopic dating of Klasies River, it turned out that Howieson's Poort was a much earlier Middle Stone Age toolkit, but one with startlingly "modern" features.

The Klasies River Howieson's Poort episode would be noteworthy if it was an isolated occurrence. It is even more so because Howieson's Poort artifacts occur not only at Border Cave and Klasies River, but in Middle Stone Age sites over a large region, from the woodlands of central Africa north of the Zambezi as far south as the Cape of Good Hope. Everywhere, the artifacts and their associated technology appear, then vanish, submerged in the long-lived and slow-evolving Middle Stone Age technology of the region. There is no obvious explanation. Perhaps, as Hilary Deacon argues, there were advantages in mounting the new, smaller blade fragments on spear shafts, to serve as weapons or knives, for a spear with jagged cutting edges causes larger wounds and heavier blood loss than a simple wooden spear. But why, then, did these superior weapons vanish suddenly? Was it because their makers were unable to develop effective ways of hafting them to wooden shafts? Did such hafting systems emerge much later in the hands of later, and technologically more sophisticated, *Homo sapiens sapiens*, about 50,000 years ago?

Hilary Deacon provides some clues from another of his meticulous excavations, this time at Boomplaas Cave in the Cango Valley north of Oudtshoorn, Cape Province. Boomplaas was first occupied by Howieson's Poort people some time after 80,000 years ago, during the early stages of the last glaciation. The people hunted relatively few game species during this arid period, until about 60,000 years ago when wetter conditions brought more mammalian forms closer to the cave. Howieson's Poort artifacts promptly vanish. As late as 30,000 years ago, the Boomplaas people were still using long flake-blades and other characteristic Middle Stone Age artifacts. Deacon's Boomplaas excavations document another cold snap, about 21,000 to 18,000 years ago. This is when blade tools again become commonplace, this time replacing Middle Stone Age technology permanently.

Deacon considers it significant that Howieson's Poort levels coincide throughout southern Africa with the variable and deteriorating climatic conditions at the beginning of the last glaciation. He believes that the new technology may have been introduced to cope with the greater difficulties in obtaining sufficient food in drier, cooler conditions. What the new technology did was to introduce more standardized artifacts, often, but not always, made from carefully selected stone such as silcrete. Some of these artifacts were hafted as spearheads and barbs. Deacon even boldly theorizes that the styles of hafting tools may have had strong social identity, at a time of increased competition for scarce resources. As stress diminished when local climatic conditions improved about 60,000 years ago, hafted weapons were less socially significant and were abandoned in favor of older forms. Thus, Howieson's Poort artifacts may represent an instance when the superior brain size and enhanced intellectual abilities of *Homo sapiens sapiens* came into play, to create a new and adaptive toolkit that went out of use just as soon as it was no longer needed.

If the Klasies River tools and fossils represent the remains of fully modern humans, how do these finds tie in with the other African evidence on the evolutionary trail to *Homo sapiens sapiens*?

Classifying the African *Homo sapiens* Fossils

At first glance, the evolutionary line between *Homo erectus* and the modern Klasies River fossils is difficult to discern, largely because there are few human remains that date to the critical millennia between about 500,000 and 120,000 years ago. What, for example, is the relationship between the robust Kabwe skull and anatomically modern humans? And can one zero in on one particular archaic *Homo sapiens* population that was the direct ancestor of modern human beings? About the only way to search for answers is to group the known finds into different degrees of anatomical modernity. This is exactly what German paleoanthropologist Günter Bräuer of Hamburg University has done. He studied every existing human fossil from Africa dating to between about 300,000 and 50,000 years ago. He followed a suggestion by a British colleague, Chris Stringer: divide the species *Homo sapiens* into various "grades" based solely on their anatomical characteristics. Bräuer's "grades" provide an interesting scenario for the emergence of anatomically modern human beings.

Bräuer's first grade ("early archaic *Homo sapiens*") includes the Kabwe individuals, another fossil from Bodo in the Afar region of Ethiopia, and some other isolated specimens from as far afield as Hopefield in the Cape Province

The location of some of the major African fossil skulls discussed in the text, and a chart showing Günter Bräuer's chronological ordering of these finds.

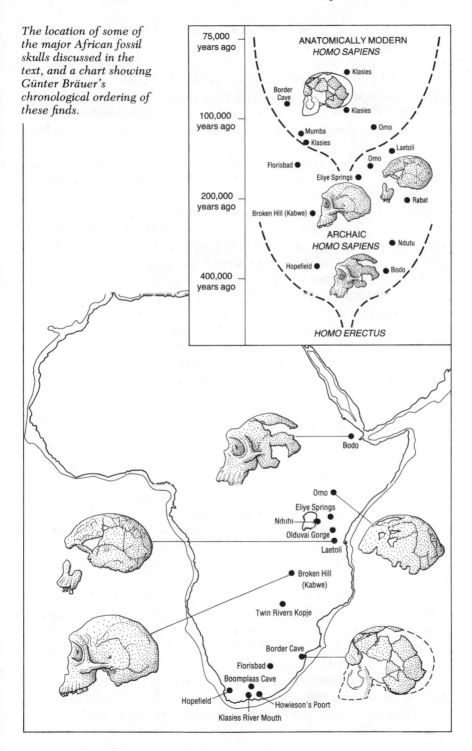

75,000 years ago

ANATOMICALLY MODERN
HOMO SAPIENS

Klasies

Border Cave

Klasies

100,000 years ago

Mumba

Omo

Klasies

Laetoli

Omo

Florisbad

Eliye Springs

Rabat

200,000 years ago

Broken Hill (Kabwe)

ARCHAIC
HOMO SAPIENS

Ndutu

Hopefield

Bodo

400,000 years ago

HOMO ERECTUS

Bodo

Omo

Eliye Springs

Ndutu

Olduvai Gorge

Laetoli

Broken Hill (Kabwe)

Twin Rivers Kopje

Border Cave

Florisbad

Boomplaas Cave

Hopefield

Howieson's Poort

Klasies River Mouth

of South Africa and Ndutu and Eyasi in Tanzania. These robust humans display considerable variation, perhaps some of it due to size differences between the sexes. They are considerably more evolved than *Homo erectus*, with larger brain capacities and other features that are closer to those of anatomically modern *Homo sapiens*. None is securely dated, but all probably lived after 300,000 years ago. Bräuer believes that these highly varied human populations may have been the ancestral forms from which later *Homo sapiens* grades evolved.

Some of the known fossils are less robust and archaic looking. Bräuer groups these into a transitional, "late archaic" grade of *Homo sapiens*. Individuals in this second, general grade combine robust, early archaic features such as sloping foreheads and some brow ridging with many anatomically modern characteristics such as rounded crania. Again, there is great variation among these fossils, which include specimens from Omo in southern Ethiopia, Eliye Springs in Kenya, Laetoli in Tanzania, and from Florisbad in South Africa. Bräuer believes that overall these fossils are anatomically closer to modern *Homo sapiens* than to Kabwe or other more robust humans of earlier millennia. These were the human beings who were widespread in tropical Africa about 150,000 years ago, having evolved slowly over the preceding 100,000 years or more. It was among these highly varied archaic *Homo sapiens* populations that anatomically modern humans evolved. Judging from the Klasies River finds, this took place before 100,000 years ago.

The Omo skull from extreme southern Ethiopia is a heavy-looking, anatomically modern skull found in a level that has been dated by a uranium/ thorium method to about 130,000 years ago. Geologist Karl Butzer believes that this level dates to the last interglacial, and that the anatomically modern skull found in it is at least 100,000 years old. This, together with Klasies River, is the best-dated, early *Homo sapiens sapiens* fossil from sub-Saharan Africa.

Bräuer believes that *Homo sapiens sapiens* could have emerged at more or less the same time over a wide area of Africa. At first, the numbers of truly modern populations may have been very small. But, by some 100,000 to 70,000 years ago, anatomically modern human beings lived everywhere in Africa.

The entire evolutionary process – the transition from developed *Homo erectus* to early archaic *Homo sapiens*, then, finally, into *Homo sapiens sapiens* – does not appear to have occurred rapidly. Rather, it was a slow and continuous development that took as much as half a million years. For this reason, it is very hard to draw a clear taxonomic boundary between *Homo erectus* and archaic *Homo sapiens* on the one hand, and between archaic and anatomically modern *Homo sapiens* on the other. Both *Homo erectus* and archaic *Homo sapiens* display considerable anatomical variation. Perhaps it is significant that the prehistoric Africans of between 300,000 and 100,000 years ago display an even more varied skeletal anatomy, especially in their skull architecture. Bräuer suspects this may be because the final "modernization" of the cranium, the ultimate enlargement of the brain and its related intellectual capacities, occurred much faster than earlier changes sometime late in this time bracket.

The Savanna People

If Robert Foley is correct (Chapter Four), then the earliest *Homo sapiens sapiens* populations in sub-Saharan Africa flourished in a varied savanna environment, where they developed distinctive anatomical characteristics, including improved communication skills and a larger brain size that separated them from their more archaic predecessors.

These people were hunters and foragers who lived in tiny bands of a few families, perhaps only encountering a handful of strangers in their short lives. Among their many skills, they developed new techniques for meat preparation. Some Middle Stone Age sites, such as Border Cave, Klasies River, and Twin Rivers Kopje in Zambia, contain layers of highly fragmented, burnt bone, as if the hunters were drying meat for later use. Similar layers have come from later rockshelters in Malawi, and have been observed at modern game poachers' camps – elongated hearths with thick, white ash and comminuted, burnt bone. The limbs and carcass are first separated, then pounded so that the bones are broken into small pieces. The meat can then be hung more easily on nearby drying racks. Drying meat concentrates the protein, increasing the food value per pound. It also allowed the hunters to store meat, making them less reliant on seasonal movements of their prey. Thus, they could organize their hunting more systematically, in a less-opportunistic way.

Game meat was not their only source of food. Without question, wild plant foods collected by the women were of paramount importance, perhaps eaten more frequently than animal flesh. By 130,000 years ago, plant grinders and pounders were in widespread use, so less-palatable meat and vegetable foods could be processed, then cooked, before consumption. Everything points to a more efficient hunter-gatherer lifeway, one based not only on game and plants, but in places on fish, shellfish, and some sea mammals as well.

In a sense, Africa was a giant nursery for modern humanity, a relatively undemanding environment where food was fairly plentiful, where Ice Age climatic changes were relatively benign. Above all, human beings here were used to relatively open habitats, that extended from North Africa to Ethiopia and the Horn of Africa, then far south toward the southern tip of the continent. For much of the last 720,000 years of the Ice Age, sub-Saharan Africa's peoples were isolated from the rest of the Old World by the arid wastes of the Sahara. But, during brief interglacial periods, much of the desert became open grassland, creating a favorable environment for animals and humans used to open country that extended far north, to the margins of the Mediterranean world. We must now examine this remarkable desert in more detail, and assess the role that the Sahara played in the evolution and spread of modern humans from what may have been their ancient homeland.

PART TWO

DIASPORA

"On the contrary, Watson, you can see everything. You fail, however, to reason from what you see. You are too timid in drawing your inferences."

Sherlock Holmes, in *The Adventure of the Blue Carbuncle*

"The data do not speak for themselves. I have been in rooms with data and listened very carefully. They never said a word."

Milford Wolpoff, 1975

CHAPTER SIX

The Saharan Pump

If the geneticists are right – and, as we saw in Chapter Five, there is archaeological and fossil evidence to support them – then anatomically modern humans had evolved in sub-Saharan Africa at least 100,000 years ago, perhaps earlier. The genetic family tree then branches in two directions. One branch is that of anatomically modern Africans, represented today by the San peoples of southern Africa and related prehistoric populations of the savanna. The other is of non-Africans, of modern humans who left Africa and settled other continents.

The Noah's Ark hypothesis is sometimes called the "Out of Africa" theory, and rightly so, for it highlights a key element in the entire argument. If *Homo sapiens sapiens* did originate in sub-Saharan Africa, how, when, and why did modern humans spread into North Africa and other continents?

The Great Desert

The word Sahara conjures up images of arid emptiness, of endless, rolling sandy plains, and of lost, verdant oases where palm trees grow and the weary traveler finds rest by unexpected, bubbling streams. This is the desert of Beau Geste, of romantic novelists and Victorian stereotypes – the greatest desert on earth. The reality is much more varied, hardly surprising when one considers what an enormous area the desert covers.

Together, the Sahara and the Nile Valley occupy about half the entire African continent, an area that is as large as the United States, including Alaska. The desert is surrounded on three sides by the ocean. Its northwestern margins end at the convoluted Atlas ranges of Morocco. To the east, the sand laps at the edge of the Nile Valley, an oasis for humans and animals since the very beginning of the Great Ice Age, or Pleistocene epoch, some 1.6 million years ago. The southern edge passes gradually into stunted grassland, then dry savanna. The frontiers of the Sahara change every year, as droughts come and go and occasional cycles of higher rainfall allow grass to grow a few miles further south than in the previous years.

Just like the Great Australian Desert, most of the Sahara's land surface is between 650 and 1,650 ft (198–502 m) above sea level, with the main highlands, the Atlas Mountains and the Ethiopian massif, on opposite corners. Other mountains rise between them, at intervals of about 600 miles (965 km). During wetter cycles of the Great Ice Age, these were the hydrographic centers from which rivers radiated, rivers that filled shallow lakes and fed into the Nile and Niger river systems at the northeastern and southwestern corners of the desert.

Today, the Sahara is one of the hottest places in the world. Dry, descending northeasterly airstreams mantle it for most of the year, raising temperatures as high as 100 degrees F (37 deg. C) on more days of the year than almost anywhere else in the world. Rainfall is less than 1.5 in (3.8 cm) annually over much of the Sahara, and even less in many areas. Evaporation losses from both surface water and vegetation are the highest on the globe. Vast tracts of the desert support no animal or human life at all, nor have they throughout historical times. The ancient Egyptians penetrated far up the Nile into what is now the Sudan, but they never braved the arid fastness of the desert. The Romans never ventured much further south than a few hundred miles beyond the fertile coastal lands of North Africa. Until the arrival of the domesticated camel enabled Berber pastoralists from the north to cross the Sahara to West Africa in the first millennium AD, tropical Africa lay outside the ken of the Mediterranean world. Judging from the large gaps in the archaeological record from the desert, it was just as formidable a barrier in earlier, arid millennia. But during wetter Ice Age interglacials, and as recently as 8,000 years ago, the Sahara was a landscape of arid grassland, where hunters and cattle herders roamed.

Scientific fieldwork in the Sahara is never easy, even with the benefits of all-terrain vehicles and modern technology. Many archaeologists have relied on the camel for transportation in the field, packing out their finds in saddlebags. Working with botanists and geologists, they have drawn back the curtain on an ancient, transient landscape. They have brought back well-preserved hippopotamus bones from the Sahara's river beds, photographed vivid rock paintings from small caves and rockshelters high in the Hoggar and other massifs, collected stone artifacts and clay potsherds from lakeside camps more than 8,000 years old. They have also found traces of far-earlier human inhabitants, of people who once hunted across the Sahara's plains tens of thousands of years ago.

The Pump Effect

In many ways the Sahara can be likened to a giant pump, one that sucked animals and people in during wetter climatic cycles, then expelled them to its fringes when arid conditions returned. The pump may have pushed out many species of African mammals and *Homo erectus* into the Mediterranean Basin and Europe, perhaps as early as 900,000 years ago, via the Nile Valley and the Sinai Peninsula. And it is reasonable to suppose that similar population movements out of an expanding desert occurred later in prehistory. Thus, the Sahara could have served as a barrier between the Mediterranean and tropical Africa for long periods of prehistoric time. During very dry conditions, about the only way to travel north would have been through the Nile Valley. However, as Victorian explorers found to their cost, the dense, swampy Sudd country of the southern Sudan makes easy movement upstream or downstream extremely difficult. "The same jungle prevails on all sides, excluding all view," wrote John Hanning Speke, who journeyed to the source of the Nile in 1862. Since the Sahara was desert when Speke made his crossing, it is reasonable to suppose that similar conditions prevailed along the Nile in earlier dry episodes. It may be, then, that the arid wastes of the Sahara bottled up *Homo sapiens sapiens* in sub-Saharan Africa for tens of thousands of years, until the gateway to the north opened up hunting grounds in the desert.

Unfortunately, we still know very little about details of the climatic fluctuations in the Sahara before about 90,000 years ago. The best way to reconstruct climatic change in the desert is by mapping the shores of shallow lakes that covered wide areas of the wilderness. French climatologists have combined such surveys with studies of ancient freshwater organisms called diatoms and also pollen taken from long-buried lake beds. They found that the water levels of Saharan lakes have fluctuated constantly during the past 300,000 years. Many of these changes resulted from local drainage and rainfall changes, but others from larger-scale Ice Age fluctuations in climate. At times, cold polar air penetrated the Sahara, bringing drier conditions to the desert. Such incursions were especially common during the last glaciation, after about 90,000 years ago.

Much of the French research has focused on Lake Chad at the southern edge of the desert on the borders of northern Nigeria, Chad, and Niger. Today, the lake is a shadow of its former self 120,000 years ago. It once filled a vast basin larger than the Caspian Sea, at a time when the southern boundary of the desert was several hundred miles further south than today. The shores of this inland sea fluctuated constantly through the Ice Age. The French studies revealed sequences of wind-blown sands, alternating with lake deposits containing diatom species that were a mirror of cooler and more humid conditions, and of rapid desertification. One particularly dry period lasted from about 20,000 to some 13,000 years ago, a span of 7,000 years that coincided with the peak of the last glaciation.

Earlier fluctuations are much harder to date and identify. A team of French geochemists led by Charles Causse of the French National Research Center have dated long dried-up deposits from Azzel Matti and Erg Chech in the western Sahara. Their researches show that the last humid period in the

Sahara ended about 90,000 years ago, and was followed by a long period of dry conditions in the desert until about 10,000 years ago, the approximate time span of much of the last glaciation. This would mean that the Sahara effectively sealed off sub-Saharan Africa from the rest of the Stone Age world for more than 80,000 years. Modern humans could have migrated north out of sub-Saharan regions before 90,000 years ago, or after 10,000 years ago – but not in between.

Fossil Evidence from North Africa

The fossil fragments that chronicle human evolution north of sub-Saharan Africa are confined to North Africa, to the fringes of the great desert. *Homo erectus* fossils have come from Ternifine, Thomas Quarries, and Salé in Morocco, dating to between 500,000 and 200,000 years ago. Here, as elsewhere, there was an evolutionary trend toward an archaic form of *Homo sapiens*. The Sidi Abderrahman quarries on the Atlantic coast of Morocco yielded a cave containing jaw fragments of archaic *Homo sapiens* and 200,000-year-old hand axes.

Fragments of archaic *Homo sapiens* have also come from other localities, mainly in Morocco. In 1939, the famous Harvard physical anthropologist Carleton Coon unearthed some juvenile archaic *Homo sapiens* fragments in the High Cave near Mugharet el-Aliya in northwestern Morocco. They were found before the days of radiocarbon dating, and are estimated to be later than 100,000 years old. The Jebel Irhoud site on the Atlantic coast of Morocco has produced two archaic *Homo sapiens* skulls and a jaw associated with artifacts made on Levallois and disc cores dating to between 60,000 and 40,000 years ago. Two other late archaic *Homo sapiens* fragments came from a 47,000-year-old occupation level in the Haua Fteah Cave in Libya in the 1950s. More skull fragments, this time to all intents and purposes anatomically modern *Homo sapiens sapiens*, from Dar-es-Soltan, also in northwestern Morocco, date to between 40,000 and 30,000 years ago. Another northwestern Moroccan site, Temara, has produced a modern-looking skull fragment estimated to date to about 30,000 years ago.

In contrast to sub-Saharan Africa, where there is at least some continuity in the fossil record, the North African finds quite clearly divide into two widely separated groups, those dating to between 500,000 and 200,000 years ago, and the much younger archaic *Homo sapiens* finds of the North African coastal region that can be assigned to the last glaciation. The latter, in turn, give way to anatomically modern specimens, at a so far unknown date. These scattered finds yield no clues as to what evolutionary processes were afoot, but there are said to be some anatomical continuities between the earlier and later fossils. Did anatomically modern humans evolve out of early *Homo sapiens* populations in North Africa, or did *Homo sapiens sapiens* develop in sub-

Saharan Africa, then spread across the Sahara during the last interglacial, between about 128,000 and 100,000 years ago? Some authorities like Chris Stringer point to the similarities between the skulls of the Ethiopian Omo I fossil of at least 100,000 years ago (Chapter Five) and the Qafzeh/Skhūl skeletons from the Near East (Chapter Eight) as evidence for replacement. In reality, however, the fossil record is simply too exiguous to provide a definitive answer. Can we, then, identify the appearance of *Homo sapiens sapiens* from artifacts and other cultural remains, specifically from evidence of dramatic technological change or radically new hunting methods?

Prehistoric Settlement in the Sahara

Like the sub-Saharan savanna, the Sahara was a highly favorable environment for hunters and foragers during the last interglacial about 128,000–90,000 years ago, the time period when *Homo sapiens sapiens* appeared south of the Sahara. The climate was wetter and cooler. Temperate vegetation covered much of the northern Sahara, with arid scrub, while Mediterranean oaks grew on the central desert massifs. The grassland and savanna at the southern boundaries of the Sahara extended much further north. Thus, it was possible for human populations to range far and wide over the desert. Pollen samples document a semi-arid climate, but one that brought a rich grazing fauna onto the Saharan grasslands. During the dry season, both humans and animals stayed close to waterholes and permanent lakes. Both moved out onto the plains when the rains came.

Veteran African archaeologist Desmond Clark bases this model on modern observations in East Africa today, where elephants have been seen moving as much as 50 miles (80 km) in 8 days to find water. It would not have been difficult for small, highly mobile hunting bands to have followed game on such movements. For example, in Kenya's Tsavo National Park, the mean home range of elephants is over 600 sq. miles (144,500 ha) in an arid environment with between 10 and 12 in (25–30 cm) of rain a year. Even in "wetter" periods, the Sahara was still considerably drier than Tsavo, so the ranges of both elephants and other game animals, as well as their human predators, must have been considerably larger than those of hunter-gatherers living in wetter environments. Under this scenario, prehistoric Saharan hunters could have moved as much as 125–200 miles (201–321 km) a year, although their actual range was probably much less. Thus, it was possible for even a sparse hunter-gatherer population to cover large areas within a few millennia.

Aterians and Tanged Points

By some 200,000 years ago, stoneworking techniques and the artifacts made with them had become more varied throughout Africa, more accommodating

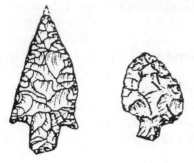

An Aterian tanged point and tanged scraper from northwest Africa.

of local needs and conditions. By now, the makers everywhere were archaic *Homo sapiens*. Just as in sub-Saharan Africa, new ways of making flakes came into use along the North African coast and in the Sahara, the distinctive Levallois and disc-core technologies among them. At first, the new methods were used occasionally, as the need arose. But by 150,000 years ago, the primeval hand axes of earlier times had largely given way to the lighter Middle Stone Age implements that relied almost entirely on Levallois and disc-core techniques.

Many Middle Stone Age peoples carefully chipped the bases of flakes and flake-blades to thin them, presumably for easier mounting in forked clefts cut in the ends of wooden spear shafts or handles. Saharan and North African hunters went further and fashioned the bases of what appear to be spear points, knives, and scrapers into crude projections, simple tangs that could be stuck into the end of a handle. The tang was an ingenious device, for it enabled the toolmaker to mount his artifact, made on a Levallois or disc core, in a wooden shaft with the working edge set to maximum advantage. These tanged artifacts are the distinctive mark of the so-called "Aterian," named after the el-Ater cave in Morocco where such tools were first discovered.

Aterian tanged artifacts occur throughout the Sahara north of a line from Dakar in Senegal to Khartoum in the Sudan. They occur all the way from the Atlantic coast to the oases of Egypt's Western Desert, but not in the Nile Valley. The Aterians who lived at Erg Tihoudaine in southern Algeria in the central Sahara, perhaps as early as 100,000 years ago, were probably typical of many groups. They took elephant, buffalo, and wild cattle from the woodland and grassland, where water was abundant. The hunters also caught fish, and ate crocodile and hippopotamus.

With small, highly mobile populations, the Sahara probably never supported more than a few thousand Aterians during the late last interglacial, dispersed in dozens of tiny family bands. When the desert dried up, probably fairly rapidly, about 90,000 years ago, Saharan populations may have plummeted, as increasingly dry conditions expelled both animals and humans to its margins.

The Aterian was probably but one of several widespread hunter-gatherer cultures in the Sahara at the end of the last interglacial, for there is also evidence of Middle Stone Age-like artifacts similar to those being made in the savannas south of the desert around Lake Chad at about the same time. Can one, however, argue that the Aterians with their tanged points were the first anatomically modern humans north of sub-Saharan Africa? The answer must be no, for not only have Aterian-like tools been found with archaic *Homo sapiens* fossils at Mugharet el-Aliya in Morocco, but also the general technology is very similar to that of Middle Stone Age (Middle Paleolithic) work elsewhere in the Near East, and to Middle Stone Age technique south of the desert. More likely, the Aterian was a local variation of an ancient and slowly evolving technology effective in open grassland environments. It may, however, have been *Homo sapiens sapiens* who introduced gradual refinements into this technology that are reflected in the greater use of hafted weapons and smaller, more specialized tools after 100,000 years ago. Such artifacts may have been especially adaptive in the cooler, drier conditions of the last glaciation.

The Nile

While early Aterian groups were flourishing in the Sahara during the last interglacial, the Nile River was flowing at a much higher level than today. Nile-dwellers caught large numbers of fish, just like their contemporaries far to the south, the Klasies River people (Chapter Five). Their stone tools include Levallois and disc cores, and points and scrapers like those found widely over the Near East and along the North African coast at this time. However, some groups also made lanceolate spear points and other artifacts that are much more like the kind of Middle Stone Age toolkits used in African environments to the south.

Desmond Clark wonders whether these latter tools formed part of a sub-Saharan hunters' technology used in wooded savanna areas where people were butchering large land mammals such as elephant, African buffalo, and wild cattle. The extension of this traditional savanna-related technology into the Nile Valley may represent the spread northward of African populations from desertic regions to the south and west during the last interglacial. Conceivably, these were fully modern *Homo sapiens* populations, though this is a matter for speculation.

"Out of Africa?"

The Noah's Ark hypothesis argues that *Homo sapiens sapiens* evolved in Africa, then spread out of this homeland into the Near East and other parts of the Old World. Such archaeological and paleontological evidence as we have

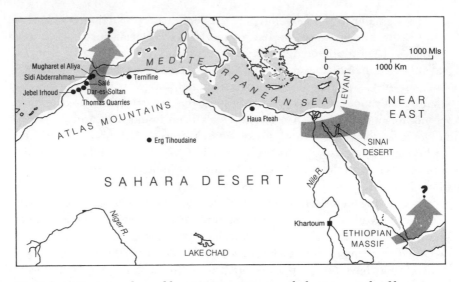

The Sahara Desert and possible migration routes north during periods of lower sea level.

from sub-Saharan Africa suggests that both early *Homo sapiens* and *Homo sapiens sapiens* evolved on the savanna over many millennia. Fully modern humans were flourishing south of the Sahara by at least 100,000 years ago, an earlier date for *Homo sapiens sapiens* than any other in the world. If we accept this proposition, we are left with two important questions. First, did *Homo sapiens sapiens* evolve only in sub-Saharan Africa, or in the Sahara and North Africa as well? Second, what role did the Sahara play in the spread of modern humans out of their homeland?

North Africa has yielded even fewer fossil hominids than the sub-Saharan savanna. Nevertheless, physical anthropologist Günter Bräuer believes that there are clear signs of at least some anatomical continuity between North African fossil hominids of before 200,000 years ago, and the scattered archaic *Homo sapiens* specimens that date to 100,000 years ago, and in turn with later *Homo sapiens sapiens* dating to after 40,000 years ago in the same general region. It has to be said, however, that this continuity is only superficially documented by the present fossils from North Africa, and may even be an illusion. There is no theoretical reason why *Homo sapiens sapiens* should not have evolved from earlier *Homo sapiens* populations throughout the African continent, but if such evolution took place, so far we have no fossil grounds for arguing it.

Whether *Homo sapiens sapiens* evolved in North Africa or not, there can be no question that the Sahara played an important part in the intermingling of human populations north and south of the desert. During the last interglacial, from about 128,000 to around 90,000 years ago, it would have been possible for people to move from sub-Saharan Africa across the Sahara to North Africa and the Nile Valley. The desert "pumped in" hitherto isolated populations that intermingled, and perhaps interbred, for thousands of years. If the dates for the Klasies River and Omo *Homo sapiens sapiens* fossils are correct at around 120,000–100,000 years ago, then at least some of these populations were probably anatomically modern.

By about 90,000 years ago, and probably a little earlier, the Sahara again dried up, and the desert pump expelled scattered populations of anatomically modern humans not only back into sub-Saharan Africa, but toward the shores of the Mediterranean and into the Nile Valley as well. If the "Out of Africa" theorists are to be believed, by at least 90,000 years ago, and perhaps considerably earlier, some of these *Homo sapiens sapiens* populations moved across the Sinai into the Near East. Before, however, we follow the evolutionary course of events in the Near East, we must take a closer look at the European Neanderthals, the indigenous inhabitants of new and very diverse environments in Eurasia, into which modern humans were now moving.

CHAPTER SEVEN

The European Neanderthals

While the Sahara was drying up rapidly 90,000 years ago, the world was in the early stages of a sustained deep freeze, the last prolonged cycle of Ice Age cold, known in Europe as the Würm glaciation. The effects of this glaciation were felt all over the world, for the oceans fell to more than 300 ft (91 m) below modern levels in places, joining Siberia to Alaska and the Southeast Asian mainland to the offshore islands. Britain was joined to France, and Turkey to Europe across the Bosphorus, making the Black Sea a lake. The Mediterranean was a chilly, Ice Age sea. Its eastern and northern shores were part of the world of the Neanderthals, descendants of ancient *Homo erectus* populations that had radiated out of Africa hundreds of thousands of years earlier.

The Neanderthal World

Between about 125,000 and some 45,000 years ago, and in some areas later, Neanderthals lived over a vast tract of the Old World, from the shores of the Atlantic in the west deep into Eurasia in the east. There were Neanderthal bands flourishing in Spain, along the northern Mediterranean coast, by the Black Sea, and in the Near East. These tough, skilled hunters displayed considerable biological and cultural diversity, and were capable of surviving extremely cold winters. They had evolved from earlier *Homo sapiens* populations during the last interglacial, and adapted successfully to the onset of the last glaciation. They lived in an Ice Age world unimaginably different from our own, and from the African homeland of early *Homo sapiens sapiens*.

Thanks to complex geological mapping projects and deep-sea core borings in many corners of the Mediterranean, we know something of that sea's shorelines during the last intensely cold cycle of the Würm glaciation, between about 27,000 and 15,000 years ago. Deep-sea core samples tell us that relatively similar cold conditions existed during earlier stages of the Würm glaciation. All indications are that the Mediterranean assumed much the same configuration then as it did during the peak of the last cold cycle. Thus, intelligent extrapolations from data for the later period are possible.

Judith Shackleton of the University of Cambridge, and her colleagues Tjerd van Andel and Curtis Runnels of Stanford University, have shown that the Mediterranean was at its smallest, about 393 ft (120 m) below modern levels, between about 23,000 and 15,000 years ago. There were large coastal plains up to 50 miles (80 km) wide off eastern Spain, and between the Pyrenees and the Alpes Maritimes of southern France. Corsica and Sardinia formed a single island. East of Tunisia and north of Libya, a large coastal plain extended toward Sicily and Europe, with only 37 miles (59 km) of open water in between. A narrow land bridge joined Sicily to southern Italy, but the Straits of Gibraltar were always open. Even at the height of the glaciation, about 5 miles (8 km) of tidal strait separated Africa from Europe.

Both 18,000 and 65,000 years ago, the northern shores of the Mediterranean were bounded by temperate and boreal forests, passing into treeless tundra at the foothills of the Alps, where the arctic landscape began. Great Alpine glaciers fingered far down the mountains toward the rolling plains of Italy, Germany, and France. Vast ice sheets had flowed south from Scandinavia, mantling not only Denmark, Sweden, and northern Germany, but the Low Countries, the North Sea, and much of Britain as well.

South of the northern ice sheets, a seemingly boundless, open landscape of scrub-covered and treeless arctic steppe-tundra stretched across Europe from the Atlantic coast as far east as the Ural Mountains and beyond. The tundra was a harsh, unrelenting place, with 9-month winters and short, warm summers. At first glance, the landscape might have appeared deserted, but a closer look would have revealed scattered herds of woolly rhinoceros, mammoth, reindeer, and other arctic animals. The topography was more broken to the south and west, where deep river valleys dissected the rolling tundra, sheltered locales that served as arctic refuges for trees, diverse animal populations, and for the human beings who preyed upon them.

This unfamiliar, immensely cold Ice Age environment was the home of the indigenous people of Eurasia – the Neanderthals.

The Rise of the Neanderthals

Between about 900,000 and 700,000 years ago, the first humans to settle in these northern lands had migrated north from Africa, together with the many species of animals they hunted. The first Europeans and Asians were small *Homo erectus* bands, originally tropical and subtropical hunters, who were adapted to live within a range of temperatures around 80 degrees F (27 deg. C). This particular temperature is the critical level at which humans neither cool nor warm their bodies, neither sweat nor shiver. We can withstand surprisingly large variations about this temperature, by maintaining an artificial microclimate around ourselves as near to this temperature as possible. For *Homo erectus* to be able to adapt to the more temperate climate of Europe and Asia, it was necessary not only to tame fire but to have both effective shelter and clothing to protect against heat loss. *Homo erectus* probably survived the winters by maintaining permanent fires, and by storing dried meat and other foods for use in the lean months.

The *Homo erectus* populations of Eurasia were no doubt sparse and scattered, but their hunting and foraging adaptation flourished with surprisingly little change for half a million years. Nevertheless a slow evolutionary trajectory propelled them toward more advanced human forms. Around 400,000 years ago, Europeans still showed a general resemblance to *Homo erectus*. Later fossils of some 300,000–200,000 years ago from such places as Swanscombe gravel pit on the River Thames near London and Steinheim in Germany show more Neanderthal-like features. Direct ancestors of the Neanderthals were living in Europe before about 130,000 years ago. By perhaps 100,000 years ago, the Neanderthals were firmly established both in Europe and Western Asia.

Who Were the Neanderthals?

The Neanderthals take their name from a fossil that came to light during quarrying operations in Germany's Neander Valley in 1856. Controversy surrounded the find from the beginning. In February 1857, anatomist Hermann Schaffhausen told the Lower Rhine Medical and Natural History Society that the recently discovered bones were those of a barbarous individual, a representative of a "very ancient human race." But other anatomists disagreed. One said that the skull was that of a Mongolian cossack from the Russian army that had chased Napoleon across the Rhine in 1814. The German scientist Rudolph Virchow, the most eminent anatomist of the day, declared the bow-legged fossil a recently deceased pathological idiot suffering from rickets.

By far the most thorough analysis came at the hands of British biologist Thomas Huxley, famous for his firm support of Charles Darwin and his theory

A 19th-century cross-sectional sketch of the cave in the Neander Valley where a fossil skull was unearthed in 1856, and after which the Neanderthals take their name.

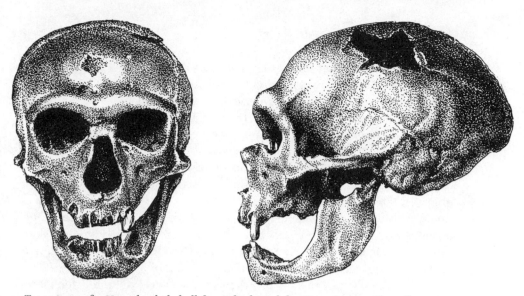

Two views of a Neanderthal skull from the burial discovered at La Chapelle-aux-Saints, southwest France, in 1908.

of evolution and natural selection. Like Schaffhausen, he realized at once that the Neanderthal skull was of a very ancient human being, not of a modern idiot. Huxley's study of the Neanderthal bones appeared in his famous essay on human evolution, *Man's Place in Nature*, published in 1863, and this brilliantly reasoned discourse started the longest running controversy in paleoanthropology: Who were the Neanderthals? Were they direct ancestors of *Homo sapiens sapiens*? What do they tell us about the nature of human evolution during the last glaciation? These questions have taken on a much greater immediacy now that both genetic and fossil clues point to tropical Africa as the cradle of modern humanity, for we know that Neanderthals were the indigenous inhabitants of Europe when *Homo sapiens sapiens* appeared in the Mediterranean world.

From the very beginning, Neanderthals have been haunted by a primitive, brutish image. Huxley's essay, and his claims of human ancestry among the apes, caused a shock of horror among devout Victorians. "Let us hope it is not true," cried one anonymous lady in distress, "but if it is, let us pray it will not become generally known." In time, science prevailed, and the Neanderthals passed into popular literature as cartoon-like, savage cave people, complete with wooden clubs and violent habits.

This crude image of the Neanderthals came in part from the researches of French anthropologist Marcellin Boule. In 1908, a complete Neanderthal burial came to light at the La-Chapelle-aux-Saints rockshelter in the Vézère Valley, southwest France. Boule studied this unique find with great care, inadvertently developing a classic caricature of a Stone Age cave man in the process. He described the La Chapelle-aux-Saints man as brutish, a hunter who slouched in a stooped position, head poked forward on a short, thick neck.

The man's brain was at least as large as that of modern people, but Boule claimed that the La Chapelle individual was slow-witted, that he lacked the developed face and forehead to give him the intellectual powers of his successors. Furthermore, he argued, the Neanderthals were not on the direct evolutionary track to modern humans: he called them *Homo neanderthalensis*, to separate them from our own species.

Boule and like-minded scientists conceived of human evolution as a series of universal stages, of a "Neanderthal Phase of Man" that immediately preceded the abrupt appearance of *Homo sapiens sapiens* in French caves. Boule considered the Neanderthals an archaic and extinct species, an evolutionary *cul-de-sac*. When the notorious (and forged) Piltdown skull came to light in England in 1912, Boule claimed that this was a representative of the "ancestor on the direct line of recent species of man, *Homo sapiens*."

Boule's so-called "Pre-sapiens" theory was widely accepted for many years, often accompanied by a prehistoric scenario that had the Neanderthals of Europe "swept aside" by superior, anatomically modern humans. Physical anthropologist Ales Hrdlička of the Smithsonian Institution in Washington was almost alone in rejecting this view. Suspicious of the "monstrous" hybrid of Piltdown's ape-like jaw and modern-looking skull, Hrdlička argued for a single line of human evolution, with the Neanderthals on the direct line of human ancestry. In proposing this scheme, he was strongly influenced by new Neanderthal discoveries from eastern and central Europe that displayed considerable anatomical variation, some appearing much more modern-like than the robust, beetle-browed western Neanderthals. Only a few scientists, among them German anatomist Franz Weidenreich, accepted Hrdlička's theory that the Neanderthals had evolved into modern humans outside Europe.

After World War II, dramatic developments in paleoanthropology and evolutionary theory ushered in a new era. New synthetic theories of evolution that called on genetics, population studies, and paleontology produced more rational thinking about hominid taxonomy. In 1953, the Piltdown skull was exposed as a forgery, while the search for early African hominids intensified. These developments caused a new generation of scientists to take another long look at the La Chapelle skeleton. They had the advantage over Boule, for they could draw on a much larger reservoir of Neanderthal remains, not only from France, but from central Europe, the Near East, and as far east as Uzbekistan in central Asia. Boule was proved wrong on the physical characteristics, but in other respects he may have been on the right track. There was no more primitive brain, clumsy walking, or short, thick neck. As for the bowed legs, Boule had not noticed the man's severe arthritis of the spine, more than sufficient reason for a stooped posture. The Neanderthals were agile, strong people, with the ability to run fast, and with at least some well-developed intellectual abilities.

To this day, physical anthropologists are still deeply divided on the Neanderthals. One school of thought espouses what has been called a compromise position between the earlier Boule and Hrdlička theories. This "Pre-Neanderthal" scheme argues that certain less-specialized Neanderthal fossils were the ancestors of both *Homo sapiens sapiens* and the anatomically more extreme Neanderthals who flourished in western Europe during the last glaciation. The Pre-Neanderthal hypothesis has been vigorously argued by physical anthropologists C. Loring Brace and Milford Wolpoff. The latter has made it a cornerstone of the Candelabra theory of modern human origins, arguing that *Homo erectus* populations living in relative isolation in both Europe and Asia slowly evolved into several archaic versions of *Homo sapiens*, one of these being the Neanderthals, and then into *Homo sapiens sapiens*. There must have been some gene flow from mixing of these regional populations, Wolpoff theorizes, otherwise they might have evolved into distinct species. Under this argument, "transitional" human beings, represented by anatomically "transitional" fossils and, culturally, by "transitional" artifact collections, can be identified in fossils from several areas, including central Europe and Southeast Asia. Thus, anatomically modern humans evolved not only in Africa, but in other regions of the world as well. Finally, argues Wolpoff, there must have been a close relationship between the Neanderthals and modern humans, because both used quite similar stone tools and ritually buried their dead.

The opposing viewpoint, espoused by scholars such as Chris Stringer and Neanderthal specialist Erik Trinkaus of the University of New Mexico, argues from the same fossils that the European Neanderthals were a specialized offshoot from the main evolutionary line to *Homo sapiens sapiens*. Stringer, Trinkaus, and others who support the Noah's Ark hypothesis, point to a unique suite of archaic anatomical features that serve to distinguish the European Neanderthals from modern humans. We must now take a closer look at these supposedly archaic features, to see whether the Noah's Ark theory is bolstered or weakened by this anatomical evidence.

Neanderthal Anatomy

In comparison with modern human skulls, Neanderthal crania are long, broad, and low, with sloping foreheads and a characteristic bun-shaped projection at the rear of the head. They contrast sharply with modern humans, who have high, domed foreheads. Thick, strongly arched brow ridges and large and projecting faces are common to all Neanderthals. Their jaws and teeth were large and robust, whereas *Homo sapiens sapiens* evolved smaller mandibles and dentition. Scholars who have studied the Neanderthals have tended to emphasize the face and skull at the expense of the rest of the body – the postcranial anatomy. Marcellin Boule and others assumed that they had a basically modern postcranial anatomy, an assumption that has proved wrong. Neanderthal movement patterns were indeed very similar to those of modern humans, as were such features as relative neck length and spine curvature, but there were significant differences in overall strength and musculature.

Erik Trinkaus has evaluated these differences by using modern functional anatomy as a yardstick for the purpose. He even compared minute muscular attachments with those of modern people. The Neanderthals had broad shoulders and very powerfully developed upper arm musculature, much more powerful than that of *Homo sapiens sapiens*. Their fingers were identical in form to modern ones, but Neanderthal thumbs were capable of exerting exceptional force during normal grips. In contrast, early anatomically modern humans had much less powerful grips.

The same difference in robusticity is found in the lower limbs. Compared with modern humans, Neanderthals had much more sturdy leg bones and powerful knees, which enabled them to generate considerable force around the knee. Judging from the few postcranial remains from earlier European humans, this was a feature that the Neanderthals inherited from archaic human forms. This robustness was an important part of the Neanderthals' biological adaptation. It enabled them to generate and sustain more strength and habitually higher levels of activity than most modern humans. However, maintaining such a body was costly in terms of energy, an important consideration for hunter-gatherer populations that, like most groups of people, were close to the limits of their energy resources. Trinkaus argues that the postcranial anatomy of all Ice Age peoples was pushed to the limits of its strength and durability during the quest for food. The decrease in robusticity in anatomically modern people suggests that they no longer needed this strong build to survive and reproduce successfully. Conceivably, substantial improvements in technology and major change in social behavior that fostered cooperation in the hunt compensated for the lighter build of the Neanderthals' modern successors.

Trinkaus has also observed other important differences in Neanderthal anatomy. They used their thumbs in different ways, and may have had more movement in their joints than we do. The range of movements they made with their thumbs was perhaps necessitated by their artifacts and the ways in which they used them. The Neanderthal pubic bone in the pelvis is unusually long, a feature which probably enabled more energy-efficient walking with a robust, heavy body.

The Neanderthals have relatively short forearms and lower legs compared with longer-limbed modern humans. Overall body proportions are similar, but the extremities – lower arms and lower legs – are shorter. This is widely believed to be an adaptation to cold climates, since a considerable amount of the body's surface area, from which heat is lost, is in the extremities. Trinkaus

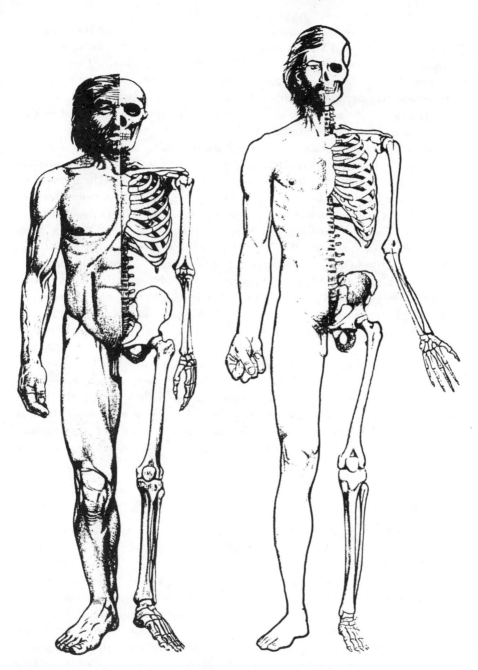

The stocky European Neanderthal physique (left) compared with that of a fully modern human.

has shown by precise measurements and statistical correlations on arctic Eskimos and tropical Africans that there is a close connection between mean annual temperature and mean proportions of the lower limbs. From this, he argues that the European Neanderthals were adapted to living in the cold, whereas the more lightly built *Homo sapiens sapiens* was heat-adapted.

Trinkaus believes that modern humans developed several key skills that more than compensated for their less-adaptive anatomy. He thinks they were more adept at generating heat than Neanderthals, internally through the metabolism of high-energy diets and/or externally with carefully controlled fires and improved dwellings. They may also have improved heat retention around the body with better, insulating clothing. Generating heat internally implies an enhanced ability to hunt game animals, especially those in prime condition that had good fat reserves. Also, modern people probably routinely constructed far more effective hearths than those of Neanderthals that both kept fires burning for extended periods of time and radiated heat efficiently. These kinds of cultural innovations were probably a major factor in the differences in limb proportions between the Neanderthals and anatomically modern humans.

Anatomical studies, then, tend to support the Noah's Ark theory that the European Neanderthals were an evolutionary dead-end, contributing little or nothing to the physical characteristics of modern humans. But, we may recall, Milford Wolpoff of the Candelabra school does not argue the case for continuity solely on anatomical grounds. He believes that there was continuity of culture, both material and spiritual – material, in the shape of technological adaptations shared by Neanderthals and modern humans; spiritual, in that both groups buried their dead. Do Neanderthal hunting and ritual practices support this contention?

Neanderthal Lifeways

Neanderthals adapted to considerable environmental extremes, everything from the temperate Mediterranean to the harsh glacial regimens in Europe and Eurasia. But their hunting never achieved the high degree of efficiency attained by later Stone Age bands. Their methods were little changed from those practiced by their more archaic predecessors, relying as they did on opportunistic kills, and momentarily favorable circumstances. While modern humans often concentrated on animals in their prime, the Neanderthals were less selective in their hunting, focusing on solitary animals, pregnant females, and other vulnerable prey. They lacked the specialized weapons such as the throwing stick and the lightweight, blade-tipped spear that allowed their successors to kill prey from a distance. There were probably many occasions when Neanderthal hunters ran down their prey in a surprise attack, stabbing it from close quarters, a dangerous practice even under the most favorable

Adequate winter shelter – as in this hypothetical reconstruction – was essential if Neanderthals were to survive harsh conditions in Europe during the last glaciation.

circumstances. It is hardly surprising that many Neanderthal skeletons show evidence of broken bones and other major injuries sustained during the chase.

The life of a Neanderthal band in the intensely cold environments of the Europe of 75,000 years ago can never have been easy. The means to survival were fire, some form of skin clothing and adequate winter shelter, and an ability to store food. It is probably no coincidence that some of the densest Neanderthal populations lay in the sheltered river valleys of the Périgord region in southwest France. The key to the successful occupation of these valleys was not the variety of game by the rivers' edge, but the predictability of certain species, especially reindeer. Reindeer are creatures of habit. They have regular, easily observed migration patterns, moving out onto the open plains in summer to graze on moss and lichens, returning to more sheltered territory in fall. Their annual migrations tend to follow the same trails through narrow defiles, through river valleys, and across favored fords. Judging from the number of reindeer bones in the Périgord's rockshelters, Neanderthals took advantage of this seasonal predictability. They also hunted other species, such as wild horse and smaller animals, when the occasion presented itself.

Modern estimates suggest it takes about 800–900 lb (363–408 kg) of lean game meat to feed 10 hunters for a month. With the European winters of 75,000 years ago lasting at least 8–9 months, there must have been long periods when hunting and trapping were restricted by weather conditions. Perhaps the Neanderthals stored up considerable amounts of energy as body fat to keep them going between kills. Other temperate species such as bison and deer do this, and even today human beings gain height in late spring and summer and put on extra weight in fall. Nevertheless, some food storage system to stockpile meat must have been essential. Such stockpiling would have been easy enough, for ice caves and pits dug into the permanently frozen subsoil (the permafrost) would have preserved deep-frozen, butchered game almost indefinitely. So far, no such Neanderthal caches have been found, except for a pit containing three rhinoceros skulls and the remains of at least five mammoths in a Neanderthal cave on the island of Jersey, off the Normandy coast of France.

Neanderthal Technology

As always with Stone Age peoples, we know more of Neanderthal stone technology than anything else. This technology, like that of Middle Stone Age peoples in Africa, was often based on Levallois and disc cores and displayed considerable variation. The distinctive stone spear points and scrapers made by the European Neanderthals are grouped into what is known as the Mousterian culture, after the famous Le Moustier rockshelter near the Vézère river in the Périgord, where such implements were first found in the 1860s.

The late François Bordes of the University of Bordeaux was a latter-day maestro of Stone Age technology, who could replicate any prehistoric stone artifact, from the earliest chopper to the most sophisticated graving tool. He could turn out a Stone Age hand axe in 2 minutes flat. Bordes was also a skilled excavator, who spent 11 years digging into the Neanderthal levels of Combe Grenal cave in the Périgord. Combe Grenal was first occupied some 150,000–125,000 years ago by pre-Neanderthal people who hunted reindeer and who used hand axes. An almost continuous record of regular, but intermittent, Neanderthal occupation follows, dating to between 90,000 and 40,000 years ago. These levels contained 19,000 Mousterian artifacts. Bordes identified no less than 60 different types of tool, made with a variety of stoneworking techniques, including the Levallois method, and with carefully prepared disc cores. Bordes identified four distinct toolkits in the Combe Grenal levels: one associated with small hand axes, another with thousands of heavy-duty side scrapers, a third with a high proportion of saw-edged flakes, and some that contained an even balance of different tool types.

Such wide variation in Mousterian toolkits is found not only at Combe Grenal, but at other Neanderthal sites throughout Europe and in the Near East, also in North Africa where other archaic *Homo sapiens* made similar tools. Bordes believed that the Combe Grenal toolkits reflected four different Neanderthal groups who all visited the same location, but who lived in almost complete isolation, and rarely had any contact with each other. Lewis Binford of the University of New Mexico, famous for his championing of scientific approaches to archaeology, disagreed. The tools were all made by one group, he averred, but a group who used them for different activities. For instance, the saw-like flakes tend to be associated with high frequencies of wild horse bones, and were perhaps used for shredding meat strips for drying or smoking. The heavy duty flakes from another well-known Périgord site, La Quina, would have been ideal for cleaning the large number of hides that were used for winter clothing.

Binford's arguments are strengthened by his own ethnographic observations among modern caribou hunters in Alaska. He observed that only five Nunamiut Eskimo families, each with their own toolkits, occupy an area the size of the entire Dordogne Province where Combe Grenal and other major Mousterian sites lie. This observation helped damp down the debate about the Combe Grenal artifacts, but it still smolders, for the toolkits may also reflect cultural diversity between different local areas, where conditions varied widely. The kind of situation encountered by Bordes at Combe Grenal has shown up in the so-called blade-levels at such widely distributed sites as Klasies River in South Africa (the Howieson's Poort tools – see Chapter Five), and in the Mount Carmel caves in the Near East, described in the next chapter. Does the appearance of such apparently exotic tools reflect a brand new technology, or simply a temporary response to local circumstances which eventually change yet again, allowing people to revert to their earlier toolkit? The accurate interpretation of what archaeologists call "artifact variability" remains one of the major issues in Stone Age archaeology.

A Concern for Life After Death?

Neanderthal subsistence and technology may have owed much to their more archaic ancestors, but these intensely conservative people were separated from their predecessors by one intellectual chasm. They were probably the first human beings to bury their dead. The Chapelle-aux-Saints man from the Dordogne was buried in a shallow trench, surrounded by stone tools. The Le Moustier rockshelter near the Vézère yielded the burial of a boy about 15 or 16 years old, lying in a trench on his right side with slightly drawn up knees, and his head resting on his forearm in a sleeping position. Some flint artifacts formed a stone pillow, and a well-made stone axe was by his hand. Charred wild ox bones lay in the grave, perhaps to provide sustenance in the next life. La Ferrassie, another nearby Neanderthal rockshelter, contained 21 mounds and pits, including 6 pits containing 4 children and 2 adults. The remaining 15 were empty, but may once have contained more human skeletons or offerings for the dead.

There are clear signs that the Neanderthals enjoyed what may have been a complex ritual life. The Monte Circeo cave on the Mediterranean coast between Rome and Naples is a deep cavern, once used by a Neanderthal group for important rituals. An inner chamber contained an inverted human skull with a hole in the base surrounded by a circle of stones. Animals were apparently an important part of Neanderthal ritual. At Régourdou near Montignac in France, the hunters buried a complete cave bear, together with the remains of more than 20 other cave bears in a rectangular pit covered by a heavy stone slab. Further afield, a Neanderthal boy who died near Uzbek in central Asia some 50,000 years ago lay in a shallow grave in a remote mountain cave. Half a dozen pairs of mountain goat horns were stuck in the ground around his head.

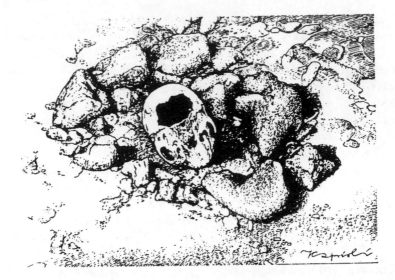

The Monte Circeo cave, on the Italian coast south of Rome, yielded this Neanderthal skull, found lying base upward within a ring of stones. The condition of the skull, and the nature of artifacts from the cave, hint at sacrificial rites.

This new concern for the dead, concern for some form of afterworld, was a major landmark in human history, for it marks the birth of an intellect capable of articulating feelings about the forces of nature, and about the mysterious powers that controlled birth, life, and death. Deliberate burial of the dead sets humans apart from animals and earlier hominids, who abandoned the infirm when they could no longer keep up, or left the deceased where they lay. Burial rituals assume an important symbolic role, for they perpetuate the idea that death is not the end of existence. Rather, it is a passage from the present world to the realm of the revered ancestors – those who have gone before.

We may never know precisely why Neanderthal rituals developed. Perhaps they were a response to the at first unfamiliar, harsh environmental conditions of the late Ice Age, of a world where hard times were commonplace, where violent death in the chase, or at the hands of other hunters, was a constant reality. Rituals reinforce close ties between kin, they seek to explain the mysterious and the unknown, and they provide continuity between one generation and the next.

Returning now to our main theme – the debate between the rival Noah's Ark and Candelabra hypotheses – we have accumulated supporting evidence on both sides. On anatomical and technological grounds the European Neanderthals appear distinctly different from modern humans, implying little or no continuity between them. On the evidence of burial of the dead, however, Neanderthals and modern humans *did* in some respects share a common outlook on life and death. But is this enough to build a theory of evolutionary continuity? Probably not. While the Neanderthals perhaps conceived of an afterlife, on present evidence they totally lacked the brilliant visual imagination of modern humans that suddenly manifests itself in the glories of European cave art after 35,000 years ago, and which we discuss in Chapter Twelve. Furthermore, there is new evidence for another archaic characteristic of Neanderthals – evidence from an unexpected quarter: human speech.

Did the Neanderthals Speak?

To a visitor from outer space, one of the most striking characteristics of modern humanity would surely be the way we communicate by emitting sounds – not just any sounds, but specific words in a multitude of languages that make up human speech. Did the Neanderthals have similar linguistic abilities? Or did a lack of them separate the Neanderthals from *Homo sapiens sapiens*, which might account for the apparently significant differences in cultural potential between them?

It might seem surprising that scientists can study prehistoric speech at all. Artifacts and fossil bones may survive for tens of thousands of years, but past human utterances disappear forever once spoken (except perhaps for those present-day listeners who believe themselves to be psychically in touch with their ancestors). Nevertheless, physical anthropologists have found two speech-linked features of the human anatomy in particular that can be studied in fossils, and measured to record differences over the millennia. The first is the human voice box – the larynx and the pharynx – whose anatomy leaves distinctive traces in the base of the skull. The second is the part of the brain known as Broca's area, which controls human speech. The shape and size of Broca's area can be deduced from casts ("endocasts") taken of the inside of the skull.

Some physical anthropologists, among them anatomist Philip Tobias of the University of Witwatersrand in South Africa, believe that *Homo habilis* was capable of articulate speech, on the grounds that Broca's area is developed in early *Homo*'s brain, but not in that of *Australopithecus*. Most experts, however, believe that speech developed much more gradually. Anatomist Jeffrey Laitman of Johns Hopkins University has studied the position of the human larynx by examining the base of hominid skulls. He found that *Australopithecus* had vocal tracts much like living apes. He was unable to study the base of *Homo habilis* crania as they are fragmentary, but *Homo erectus* had a larynx with an equivalent position to that of an 8-year-old modern child. He believes that it was only after 300,000 years ago, with the appearance of archaic *Homo sapiens*, that the larynx assumed its modern position, giving at least mechanical potential for the full range of speech sounds used today.

Anatomist Philip Lieberman of Brown University believes that fully articulate speech evolved even later, with *Homo sapiens sapiens*. He has carried out comparative studies on the Neanderthal La Chapelle-aux-Saints skull, comparing its anatomy with that of chimpanzees and modern infants. Computer modeling of the upper airway based on these comparisons suggested that this Neanderthal individual was capable of a phonetic output quite similar to non-human primates and modern newborns. Thus, Lieberman believes that the Neanderthal vocal tract could not produce some vowels, that its output was very nasal, and speech subject to many errors. He points out that a Neanderthal would need a vocal tract with a curved tongue body and sufficient space between the base of the skull and the spinal column to generate the full range of human speech sounds. This Neanderthals did not possess.

Lieberman is convinced that the Neanderthals had less-advanced linguistic and cognitive skills than *Homo sapiens sapiens*. Their speech was not only nasal, but probably slowly delivered. Neanderthals would have been unable to put together or to understand complex sentences. If Lieberman is right, fully articulate speech was an attribute of *Homo sapiens sapiens*, which may have given modern humans a major evolutionary advantage in communicating and in competing for food. Fully developed speech could have been one of the most significant factors in the rapid colonization of the globe by anatomically modern people.

An Evolutionary Dead End?

The European Neanderthals were skilled and successful hunters. They had to be to survive at all in the hazardous conditions of the Ice Age. They shared

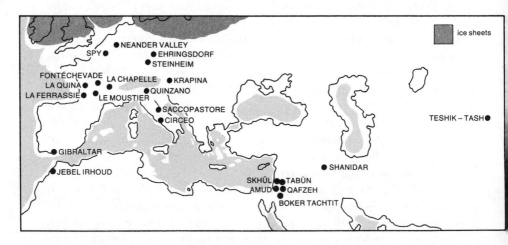

Sites referred to in Chapters Seven and Eight.

with modern humans a concern for the dead, something that sets them apart from all their predecessors. But – these abilities and attributes notwithstanding – in every other respect they seem to be on an evolutionary byway of prehistory. Anatomically they show a specialized physical adaptation to extreme cold that sets them apart from *Homo sapiens sapiens*. Intellectually they lacked the ability of their successors to devise new lightweight technologies, to conceptualize visually, and to communicate with fully articulate speech. This evidence, taken together with the new archaeological and genetic arguments for the evolution of modern humans in Africa, suggests strongly that the European Neanderthals were not on the direct line of evolution to modern humans. In time they became extinct, overtaken by a new, faster-moving Stone Age world.

Their cousins in the Near East are a different matter, however. Here there is intriguing evidence for Neanderthals with less specialized physical characteristics. Who exactly were these people? Might they conceivably be the ancestors of modern humans in the region?

CHAPTER EIGHT

Qafzeh and Skhūl

Proponents of the Noah's Ark hypothesis believe that *Homo sapiens sapiens* had moved out of Africa by at least 90,000 years ago, by which time the Sahara was an arid barrier between the Mediterranean and African worlds. As the Sahara supported open grassland during the last interglacial, it is reasonable to assume that anatomically modern humans hunted their way into North Africa and the Nile Valley well before the deepening drought in the Sahara expelled their descendants to the margins of the desert. Even the existence of such a population movement is questioned by supporters of the Candelabra theory, who believe that modern humans evolved in many different areas of the world.

The most obvious route from Africa to Eurasia is from northeast Africa into the Near East via the Nile Valley, along the shores of northern Sinai and from there into the Levant, the regions bordering the eastern Mediterranean in present-day Israel, Lebanon, and Syria. After 100,000 years ago, as we have seen, falling Mediterranean sea levels would have opened up a broad, low-lying coastal plain that extended from Libya to the Levant, making the journey even easier. There is, of course, always the possibility of an open-water crossing, across the Strait of Gibraltar, but there is no evidence that any Ice Age humans, however anatomically modern, had the necessary water-craft to make this often windy and current-racked crossing. As any sailor knows, the Mediterranean can be a dangerous ocean, with sudden wind shifts and unexpected storms, and it must have been even more hazardous in the cooler millennia of the Würm glaciation. The earliest proven Mediterranean seafaring dates only to about 8,000 years ago, to a time when human technology was much more sophisticated. Almost certainly, both *Homo erectus* and *Homo sapiens* crossed into the Near East and Europe by a circuitous land route that took thousands of years to traverse.

The earliest documented human occupation of the Near East dates to about 700,000 years ago at Ubeidiya in Israel, some time after *Homo erectus* is thought to have radiated out of Africa. For hundreds of thousands of years, the human population of western Asia was probably very sparse, despite very diverse, often-fertile grassland, oak forest, and open parkland environments and a great abundance of fine-grained flint, ideal for making stone implements of every shape and size. This magnificent stoneworking material was much favored after 100,000 years ago, when more varied Levallois, disc-core, and sometimes blade technologies came into widespread use. This was the time when local populations increased, when, apparently, newcomers arrived in the Near East. The identity of these newcomers has been the subject of vigorous controversy ever since the first large-scale excavations of Stone Age sites in the Levant during the 1920s and 1930s.

Mount Carmel: et-Tabūn and Mugharet el-Wad

In 1929, Cambridge University archaeologist Dorothy Garrod came to what was then Palestine to excavate a series of caverns in the slopes of Mount Carmel near Haifa. She came with a thorough training in Middle and Upper Paleolithic technology, in the minutiae of artifact classification and long experience of cave excavation in temperate climates. Her excavations centered on three major caves: et-Tabūn ("the cave of ovens"), Mugharet el-Wad, and es-Skhūl ("the cave of young goats"). Her hectic digging seasons, conducted on a shoestring, with often an improvised budget, produced trend-setting, unanticipated results.

She began by excavating deep into Mugharet el-Wad, a huge cave occupied not only by anatomically modern humans making fine blade tools, but by even earlier, Middle Paleolithic hunter-gatherers as well. A level with "small, and delicate, and not at all primitive" artifacts marked the beginning of the Upper Paleolithic. The tools included small spear heads made of a triangular flake with thinned base, which Garrod named "Emiran points" after Emireh cave, where they were first found. The earliest inhabitants of el-Wad had been Middle Paleolithic hunters using the Levallois technique to make spear points.

Nearby et-Tabūn continued the long cultural sequence much further back into prehistory. Garrod identified no less than three layers of Middle Paleolithic occupation, a culture she called "Levalloiso-Mousterian," for it contained enormous numbers of Levallois cores, as well as familiar Mousterian artifacts like those made by Neanderthals in distant western Europe. (Modern researchers prefer the term "Mousterian" to Levalloiso-Mousterian, and we will use this from now on.) The uppermost Mousterian level (level B) Garrod labeled "Upper," the other two (C and D) she labeled "Lower," distinguishing between them on the basis of improved flaking technique in the later levels, and more use of the Levallois technique in the lower. Since the Mousterian was commonly associated with the Neanderthals of western Europe, no one was surprised when Garrod found a single Neanderthal burial in level C.

The thick occupation layers at Mughâret el-Wad and et-Tabūn covered the critical transition between the Middle and Upper Paleolithic, the conventional moment when everyone assumed *Homo sapiens sapiens* first appeared in the Near East. But nothing prepared the archaeological world for the remarkable discoveries that came from es-Skhūl, the smallest and least impressive of the Mount Carmel caves.

Mount Carmel: es-Skhūl

The site of es-Skhūl lies only about 300 ft (100 m) east of Mughâret el-Wad. It is actually more of a rockshelter than a cave, and is an unprepossessing site at first glance. Garrod handed over the excavations there to physical anthropologist Ted McCown of the American School of Prehistoric Research in Cambridge, Massachusetts. McCown's 1931 excavations yielded an infant skull in hardened cave earth, associated with Mousterian tools identical to those from nearby Tabūn, and also other fragmentary human remains. These finds, and some test trenching, convinced McCown that the more intensive occupation had been on the terrace fronting the cave.

The 1932 excavations shifted to the terrace and soon yielded more human remains, but in such quantities that they were obviously far more than scattered finds. During two exciting months of careful excavation, McCown recovered the remains of eight more individuals, all of them burials, from what he called "this most ancient prehistoric necropolis." They were associated with stone tools very similar to those found in Tabūn layer C – Garrod's Lower Mousterian. By 1935, 10 burials had been unearthed from es-Skhūl.

There was no doubt that es-Skhūl had been occupied over a long period of time, and that it had also served as a burial place on several occasions, to the point that the inhabitants had disturbed earlier interments while burying more dead. All the skeletons in the cave were deliberate burials. "Skhūl IV," for example, was "a deliberate, if carelessly made burial," McCown wrote. "At the side of the shelter a shallow, concave hole must have been scooped out of the then soft deposit and the body placed in it, the head resting on the downward curving eastern side and directed in such a way that it looked up the valley. The arms were folded, the hands placed in front of the face, and the legs folded back upon the buttocks." Not that the burial practices were standardized. Each skeleton was crouched up into a grave, but they faced in different directions.

All of this was not unexpected, for similar Neanderthal burials had come to light in French caves. But were these Mousterian skeletons those of Neanderthals? McCown studied the bones in collaboration with the great British anatomist Sir Arthur Keith. They concluded that the Skhūl people were "a curious combination of Neanderthal and Neanthropic man: perhaps it is more accurate to say a form of Palaeoanthropic man with many physical features hitherto most commonly met with in *Homo sapiens.*" In other words, Skhūl appeared to straddle the critical evolutionary transition from archaic to modern human beings.

McCown and Keith noted that no such transitional skeletons, showing the features of both Neanderthals and *Homo sapiens sapiens*, had been found in France or other parts of Europe. There seemed to be a good chance, then, that the Near East was the place where the Neanderthals had evolved into anatomically modern people, that Mount Carmel was close to the cradle of *Homo sapiens sapiens*. The two scientists, one an anatomist of vast experience, the other a comparative neophyte, also assumed that the Neanderthal-like Tabūn burial and the Skhūl individuals were part of a single, highly varied population in the process of evolving into modern humans.

Emiran Points and the Upper Paleolithic

Certainly, the tens of thousands of stone artifacts from the Mount Carmel caves tended to support this viewpoint. Mugharet el-Wad and et-Tabūn's deep occupation layers chronicled a dramatic shift in artifact forms and prehistoric technology over a long period of time. El-Wad's Upper Paleolithic levels contained fine blade artifacts that looked quite like those from contemporary French and central European caves. The brief, earliest Upper Paleolithic layer below these horizons featured both new, more delicate blade artifacts and the distinctive Emiran point that Garrod considered a sign of a technological transition from Middle to Upper Paleolithic in the Near East. Then the lowermost el-Wad horizons and the thick Tabūn deposits documented "remarkable continuity" during the Middle Paleolithic. Finished artifacts identical to those from Tabūn level C – Garrod's Lower Mousterian – were associated with a Neanderthal burial at Tabūn, and with much more anatomically modern people at nearby Skhūl. Thus, Garrod not unreasonably argued, *Homo sapiens sapiens* had evolved from Neanderthal roots in the Near East, then spread from there, moving north and west into Europe, carrying new blade technologies.

Emiran points from Mugharet el-Wad.

Dorothy Garrod's excavations were a remarkable achievement for her day. Conducted at a time when almost nothing was known of Stone Age archaeology outside the narrow confines of western Europe, she, and a contemporary, German archaeologist Alfred Rust, revolutionized Ice Age archaeology. Rust excavated at the Jabrud cave in Syria, where he found a sequence of Stone Age occupations very similar to those at Mount Carmel. His funds were even more limited than Garrod's. He is said to have bicycled from Germany to Syria and back to save money! Frenchman René Neuville also contributed to the revolution by trenching into the huge Qafzeh cave inland of Haifa, where he recovered seven anatomically modern skeletons like those from Skhūl, in another Mousterian level.

Qafzeh

At first, most anatomists agreed with McCown and Keith that the Skhūl burials, the Qafzeh skeletons, and the Tabūn individual were members of a single, highly variable Near Eastern population in process of evolving toward anatomically modern people. Then, more pure Neanderthal burials came to light, from such caves as Amūd and Kebara in Israel, and, notably, Shanidar in Iraq, where eight individuals were found in 1959, including a 30-year old man with a withered right arm, who died under a rock fall from the cave roof. These discoveries, and more detailed studies of all Near Eastern fossils, now convinced the experts that the Tabūn burial belonged with the Neanderthals, while the Skhūl and Qafzeh individuals were quite separate populations of anatomically modern people. Furthermore, Skhūl and Qafzeh were now thought to date to about 40,000 years ago, somewhat later than the Mousterian occupation at nearby Tabūn. No longer did people think in terms of a transitional population, but of a process of local evolution from Neanderthals to *Homo sapiens sapiens* shortly before 40,000 years ago.

There matters stood until 1965, when French archaeologist Bernard Vandermeersch began new excavations at Qafzeh. Vandermeersch's prospects did not look good at first, for the British had blown up the cave as a suspected ammunition dump in the 1940s. He spent six weeks removing rubble from the explosion, then promptly discovered two beautifully preserved anatomically modern skeletons under the fallen rock. In 13 subsequent years of careful excavation, Vandermeersch and his colleagues uncovered nearly 15 ft (4.5 m) of Mousterian deposits. The lowermost 6 ft (1.8 m) of the deposits contained evidence of intensive occupation, thousands of stone fragments, and animals, including extinct species of rodents, associated with hearths. The artifacts from these layers resembled Tabūn layer C's Lower Mousterian. Above these dense and rapidly accumulated layers followed about 8 ft (2.4 m) of intermittent occupation. Here Vandermeersch recovered the remains of at least six more people, all of them, like the original

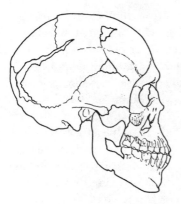

One of the anatomically modern skulls recovered from the site of Qafzeh.

finds, of anatomically modern appearance, and all of them associated with Mousterian artifacts.

At first, the Qafzeh skeletons appeared to be about the same age as the Skhūl burials – about 40,000 years old. Thus, they fitted in with the prevailing notion at the time of a gradual evolutionary transition from the Neanderthals to *Homo sapiens sapiens.*

Jelinek at et-Tabūn

If there had been a slow evolution from the Neanderthals to *Homo sapiens sapiens* in the Near East, could one, then, pick up any signs of cultural change in the thick Mousterian levels at Tabūn and elsewhere? While Bernard Vandermeersch dug into Qafzeh, Arthur Jelinek of the University of Arizona went back to Tabūn to take a closer look.

Dorothy Garrod had identified six layers in Tabūn, three of them Mousterian. Her excavation methods were excellent for the early 1930s, but not as detailed as the more refined techniques that Jelinek brought to bear on the same levels. For six years, he excavated through Tabūn's Mousterian levels right down to bedrock, studying not only artifacts and stoneworking debris, but animal bones and the cave deposits themselves. He identified not just six layers, but no less than 85 geological layers in a 32-ft (9.8-m) stratigraphic section, recovering more than 44,000 stone fragments and over 300 finished artifacts. According to the new evidence, Mousterian occupation of Tabūn may have begun as early as 90,000 years ago.

Jelinek studied the Tabūn stone tools in minute detail, tracing small changes in the different artifacts over long periods of time. He was impressed, as was Garrod before him, by the general continuity in stone technology. There were, however, significant changes that began with a dramatic reorientation from the making of heavy bifaces and scrapers to the thin-edged Levallois flakes and points that are typical of the later Tabūn levels.

Jelinek's measurements also showed that Mousterian flakes became ever thinner relative to their length as time went on. This immediately raised a fundamental question: were these changes the result of purely local phenomena, or were they a reflection of enhanced manual dexterity and control, perhaps by anatomically more advanced human beings? Jelinek compared his thickness measurements with Mousterian collections from other Middle Paleolithic caves in the Levant. He included Kebara cave, south of Mount Carmel in Israel, where a Neanderthal infant burial was found by Israeli archaeologist Ofer Bar-Yosef; Qafzeh with its anatomically modern burials; and also Skhūl. The thickness–length ratios of Tabūn C and Kebara with their Neanderthals were very similar, while those from the apparently later Skhūl and Qafzeh occupations were lower. After years of laboratory measurements, Jelinek became convinced there was an orderly and continuous progress of Mousterian technology over thousands of years of human occupation in the Near East. Perhaps the diminution in flake thickness toward the end of the Mousterian reflected the emergence of a new, "qualitatively different" behavior. Perhaps, too, this was associated with the appearance or emergence of modern humans in the area.

Boker Tachtit

The technological picture was enhanced by a series of studies at Stone Age sites in Lebanon, where Mousterian toolkits became more and more refined over time. But it was the work of Southern Methodist University prehistorian Anthony Marks at Boker Tachtit, in Israel's Negev Desert, that showed just how complicated the technological transition was.

Boker Tachtit, excavated by Marks from 1977 to 1980, lies on an ancient river terrace in the central Negev, a stratified chronicle of Stone Age culture change between 47,000 and 38,000 years ago. The four occupation levels contained sealed collections of stone artifacts and toolmaking waste that lay exactly where their makers had dropped them thousands of years before. Marks set himself the task of fitting the many flakes and cores back together – retrofitting the stones as a way of reconstructing ancient toolmaking practices. By completing this task for each brief occupation, he had a measure of technological change over more than nine critical millennia.

The first visitors to Boker Tachtit around 47,000 years ago made triangular flakes with Levallois cores far more economically than the Mousterians at Mount Carmel and elsewhere. They used a special Levallois process, aimed at producing spear points, but also such tools as scrapers, skin perforators, and simple graving tools. Almost 60 percent of the tools were made on blade-shaped pieces. As time went on, the process of making spear points became more refined, until, about 38,000 years ago, the Levallois point core vanished. Now the stoneworkers used pyramid-shaped cores, producing simple

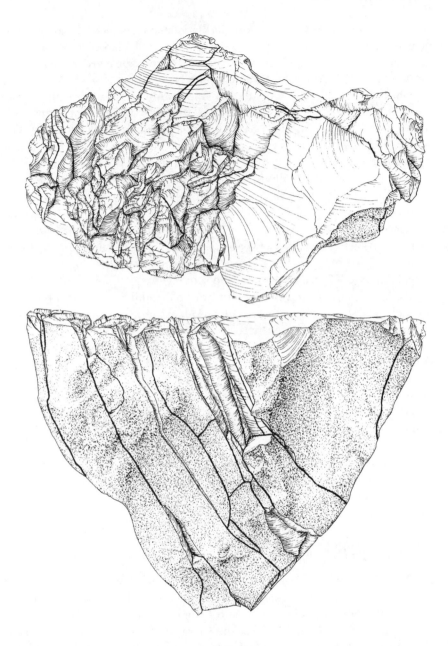

The art of retrofitting: painstaking work by Anthony Marks at Boker Tachtit has allowed him to fit flakes from the site back on to the cores from which they came. This increasingly important method in archaeology makes it possible to reconstruct ancient toolmaking practices. The top and side views here of one group of refitted pieces show how the stoneworkers began with a core shaped like an inverted pyramid.

triangular points from the same cores as blade-shaped pieces. This production of everything from thick flakes to large and small blades from the same general core forms was to become a common technological artifice of the later Upper Paleolithic cultural traditions of the Near East.

Marks' research brought out two important details. First, the actual technological change from the early to the late levels of Boker Tachtit is small, merely a shift from a Levallois-based technology to a non-Levallois one. This latter technique still involved the use of the hard stone hammer. There are no signs that the Boker Tachtit stoneworkers had starting using soft hammers of bone or wood – traditionally seen as necessary for Upper Paleolithic blade production – even though they were creating Upper Paleolithic-type blades. Second, what is surprising is that this technological shift resulted in so few changes to the artifacts. There was a limited elaboration of Upper Paleolithic tool types such as blade scrapers and gravers through the 9,000-year occupation of Boker Tachtit, but spear heads characteristic of the Middle Paleolithic also feature throughout the sequence.

Marks' retrofits from Boker Tachtit are a breakthrough in studying the technological shift from Middle to Upper Paleolithic in the Near East. Instead of an abrupt transition from hard-hammer to soft-hammer stoneworking, there was an important intermediate period when blade technology assumed ever greater significance within a general context of *hard*-hammer work. This blade technology was the earliest true Upper Paleolithic in the Near East, and eventually developed into the versatile soft-hammer technology used by *Homo sapiens sapiens* all over temperate and arctic latitudes. Once soft-hammer blade technology came into widespread use, its sheer effectiveness and efficiency submerged older technologies rapidly.

Important as the stone tools are to an understanding of the complex changes leading to the evolution of modern humans, we come back to the fossil bones as our most crucial source of evidence. Here, new work at Qafzeh has produced astonishing results.

New Dates for Qafzeh

In 1988, a team of French and Israeli scientists headed by Hélène Valladas of Gif-sur-Yvette's Institute for Low Level Radiation delivered an academic bombshell. They took a sample of burnt stone flakes from the Qafzeh burial layers and reheated them to release the energy of the electrons trapped inside since the stone fragments were last heated accidentally by a prehistoric camp fire. When the stored energy was released, the scientists measured its visible light rays, known as thermoluminescence, obtaining a date for the stones' original heating, at the time when the Qafzeh people were laid to rest. To everyone's astonishment, the samples gave a mean reading of $92,000 \pm 5,000$ years ago – at least 50,000 years earlier than previous estimates!

The implications of the new Qafzeh dates sent shock waves through the small world of human paleontology. Since the dated stone fragments were associated with the bones of anatomically modern people, they meant that *Homo sapiens sapiens* populations were living in the Near East over 90,000 years ago. Among the most jubilant recipients of the Qafzeh dates was physical anthropologist Chris Stringer of London's Natural History Museum, a strong supporter of the Noah's Ark hypothesis. He and his colleague Peter Andrews boldly stated in the widely read pages of *Science* magazine that the collective evidence, including the Qafzeh dates, now "favors a recent African origin of *Homo sapiens.*" Now, Stringer and Andrews wrote, both genetics and fossil remains point to Africa as the ultimate homeland of modern humans, even if the details of what actually transpired remain a mystery. They pointed out that the new Qafzeh dates place *Homo sapiens sapiens* in the Near East almost as early as modern humans are known to have flourished in southern Africa (Chapter Five).

As proponents of the Noah's Ark hypothesis freely admit, the new Qafzeh dates leave many puzzling questions unanswered. On the face of it, they suggest that Neanderthals and anatomically modern humans coexisted in the Levant for many thousands of years. Were they close enough biologically to intermarry? And if Arthur Jelinek's and Anthony Marks' analyses at Tabūn and Boker Tachtit are correct in charting a slow evolution of stone tools right through the Mousterian, from 100,000 up to 40,000 years ago, did both Neanderthals and modern humans make these tools? Milford Wolpoff believes the uniformity in tool technology supports the Candelabra hypothesis. To him, the Neanderthals and early modern humans were no more than different races of the same archaic species, which interbred to produce fully modern *Homo sapiens sapiens*. Bernard Vandermeersch and others, such as Ofer Bar-Yosef, take a quite different view. They believe that the Neanderthals arrived in the Levant perhaps as late as 50,000 years ago – driven south from Europe by severe climatic conditions into hunting grounds already occupied by sparse populations of anatomically more advanced people.

The early human story in the Near East is currently in a state of flux. Until we have more evidence and reliable early dates, the issues are unlikely to be resolved. The Tabūn material suggests that the Neanderthals *were* in the Levant before 50,000 years ago, and therefore overlapped with modern humans there. Did both groups make the same tools? As we have already seen, it is notoriously difficult to link specific technologies with specific groups of people. One kind of evidence deals with evolution in stone tools, the other in fossil bones. But there is nothing archaeologically impossible in the idea that different human species may have used similar artifacts when faced with similar environmental conditions. What is significant is that, after 45,000 years ago, blade technologies associated with anatomically modern humans became dominant. Perhaps it was not until these technologies were developed that fully modern people had the competitive edge enabling them to move north into Ice Age Europe. There is otherwise the puzzling question as to why modern humans lived successfully in the Levant as early as 90,000 years ago, but took another 50,000 years to reach the Neanderthal heartland in continental Europe. Later, in Chapter Eleven, we discuss some of the other theories put forward to explain this extraordinary hiatus. First, however, we must turn to the remarkable story of early humanity to the east, in Asia and Australasia.

PART THREE

BAMBOO AND BOATS

"It is a capital mistake to theorize before one has data. Insensibly, one begins to wish facts to suit theories, instead of theories to suit facts . . ."

Sherlock Holmes, in *A Scandal in Bohemia*

CHAPTER NINE

The Primeval Asians

"Migration" is somewhat of a dirty word in modern archaeology, for it implies simplistic explanations of complex prehistoric events. It is small wonder that archaeologists are cynical about large-scale population movements, for they spend their careers refuting pseudoarchaeologies that bring ancient astronauts to earth to found civilization, the ancient Egyptians to North America, and Chinese junks to the Pacific more than 3,000 years ago. Perhaps this is one reason why so many scientists are cautious when it comes to the Noah's Ark hypothesis, of locating the origins of modern humans in one place, then following their complex movements out of their original homeland to all parts of the globe.

On superficial acquaintance, the Noah's Ark hypothesis tends to conjure up images of small bands of hunter-gatherers marching from continent to continent, taking revolutionary new technologies and hunting methods with them. In fact, the population movements associated with any radiation of *Homo sapiens sapiens* from Africa should not be thought of as migrations, certainly not in terms of the kind of mass population movements that characterize later migrations in human history. These millennia-long population movements were gradual, dictated in large part not by the innate human curiosity about what lay over the next horizon, but by a myriad of complex environmental, climatic, and entirely pragmatic factors.

It would certainly be a mistake to think of these steady radiations as deliberate long-term plans. Rather, they were short-term responses to everchanging local conditions, often triggered in turn by larger global climatic fluctuations throughout the last (Würm) glaciation. In a real sense, our remote modern ancestors were part of a complex world ecological system that affected all animal species on earth. When modern people emerged some 100,000 years ago, they were certainly incapable of influencing or altering their surroundings in the way we can (for good or ill) today. Thus, one should conceive of them as an integral part of the ecological systems in which they lived. And invariably the way for humans to survive in such systems was to keep on the move, and to cover large areas. Such movements brought human groups into contact with each other, broke down barriers of isolation, and increased chances for interbreeding.

If one accepts the general proposition that anatomically modern people radiated out of sub-Saharan Africa somewhere around 100,000 years ago, it would be naive to think that this radiation was just across the Sahara Desert and into the Near East, where people then ceased their wanderings. It would be naive, too, to think that the complicated evolutionary processes that took place in the Near East did not repeat themselves outside that narrow geographical compass, as far afield as southern Asia or even in the temperate zones of central Asia. How did our remote ancestors radiate into these large regions and into tropical Southeast Asia? Unfortunately, Arabia is almost virgin archaeological territory, and the Stone Age archaeology of the Indian subcontinent is barely known. In taking up the story of *Homo sapiens sapiens* in these latter regions, all we can rely on is some preliminary genetic evidence, some logical reasoning, and the incomplete archaeological and paleoanthropological record from Southeast Asia and Australasia. Ironically, Asia has yielded the most complete record of *Homo erectus* anywhere in the Old World. It is with these primeval humans that we must begin, for their anatomical relationship to the modern Australasian population lies at the crux of our narrative.

Homo erectus in Asia

The antiquity of humankind in Asia lags far behind that of Africa. Despite many years of search, no one has found fossils of either *Australopithecus* or *Homo habilis* in this vast region of the Old World. Although there are disputed claims of 2-million-year-old stone tools in Pakistan, perhaps the work of *Homo habilis*, most paleoanthropologists agree that *Homo erectus* was the first human species to settle in the eastern Old World, and that this settlement coincided, in general, with the radiation of archaic humans out of sub-Saharan Africa between about 1 million and 700,000 years ago. These archaic humans developed a distinctive adaptation to the forest environments of tropical and temperate Asia. This adaptation was to persist until long after modern people had appeared in the east.

Back in 1891, Dutch surgeon Eugène Dubois unearthed the primitive skull of an early human being in a terrace of the Solo River near Trinil, Java. The year after, he recovered the thigh bone of another fossil human a short distance away, in the same levels as bones of deer, pig, and rhinoceros. Dubois' new human had a thick-walled skull, receding forehead, and prominent brow ridges over the eyes. The thigh bone was proof, however, that these people walked upright, like modern humans. The enthusiastic surgeon named his find *Pithecanthropus erectus* ("erect-walking apeman").*

° The term *Pithecanthropus* was abandoned in favor of *Homo erectus* in the 1950s. By then it was clear that these, and other *Pithecanthropus* fossils, were more human than ape-like.

13 Belief in an Afterlife? The Neanderthals were the first humans to bury their dead. This scene reconstructs the burial of a Neanderthal child at Teshik-Tash in central Asia some 50,000 years ago.

14,15   The Harsh World of the European Neanderthals   With their powerful musculature and robust physique, the Neanderthals were specially adapted to the severe conditions of central and western Europe during the last glaciation. But they may have lacked the manual dexterity and fully developed speech which gave more lightly built modern humans the competitive edge after 40,000 years ago.

16–19　**Excavations in the Near East**　The British archaeologist Dorothy Garrod was a pioneer of Stone Age studies. Her excavations in the caves of Mount Carmel, near Haifa, during the 1920s and 1930s (*above*) revealed remains of both Neanderthals and anatomically modern people (*below*).

Bernard Vandermeersch's work at the site of Qafzeh, inland of Haifa, during the 1960s (*left* and *below*) produced modern-looking skeletons that have recently been redated to as early as 92,000 years old.

20–24 **A World of Bamboo** In Southeast Asia the first human colonizers – *Homo erectus* – encountered an environment dominated by tropical rainforest (*opposite page*; and, *inset*, a 700,000-year-old hearth being excavated at the site of Kao Pah Nam in northern Thailand). One forest product, bamboo, proved so versatile that the only stone tools needed were simple choppers (*above right*). Thus was born a bamboo technology that still flourishes today in the shape of scaffolding (*above*) or basketry (*near right*).

25 The First Australians The distant forebears of this Aborigine and his young son began to settle in Australia from Southeast Asia at least 40,000 years ago – just about the time similarly modern people were moving into Europe from western Asia.

Subsequently, similar archaic human fossils have come to light elsewhere in Java, notably from Sangiran (Chapter Ten). Many scientists remained skeptical about Dubois' discoveries until 1929, when Chinese archaeologist Bei Qen-Xung unearthed a skull cap of *Homo erectus* from the depths of the fossil-filled Zhoukoudian (formerly Choukoutien) Cave about 30 miles (48 km) from Beijing (Peking). By the outbreak of World War II, Zhoukoudian had yielded more than 14 fossil skulls, about 150 teeth, and various other body parts. The total remains represent about 40 individuals, who had died in the cave over a period of several hundred thousand years. Subsequent discoveries and excavations at Lantian and elsewhere have yielded more *Homo erectus* fossils to add to the Zhoukoudian collections. *Homo erectus* from Zhoukoudian (better known perhaps as "Peking Man") was, to all intents and purposes, anatomically identical to the Java finds.

Zhoukoudian Cave was originally an enormous cavern, measuring 460 ft (140 m) across at its widest, and 130 ft (40 m) from floor to ceiling. Recent estimates place its intermittent occupation between about 600,000 and 200,000 years ago, during a long period when the climate fluctuated between being somewhat warmer than today and more temperate conditions with cold winters and very hot summers. The cave may have been an intermittent winter camp, for thick layers of ash with burned and charred bone occur throughout the deposits from the very earliest times. These ashy layers are up to 20 ft (6 m) thick, and are some of the earliest good evidence for fire in prehistory – although some scholars believe that even this ash may be from natural fires or other phenomena. The bands of people that visited Zhoukoudian were able hunters, preying off bison, deer, and other animals. The cave lay in the midst of a mosaic of forest, riverside, and wooded grassland environments, and the animal bones reflect this diversity. Judging from the hackberries and other edible plants found in the cave, *Homo erectus* exploited many vegetable foods as well. This enormous site gives, however, a strong impression of biological and cultural homogeneity that has exercised a profound influence on thinking about the emergence of modern humans in Asia.

Some of the Java *Homo erectus* fossils may date to around 900,000 years ago or even earlier, with others dating to an estimated 700,000 to 500,000 years ago. Thus, they span much the same time frame as the Chinese specimens from Zhoukoudian, Lantian, and elsewhere. Together, the Asian *Homo erectus* individuals are remarkably homogeneous. They have broad-based skulls, low and receding foreheads and protruding (prognathous) faces, thick upper skull bones, and a massive chewing apparatus. These general characteristics, and many others, appear on all Asian *Homo erectus* fossils. Their brain capacity was between 775 and 1,300 ml, and they stood up to 5 ft 6 in (1.67 m) tall. Like African *Homo erectus*, these humans made tools and were skilled hunter-gatherers.

Peking Man: one of the Homo erectus skulls from Zhoukoudian, and an artist's impression of what this male may have looked like.

We have an impression, then, of a relatively homogeneous, biologically conservative *Homo erectus* population, known from fossil finds in China, Java, and from Narmada in India, that flourished in Asia for hundreds of thousands of years. Unfortunately, the latest *Homo erectus* Asian fossils are far from accurately dated, but the Dali cranium from China's eastern Shaanxi Province may be about 200,000 years old, and another find at Hexian has uranium dates between 200,000 and 150,000 years ago. There are traces of archaic *Homo sapiens* in fissures at Jinniushan in Liaoning Province, northeast of Zhoukoudian, uranium-series dated to an average of 263,000 years ago (see Chapter Fourteen). There are also reports of archaic *Homo sapiens* from other locations such as Dingcun, Tonzhi, and Maba in the 200,000-to-100,000-year range, with the Xujiayao finds having uranium dates that range as late as 131,000 to 83,000 years ago. There is said to be considerable anatomical continuity between *Homo erectus* and early *Homo sapiens* on the basis of these finds, including an increase in brain size, but the fossils are very incomplete and only dated within very broad ranges. The earliest dated anatomically modern human skull comes from Liujiang, uranium-series dated to about 67,000 years ago. Thereafter, there is a chronological gap until about 35,000 years ago, by which date *Homo sapiens sapiens* occurs at Salawasu in Mongolia.

Choppers and Chopping Tools

Back in 1948, Harvard University archaeologist Hallam Movius pointed out that the archaic world of *Homo erectus* could be divided into two great cultural provinces. For hundreds of thousands of years, hand-axe makers flourished in the grassland and woodland environments of Africa and Europe, in the Indian subcontinent and far into Eurasia. A second province lay in the east, an enormous region of woodland and forest and great environmental diversity where hand axes were never made, where stone technology was far cruder, more conservative, and apparently unchanging not only in the hands of *Homo erectus*, but in those of *Homo sapiens* as well. In southern China, indeed, such a simple stone technology may have remained in use until the beginnings of farming, between 6,000 and 10,000 years ago.

Movius worked at a time when archaeology was seen as a descriptive science, when prehistorians relied heavily on stone tools to trace human cultural evolution. He supposed that a primeval stone technology based on choppers and "pebble tools" (artifacts made on river pebbles) spread through the inhabited parts of the Old World in very early prehistory. In the west, this age-old tradition evolved not only into a wide variety of hand-axe traditions, but, subsequently, into disc and Levallois core-based technologies reflective of far more varied and innovative cultures. In the east, however, the old ways persisted without major change, as if something inhibited cultural change.

Movius and other investigators pondered these crude artifacts and assumed from their rough appearance that Asia was an area of cultural retardation. It could never have played "a vital and dynamic role in early human evolution, although very primitive forms of Early Man apparently persisted there long after types at a comparable stage of physical evolution had become extinct elsewhere," Movius wrote in 1942. For generations, the chopper-chopping tool complex was taken as evidence of racial isolation and cultural backwardness.

More recent interpretations have developed from a very different line of reasoning, which assumes that the early Asians, like other prehistoric groups everywhere, were opportunists. They relied most heavily on those raw materials that were most conveniently to hand. In the Asian forests, such materials were primarily wood, bamboo, and fiber, all of them organic materials that survive poorly in the archaeological record, especially from sites several hundred thousands of years old. In other words, our view of the Asians is biased, simply because we lack evidence of the whole range of their forest culture.

Nevertheless, the biological and cultural conservatism of early Asian prehistory is very striking. Why did technological traditions in east and west diverge so sharply? Was it an accident of human evolution or migration? Or was it the result of some unexplained ecological phenomenon? Could, for example, the dense tropical forests of Southeast Asia have served as a barrier against the diffusion of the hand axe and other butchering artifacts from the west?

Anthropologist Karl Hutterer of the University of Michigan has argued that tropical forests are rich in plant and animal foods, but they are widely dispersed through the forest. Thus, human groups subsisting off forest foods have to move constantly, carrying their artifacts with them. Under these circumstances, it would be logical to make use of the most economical and easily processed raw materials available – bamboo, wood, and other fibrous products. There was no need for the specialized, often complicated artifacts that were required in more open country in the west, either for spear points or for butchering large animals such as bison or large antelope.

Modern hunter-gatherers of the Southeast Asian rainforest, such as the Semang of Malaysia, still rely heavily on vegetable foods. They hunt only smaller forest animals such as rats, squirrels, lizards, and snakes. Japanese archaeologist Hiroshi Watanabe of the University of Tokyo believes that the same predominantly vegetarian diet was commonplace in early prehistory, and that the very earliest humans in Africa still relied predominantly on plant foods. The appearance of hand axes and cleavers in the west may, then, be connected with the emergence of big-game hunting in more open environments. When prehistoric hunter-gatherers adapted to the forest, as they did in Central Africa, for example, they stopped making hand axes and cleavers and turned to choppers and flake tools, which were better adaptations to forest living. Watanabe believes that the chopper-chopping tool complex was a readaptation by the makers of hand axes to the Asian rainforest, for the apparently simple tools were more efficient in coping with a forest environment than the hand axes and cleavers of more open country. This process of readaptation may not have taken place uniformly over all of southeastern and eastern Asia. Local ecological conditions may have determined the elaborateness of artifacts, with crude hand axes being used in some areas but not in others.

There is little difference between the chopper-chopping tools of Southeast Asia and those found much further north, in, for example, the Zhoukoudian region. There, *Homo erectus* hunted the rhinoceros and other large mammals, yet still used the chopper-chopping tool technology. Conceivably, this is a hint that Asian *Homo erectus* spread from the forested tropics into climatically more diverse and extreme environments.

The Bamboo Line

When archaeologist Geoffrey Pope of the University of Illinois, Urbana, studied the bones of Pleistocene animals from the Southeast Asian mainland and the offshore islands, he was surprised to find that open-country species such as camels, horses, and relatives of the giraffe family were absent. For long glacial periods of the Ice Age, when sea levels were much lower, the offshore islands were connected to the mainland by dry land. If open grassland animals were absent, then the entire area was forested. As if to prove the point, orang-utans, tapirs, and gibbons did occur in Pope's fossil assemblages.

Nearly all writing about early human evolution tends to emphasize the importance of open savanna woodland in hominid evolution. Over millions of years, our remote ancestors changed from living in forests to living in more open country, with the accompanying development of the bipedal posture and toolmaking that ultimately led to the emergence of anatomically modern people. If sub-Saharan Africa was the cradle of *Homo erectus* and of *Homo sapiens sapiens*, and both then spread into Asia, then at some point both would have had to adapt to forest living. Geoffrey Pope noticed that the area of Asia where forest animals were found in fossil beds coincided remarkably well with the distribution of chopper-chopping tools and other crude stone artifacts. And the distribution of chopper-chopping tool industries, from the Beijing area in the north to extreme Southeast Asia, coincides generally with the distribution of bamboo. Significantly, as you travel to the edges of bamboo country near the Chinese/North Korean border, artifacts somewhat like hand axes appear, as if their makers were adapting to somewhat different environmental conditions.

Map of Southeast Asia, showing how the distribution of chopper-chopping tools coincides broadly with the natural range of bamboo.

Bamboo grows in tropical environments all over the Old World, but the greatest diversity of species, more than 60 percent of them, occur in Asia. It is a raw material that archaeologists have ignored, for it is rarely, if ever, preserved in Stone Age sites. But this grass still provides an incredible diversity of artifacts. The stalks alone are easily fashioned into spears and knives, projectile points, containers, fiber ropes, clothing, even dwellings. The seeds and shoots of many species can be eaten. This versatile material is durable, incredibly strong, and forms sharp points and edges. Even today, many building contractors in the Far East use bamboo scaffolding when erecting skyscrapers. Besides being so functional, bamboo is also fast growing, some species regenerating at the rate of a foot or more a day.

Bamboo is not the most effective raw material for making lethal spears and projectile points. Sharp-edged, flaked stone is vastly superior for this purpose. However, such weapons may have been relatively unimportant in Asia, where prehistoric forest hunters, like their modern successors, probably relied on traps and snares to catch the small and medium-sized animals in which their environments abounded. Many anthropologists record seeing forest hunters snare small animals, then roast them whole in the ashes of a fire. The same must have been true in prehistoric times.

We should not think of the early Asians as bamboo users to the exclusion of other conveniently available raw materials such as llanas, rattan, and many forms of grass and reed. The forest itself, like the African savanna, is highly varied in its composition, with tropical rainforest in parts of the southeast, drier forests elsewhere, deciduous monsoon forest in northern Thailand, and boreal woodland forest in northern China. About the only tools that could not be fashioned from bamboo and other forest plants were axes and adzes. Crude stone tools and flakes were needed to fabricate and maintain bamboo and other artifacts and weapons. For these weapons, sharp-edged flakes would have been especially useful.

The chopper-chopping tool technology is the simplest imaginable, as simple and versatile as the rudimentary stone artifacts fashioned by *Homo habilis* in Africa. These early hominids also probably made simple wooden tools for use in the chase and for digging up plant tubers and roots. One does not necessarily have to argue that the Asian chopper-chopping tool technology evolved from the earliest of African tools and was then carried all the way to eastern Asia. Rather, it represents a remarkably simple and effective way of unlocking the potential of abundant, versatile, and easily renewable forest resources such as bamboo. And the great advantage of bamboo and other forest materials over fine-grained stone is that they are ubiquitous, and easily obtainable without a constant search. Nor is there a need to conserve raw material.

Homo erectus had another valuable artifact to hand – domesticated fire, probably in use at Zhoukoudian Cave from the earliest times of its occupation. As we have seen, fire was a vital element in the peopling of the globe, for it allowed people to settle in climates with very sharp seasonal contrasts, to cook food, and to protect themselves against predators. Fire is a valuable artifact in forest environments, for it enables people to burn off dense undergrowth during the dry season, especially in such areas as northern Thailand, where many hardwood trees are fire-resistant, and so are little affected by fast-moving seasonal burns. Indeed, fire may have helped humans to settle forested environments for the first time, for it enabled them to clear undergrowth, thereby making it possible for bands to walk through the trees.

Since the time of earliest settlement, there has been a close relationship between people, fire, and the forest in Asia, just as there has been a similar relationship in Africa, the Americas, and elsewhere. Today, whether you are traveling in tropical savanna, or deep in a Burmese forest, dark smoke and drifting ash darken skies during the dry season. The newcomer to an Asian forest may be startled by the explosive bursting of a dense bamboo thicket, but both animals and humans ignore this familiar sound. They are sounds and smells that have been part of the world for hundreds of thousands of years.

Kao Pah Nam

Geoffrey Pope has been excavating deep in the northern Thailand forest, in caves in a heavily eroded limestone landscape, caves once used by early prehistoric inhabitants of the forest. One rockshelter at an outcrop named Kao Pah Nam had yielded animal bones, stone tools, and the remains of a crude, basalt boulder-ringed hearth. The basalt was imported to the site by the people who once sat around the fire, for they knew that burning limestone creates quicklime, a dangerous, caustic substance. The inhabitants took large hippopotamus, and giant forms of ox, deer, bamboo rat, and porcupine – all forest animals. The people also consumed considerable numbers of fresh-water oysters and piled up the empty shells against the nearby cave wall. Kao Pah Nam is estimated to be about 700,000 years old, a date confirmed by radiometric and paleomagnetic studies at other sites, where volcanic basalt flows can be dated with some accuracy.

Kao Pah Nam was far from unique 700,000 years ago, and similar sites and adaptations persisted for thousands of years throughout the thickly forested regions of Asia. Of course, there were minor variations in artifacts between different areas, just as there were also wide differences in the animals and plants that formed local diets. The keys to these many and conservative adaptations were a simple stone technology, bamboo and other easily worked forest materials, and the taming of fire that helped people penetrate the remote corners of the forest. These highly effective forest cultures were to flourish and evolve slowly over hundreds of thousands of years, quite independently of the evolutionary changes in humankind in Africa and Europe. And, in time, the same adaptations took human beings across open water to the uninhabited coasts, forests, and deserts of New Guinea and Australia.

CHAPTER TEN

The First Seafarers

For hundreds of thousands of years, from over 900,000 years ago until perhaps later than 200,000 years ago, tiny *Homo erectus* populations flourished in Southeast Asia. These archaic humans adapted to a great range of environments throughout Asia, but in the southeast they were predominantly forest-dwellers, adept at subsisting off small game and a great variety of plant foods. This was a conservative region of the prehistoric world, both biologically and culturally, and *Homo erectus* survived here for perhaps 200,000–300,000 years longer than in Europe and Africa.

Mainland Southeast Asia faces a complex archipelago of offshore islands large and small, which extend southeastward toward even remoter land-masses, those of New Guinea and Australia. Java, Borneo, and the Philippines lie relatively close offshore today, but during intervals of lower sea levels, among them much of the last glaciation, they were joined to the mainland by a low-lying continental shelf. New Guinea and Australia, on the other hand, were always separated from the mainland by considerable stretches of open sea. Therein lies one of the most fascinating questions of human prehistory – when and how did humans first cross open water, journey out of sight of land to colonize New Guinea and Australia? We know that *Homo erectus* reached Java, which is but a short distance from the mainland, presumably during a period of lower sea level. But did these humans, or archaic *Homo sapiens*, ever penetrate further offshore? Were these early people the first seafarers, or was it *Homo sapiens sapiens* who first colonized Australasia? As always in archaeology, these issues have caused controversy, and sometimes passionate debate.

Ngandong and Niah

The Southeast Asians of 100,000 years ago – we do not know their identity – lived in much the same way as their predecessors had done for more than half a million years. They subsisted off forest foods, hunted game, and occupied a mosaic of forest environments that served to isolate tiny human populations not only from one another, but from the prehistoric world far to the west.

While physical anthropologists argue over the anatomical differences between different Asian *Homo erectus* fossils, no one doubts that there were gradual changes in the morphology of these humans, in particular associated with an increase in brain capacity. As we saw in Chapter Nine, however, an enormous chronological gap separates the early Java *Homo erectus* finds, dated to over 700,000 years ago, from more recent fossils dating to within the past 200,000 years. The most important later fossil discoveries come from a late Ice Age river terrace on the banks of the Solo River at Ngandong in central Java. Some 25,000 mammalian bones of such grassland species as wild cattle, elephants, and deer came from the same level as 11 undated human skulls and 2 upper leg bones. None of the Ngandong crania retain their faces or bases, but the relatively flat, bun-shaped skulls are regarded by some authorities as being from an advanced form of *Homo erectus*, by others as an early *Homo sapiens* – *Homo sapiens soloensis*.

These somewhat archaic crania were long undated, except for a statistical estimate of age based on cranial capacity that placed the fossils at about 265,000 years old, hardly a reliable method of dating an archaeological site! Fortunately, the original excavators left a control column of unexcavated deposit at the site, which was recently reexamined. Uranium-thorium dates from a bone layer thought to coincide with that of the human remains lie between 100,000 and 75,000 years ago, or may be even later. If correctly dated, Ngandong may be evidence for the survival of late forms of *Homo erectus* in Southeast Asian forests at least 300,000–200,000 years later than in Europe or Africa. Alternatively, if the bones are those of early *Homo sapiens*, then the same general evolutionary trends were appearing in Southeast Asia as elsewhere. There is, however, absolutely no evidence whatsoever for anatomically modern humans in mainland Southeast Asia 100,000 years ago, when they were already flourishing in Africa and about to appear in the Near East as well.

The only known *Homo sapiens sapiens* fossils are much later. As early as 41,000 years ago, people visited the vast Niah Cave in Borneo, and left their tools behind. But the identity of the toolmakers remains a puzzle. Anthropologist Tom Harrisson of the Sarawak Museum excavated Niah on a large scale in the 1950s and found a modern-looking skull and associated limb bones in the West Mouth of the cave, a burial subsequently radiocarbon-dated to about 40,000 years ago. There are serious doubts about the precise location of these remains, which may have been deposited in a later grave that was dug into 40,000-year-old tool-bearing levels. Significantly, many burials from the same cave date to between about 14,000 years ago and the time of Christ; the purportedly ancient skeleton may be one of them. Tabon Cave on Palawan in the Philippines has yielded the frontal part of an anatomically modern human skull, also a mandible claimed to have "Australoid" features. The cranium has been radiocarbon-dated to between 24,000 and 22,000 years ago.

When did *Homo sapiens sapiens* appear in Southeast Asia? Did anatomically modern humans spread into southern Asia and then further southeast from Africa and the Near East after 90,000 years ago, as Noah's Ark theorists would have us believe? Or, as Candelabra proponents argue, did *Homo sapiens sapiens* evolve from ancient local roots over hundreds of thousands of years? In the absence of fossil discoveries, we must fall back on theoretical arguments, and on studies based on fossils that are hundreds of thousands of years apart in time.

Multiregional Evolution: Sangiran and Kow

Homo erectus was an archaic human being, with considerable brain capacity, and quite impressive, if limited, cultural capacity. Those who argue for regional continuity argue for parallel evolution in the direction of *Homo sapiens sapiens* among widely distributed Asian *Homo erectus* populations.

Faced with a paucity of fossils, two proponents of the regional theory, Milford Wolpoff of the University of Michigan and Alan Thorne of Australian National University, Canberra, came up with a bold approach to the problem. They compared fossils separated by over 700,000 years of prehistoric time, on the argument that this provides at least some basis for evaluating the continuity hypothesis. At one end of the timescale was a *Homo erectus* skull found at Sangiran in Java in 1969, estimated to be over 700,000 years old, with, unusually, the face preserved. At the other end was a fairly large sample of Australian *Homo sapiens sapiens* skeletons from Kow Swamp in northern Victoria, which date to between 14,000 and 9,500 years ago.

The Sangiran skull closely resembles other Indonesian *Homo erectus* fossils, but displays some differences from the Ngandong fossils from Solo River, which may date as late as 75,000 years ago. Thorne and Wolpoff found that both the Sangiran *Homo erectus* and the much more modern Kow

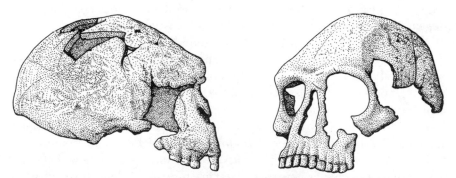

Skulls from Sangiran (left) and Kow Swamp (right) both show prognathism – a jutting forward of the face – even though they are separated in time by over 700,000 years.

specimens display marked prognathism, a jutting forward of the face that was a persistent feature in human populations in Southeast Asia for hundreds of thousands of years. On the basis of this, and other selected anatomical features, they claimed there was evidence of some continuity between *Homo erectus* and much more recent Australian populations.

Wolpoff and Thorne, like other Candelabra supporters, agree with Noah's Ark proponents that early *Homo erectus* was the first hominid form to migrate out of Africa. They hypothesize that the basic differences between Asian and other human populations were established when *Homo erectus* first settled in this region. These Asian populations were relatively homogeneous and this homogeneity was maintained over a very long period of time. This dynamic balance accounts for the marked prognathism and other more apparently archaic physical features that researchers see among modern Australian Aboriginal populations.

Thorne, Chinese scholar Wu Zin Xhi, and Wolpoff believe that there was interbreeding of *Homo sapiens sapiens* populations from "centers" of greater morphological variation like the Near East with more archaic humans further east. The further one got from the "centers," they argue, the later the appearance of modern humans. One of the later regions was mainland Southeast Asia, where *Homo erectus* apparently survived far longer than in Africa and Europe.

Noah's Ark critics of this regional hypothesis base their arguments both on the rapidly accumulating genetic evidence for a *Homo sapiens sapiens* African-based family tree, and what they perceive as serious deficiencies in Thorne and Wolpoff's studies of Asian and Australian fossils. They argue that Thorne and Wolpoff's research is based on a careful selection of anatomical features, some of which may represent primitive retentions. They reason that such anatomical characteristics are inappropriate for linking widely separated geographical populations that are hundreds of thousands of years apart in prehistoric time. In fact, the paucity of late *Homo erectus* and early *Homo sapiens* fossils from anywhere in Asia makes any detailed consideration of the regional hypothesis virtually impossible, and must place the quite ambitious conclusions of Thorne and Wolpoff's Sangiran-Kow study in some doubt.

There is now a widespread consensus that in many respects the Noah's Ark school are broadly correct, that *Homo sapiens sapiens* spread into Southeast Asia from outside. But it has to be admitted that the date and the processes by which this development took place are still a mystery. Perhaps both Noah's Ark and Candelabra are too extreme as hypotheses. Perhaps there was some anatomical continuity between *Homo erectus*/archaic *Homo sapiens* and modern humans in Southeast Asia, as a result of gene flow between populations. But equally, any such gene flow must surely have taken place in the context of a *replacement* of archaic humans by *Homo sapiens sapiens* populations coming from western Asia and, ultimately, "out of Africa."

A crude blueprint is suggested by the Cavalli-Sforza genetic tree (Chapter Three), which has Southeast Asians and Northeurasians bifurcating somewhere around 40,000 years ago. Still later, there were further splits – of mainland Asians from the primeval inhabitants of New Guinea and Australia, and of Pacific islanders from mainland populations (the latter discussed in Chapter Sixteen). These, and other genetic studies, strongly imply that anatomically modern humans spread into Asia from elsewhere, creating the varied modern populations of the region.

Cultural Innovation

If we cannot identify early populations of *Homo sapiens sapiens* from fossil evidence in Southeast Asia, are there cultural signposts? In Chapter Nine, we described the long-lived forest lifeway of *Homo erectus*, an adaptation based on the simplest of technologies that changed but little over many millennia. One has an overwhelming impression of simplicity, with, perhaps, a slight trend toward a greater use of smaller tools, and more sharp-edged flakes in later times. Even at the end of the Ice Age, long after the arrival of modern people, many Southeast Asian groups were still using a technology largely based on pebbles, many of them carefully trimmed to make choppers, with flakes and rare blades that may have served as convenient tools without further retouch. There can be no doubt that this simple toolkit had roots in much earlier cultural traditions. It continued in use in some mainland and island areas until at least 6,000 years ago, with, however, greater regional variation and a larger inventory of more specialized artifacts.

This technological conservatism is in sharp contrast to the situation in the more open river valleys, deserts, and plains of India and other parts of southern Asia west of the so-called Movius Line. Here one finds the characteristic and familiar Levallois and disc-core technologies of the Near Eastern Middle Paleolithic. Here, after 40,000 years ago, there are hints of the same kinds of technological change that occurred in the Near East, of more refined core preparation and ever more precise flaking that evolved, eventually, into the familiar Upper Paleolithic blade technology. To the east, in the forests and woodlands of Southeast Asia, Stone Age peoples continued to use the simplest of stone technologies. There are no signs yet of the kinds of gradual technological change chronicled by Jelinek and Marks at Tabūn and Boker Tachtit in the Near East (Chapter Eight), nor of an emerging blade technology in the forest zones this early, merely of a slow trend toward smaller, more varied toolkits. Perhaps blade technology was unnecessary in environments where bamboo was plentiful and other easily sharpened woods could be used.

If there were technological changes associated with *Homo sapiens sapiens*, they may have been reflected in perishable materials, and, more importantly, in more efficient ways of exploiting the rich, and highly varied environments of not only the mainland, but landmasses offshore. Only two categories of artifact hint at significant invention. A few simple bone tools appear in occupation levels dating to about 40,000 years ago (see below), and a simple form of "waisted" stone axe blade designed to be bound to a wooden handle was in use in some areas by about the same time. We can only guess at these and other innovations, but they may have included an ability to journey over open water, to hitherto uninhabited lands far from the familiar forests of the Asian mainland.

Sunda, Wallacea, and Sahul

Just like the rest of the world, Southeast Asia experienced major fluctuations in sea levels that coincided with Ice Age glacial and interglacial cycles. At intervals during the long sojourn of *Homo erectus* in Southeast Asia, the continental shelf extended far out from the present-day mainland coasts, most recently during the last (Würm) glaciation. The sea-level fluctuations of this final cold cycle give us at least a general impression of what the coastal geography of Southeast Asia might have been like during earlier glaciations too. At the height of the last glaciation some 20,000 years ago, sea levels were as much as 400 ft (122 m) below modern levels. Dry land joined Sumatra to Borneo, the Philippines and Malaya to the Southeast Asian mainland. Great rivers dissected the now-sunken plains, known to geologists as Sundaland, or Sunda for short. Further offshore, nearly 19 miles (30 km) of open water separated Sunda from Wallacea, another large island that comprised modern Sulawesi and Timor. During the glacial maximum, another 62 miles (100 km) of open water separated Wallacea from another enormous landmass, Sahul. This was a combination of Australia, New Guinea, and the low-lying and now-flooded shelf between them.

It should be stressed that these coastlines were those of the last glacial *maximum* 20,000 years ago. For most of the many millennia when global climatic conditions were colder than today, sea levels were probably considerably higher than at this maximum. It is difficult to estimate the heights of earlier coasts, but a fortunate discovery of some late Ice Age reefs uplifted by earth movement on the Huon Peninsula in New Guinea has enabled scientists to correlate geological sequences of raised beaches from earlier in the Würm glaciation with oxygen isotope curves from deep-sea cores. Between about 110,000 and 30,000 years ago, they estimate that the sea level may have averaged around 131 ft (40 m) below modern levels, giving a very different coastal configuration than that of 20,000 years ago – and, for that matter, of today. This means that, for most of the Würm glaciation, people moving from Sunda (linked to the mainland) to Wallacea and from Wallacea to Sahul would have needed to cross much wider bodies of open water than they would around 18,000–20,000 years ago. And even at the height of a glacial cycle, the colonization of Wallacea or Sahul would have required some form of watercraft, and the technology to build them. This raises one of the most fascinating questions surrounding the origins of anatomically modern people – who were the first Southeast Asians to build rafts or boats and cross open water to new lands over the horizon? Was it *Homo erectus* before perhaps as late as 75,000 years ago? Or did early *Homo sapiens* make the first crossing to a virgin Sahul? Or were anatomically modern people the primeval settlers of New Guinea and Australia? The only clues can come from archaeological sites from the mainland and from the islands close offshore, and from the surviving portions of Sahul itself.

Archaeological Sites on Sunda

Every expert agrees that Wallacea was first colonized from the Southeast Asian mainland by way of Sunda, but currently our knowledge of this mainland stock is virtually non-existent. If the Noah's Ark hypothesis is correct, then *Homo sapiens sapiens* would have been capable of colonizing mainland Southeast Asia some time after about 90,000 years ago. If the new Ngandong dates of between 100,000 and 75,000 years ago for archaic *Homo sapiens*/advanced *Homo erectus* are to be believed, then modern humans may have arrived somewhat later. There is a gap of at least 45,000 years between the youngest Ngandong estimate and the earliest indisputable fossil evidence for *Homo sapiens sapiens* in the region, which dates to about 30,000 years ago. As we shall see, that evidence comes from Australia, far offshore in what was once southern Sahul. The earliest modern human fossils from Sunda are the doubtful Niah burial from Borneo and the Tabon find from the Philippines, both of which postdate the earliest dated archaeological sites from Sahul.

Culturally, we can assume that the mainlanders of 100,000 years ago still relied heavily on bamboo and other forest materials for their artifacts, and that they used some form of simple chopper-chopping tool technology, as no other toolkit has yet been found in the region. The earliest dated site that might be attributed to *Homo sapiens sapiens* is the Long Rongrien cave, on the west end of the Thai–Malay Peninsula in the thick rainforest. The lowest occupation levels, which date to at least 37,000 ± 1780 years ago, are marked by small scrapers, some worked pebbles, and three antler or bone tools. After 27,000 years ago, a limestone collapse sealed these layers under rocks. There are no signs of dramatic cultural innovation.

Offshore, the environment of the time may have been more varied. Many people think of Sunda as a broad forested plain 40,000 years ago, with a dense canopy of trees extending out from the mainland all the way to the open sea. In fact, the climate of Sunda was probably drier and more seasonal, with many areas of open vegetational cover unlike the dense rainforest of today. Thus, it would be a mistake to think of late Ice Age human settlement in this vast region as merely a variation on the forest adaptations that flourished further north, even during drier glacial periods. There may well have been ample opportunities for more specialized hunting and gathering adaptations, for fishing and hunting of sea mammals.

Not that the archaeological record reflects any such specialization. Niah Cave on Borneo was occupied intermittently over a long period from 40,000 to 15,000 years ago. Niah's first occupants exploited local forests and rivers, hunting deer, monkeys, pangolins, pigs, and other forest animals. They also collected freshwater mollusks, gathering bivalves from coastal mangrove swamps at least 12 miles (20 km) away. Their toolkit was rudimentary – mainly stone flakes from shattered pebbles, and a few spatula-like bone tools. The latter became more common after 30,000 years ago. Leang Burung 2 cave on Sulawesi was occupied from about 31,000 to 10,000 years ago, and has yielded the simplest of stone toolkits, mostly flat, pointed flakes and steep-edged scrapers, many showing silica polish from plant processing.

With so little evidence to go on, we can only hypothesize about the inhabitants of Sunda between 100,000 and 40,000 years ago, extrapolating forward from early prehistory and backward from the scanty archaeological signature at Long Rongrien and Niah. In the forests, there was little need for sophisticated stone artifacts, when easily split and sharpened bamboo and other woods would suffice for weapons and knives. If the Ngandong dates are to be believed, then a late form of *Homo erectus*, perhaps archaic *Homo sapiens*, was flourishing in some of these forests well into the Würm glaciation. We do not know when *Homo sapiens sapiens* colonized mainland Southeast Asia and Sunda, but an intelligent guess (that relies perhaps too heavily on the Ngandong chronology) would be after 75,000 years ago.

During the early millennia of the last glaciation, sea levels were below modern levels, even if they were still substantially above those of the glacial maximum some 20,000 years ago. Human settlement was probably concentrated on areas such as coasts, lake shores and river valleys with more diverse and predictable food resources. As in the rainforests, easily split bamboo and other woods sufficed for many tasks. Elaborate blade technology was unnecessary.

The coastlines that faced toward Wallacea and Sahul were lapped by relatively benign waters and probably offered a bounty of easily taken shallowwater fish and shellfish to supplement game and plant foods. Without invoking a full boatbuilding technology, one can speculate that the people living along these shores could easily fashion simple bamboo and mangrove wood rafts, stout logs lashed together with lengths of forest vines. Archaeologist Rhys Jones of Australian National University has observed people on the Sepik River in New Guinea using large rafts of layers of vine-lashed poles with bark decks, made with a minimal technology. He believes, probably correctly, that such rafts would last quite a long time in moderate seas. Such rafts would have been an ingenious way of reaching offlying bivalve sites, and have served as a platform for shallowwater bottom fishing, or for riding tides to nearby inshore islands and sand bars. At some point, long before the climax of the last glaciation some 20,000 years ago, some of these coastal peoples crossed to Wallacea and Sahul and colonized virgin lands.

The First Settlement of Sahul

At its maximum extent some 20,000 years ago, the continent of Sahul (New Guinea and Australia) was a landmass of dramatic contrasts. What is now New Guinea in the far north was a landscape of rugged mountain chains and highland valleys with regular rainfall and sharply contrasting local environments. The remainder of Sahul (that is, the Australian continent) was far drier, much of it rolling, semi-arid lowlands. Sahul has distinctive marsupial mammals, a fauna that evolved separately from the rest of the world for more than 50 million years. The most dramatic Ice Age climatic changes were sea-level changes, and a rise or fall of about 100 ft (31 m) severed or joined the two lands. In the higher country of New Guinea and southeastern Australia, temperatures were considerably lower during the late Würm glaciation, and areas of New Guinea now covered by lowland rainforest may have been open forest. Not that all the changes were natural ones, for there is clear evidence that firing by humans was responsible for considerable vegetational change in later prehistoric times.

The first human settlement of Sahul remains one of the controversial questions of prehistory, for to settle this isolated land people would have had to have crossed a minimum of 62 miles (100 km) of open water, and, if they settled Sahul earlier than the last glacial maximum about 20,000 years ago, which they certainly did, a lot more water than that. Two routes were possible. One led from southern Sunda to the island of Timor, part of Wallacea, and then across to the Australian shore. The other was from Vietnam, across northern Sunda and Borneo, and into New Guinea via Sulawesi. Whichever general route was used, the process of colonization involved considerable distances of island hopping and open-water travel – the first instance of seafaring by human beings.

Even during the Würm glaciation, the oceans of Southeast Asia were relatively warm, compared with those of more northern lands. They were seas that were generally benign, except during the seasonal monsoons that brought rainfall and high winds. Simple watercraft, such as bamboo rafts, can support a few people and carry them across open water on the arms of a favorable breeze or ocean current, even if they have little control over their course. It may be that the first Sahulians were small bands of coastal people,

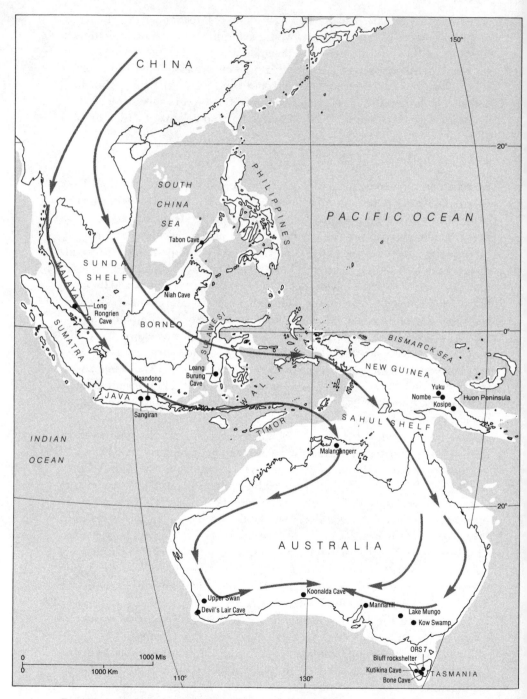

Possible migration routes to New Guinea and Australia at periods of lower sea level, when the Sunda and Sahul shelves were exposed.

living, say, in southern Sunda, who were accustomed to fishing in shallow water from simple rafts. Inevitably, perhaps during the months when summer monsoon winds blow strongly from the north and toward invisible Sahul, occasional rafts were carried into deeper water, then offshore, out of sight of land. A few days later, prevailing winds and currents cast them ashore in a deserted, and hitherto unknown land, where they settled, moving inshore in search of more favorable environments. Computer simulations show that under these conditions there are moderate chances of a raft traveling from the Timor coast to northern Australia in about seven days.

As is always the case with such colonizations, however, scholars debate endlessly over whether the settlement could have been accidental or deliberate, the result of some compelling curiosity that took a small band of hunter-gatherers over the horizon, presumably with the expectation that they would return. To undertake a deliberate voyage with the intention of returning would have required not a raft, but very seaworthy bark or dugout canoes capable of being paddled against prevailing winds. And how would people find their way across open ocean? Were they capable of using sun and stars, or other natural phenomena, to set a course out and to return? We have no means of knowing if such skills were within the capabilities of late Ice Age Southeast Asians, for the watercraft they used are not preserved in the archaeological record. We can only hope that one day someone will discover a waterlogged coastal site where such artifacts as canoe paddles might be found. Many scholars have argued that there was an easy "voyaging corridor" from mainland Southeast Asia out to New Guinea and the closer islands of Melanesia. Many parts of Sahul may have been reached quite frequently, along short routes where high land was visible from one island to the next. This was also a corridor where winds and currents reversed from one season to another, with a sheltered equatorial position between the usual northern and southern cyclonic belts. Geoffrey Irwin of the University of Auckland has studied the currents, distances, and winds in detail and believes this entire region was an ideal location for people to develop the seagoing skills required to colonize both near Melanesia, and, much later, the more remote islands of the Pacific as well.

It seems likely that the initial settlement was a combination of both accidental and deliberate voyaging by tiny numbers of people over a period of millennia. Undoubtedly, many of these journeys, ending on a large land target of more than 1,850 miles (3,000 km) of coastline, ended in the group dying out. A successful colonizing group requires several individuals of both genders. Simulation modeling of the chances of long-term reproduction success of small founding groups show the chance of success was very small. There may have been many accidental colonizations over the millennia before a viable population was established. The date when such a population or populations became permanent residents is still highly uncertain, but hunter-gatherers were living throughout much of New Guinea and Australia at least 40,000 years ago, and possibly as early as 50,000 or 60,000 years ago.

New Guinea and Offshore Islands

Many of the important sites that would chronicle the first settlement of Sahul are buried, as they are in the far north, under high modern sea levels. Only in a few exceptional locations where the forces of nature have uplifted the land such as the Huon Peninsula in New Guinea, already mentioned, can we obtain firm evidence for early human occupation. At Bobongara on the Huon, Australian archaeologist Les Groube of the University of Papua New Guinea found waisted ground axes and a single stone flake sealed under volcanic ash that dates to at least 40,000 years ago. Groube believes that these waisted axes were used to ring trees and clear forest, perhaps to encourage the growth of plants on the forest fringes – a form of deliberate manipulation of wild plants to enhance growth of wild plant foods such as yams, sugarcane, and perhaps taro and tree fruits. The Huon discovery is reliably dated, and the artifacts are unquestionably of human manufacture, and of impeccable association. They provide incontrovertible evidence that Sahul was settled by humans when Neanderthals were still flourishing in distant Europe. As we have seen, there is no fossil evidence of this date to tell us whether the Huon axe makers were anatomically modern in appearance.

The Huon Peninsula faces the Bismarck Sea, with the island of New Britain only a 30-mile (51-km) passage or so offshore. From there, it is but a short voyage to New Ireland. Although both islands are visible targets navigationally speaking, they are "oceanic" islands, separated from New Guinea by deep-water straits, not by submerged continental shelf. So open-water voyages were necessary to colonize them, even in times of lowered sea levels. Excavations in four limestone caves on New Ireland have yielded traces of human occupation at least 32,000 years ago. These were expert fishermen, who took crustacea, fish, and shellfish from nearby reefs, and they hunted bats, reptiles, birds, and rats as well. By 20,000 years ago, their successors were regularly trading obsidian across 19 miles (30 km) of open water from west New Britain, from a source 217 straight-line miles (350 km) from their home.

The Kilu rockshelter on Buka Island in the northern Solomons to the south contains human occupation dating to between 28,000 and 20,000 years ago, as revealed by radiocarbon dates from shells brought into the site. Kilu was first occupied when the sea level was about 150 ft (46 m) below modern levels, and before the last glacial maximum. Open-water crossings of at least 81–112 miles (130–180 km) would have been required to settle on Buka, depending on the route selected. (One's destination is invisible from either end, although both New Ireland and Buka can be seen when far from land.) Voyaging over this distance would certainly have required some form of open-water craft, also foods that could be preserved for use aboard during relatively extended voyages. The crews would need some form of bark, wild gourd, or skin containers, too, to carry water – not that these were a revolutionary innovation, for they would have long been used on land. From Buka it would have been an easy matter to colonize the rest of the Solomon chain, for the islands are separated by but short distances.

The Kilu people exploited both marine and forest resources, and used a stone technology that relied on core tools and scrapers, such as was widely used throughout the settled areas of Sahul during the late Ice Age and into postglacial times. Some of the flakes display microscopic traces of starch grains, good evidence for the exploitation of plant foods.

All the data point to a relatively rapid spread of hunter-gatherer peoples through Sahul by at least 40,000 years ago, with a few bands settling on the northern Solomons at about the time that other groups were reaching the southern shores of Australia. Judging from the Kilu site, these people had probably developed some more effective forms of watercraft than the raft for inter-island passages by 30,000 years ago.

Highland New Guinea does not yet boast of such early settlement, but the Kosipe site in the eastern highlands dates to 24,000 years ago. This small open site may have been a base for collecting fruit from the palm-like pandanus (screw-pine) trees in a nearby swamp. Other sites such as the Nombe and Yuku rockshelters are proof that people were exploiting the tropical highlands during the last glacial maximum, between 20,000 and 15,000 years ago. There is good reason to believe that they were also doing so at least 30,000 years ago, and conceivably at least 10,000 years earlier than that.

Australia

After about 60,000 years ago, Australia, which formed the southern part of Sahul and was intermittently joined to New Guinea, was colder and drier than today. Between 40,000 and 30,000 years ago northeastern Australia became even more arid, while lakes filled in the southern areas of the continent, perhaps as a result of reduced evaporation rates. The sunken parts of Sahul are now covered by the Arafura Sea, which, during the coldest millennia of the Würm glaciation, was a flat, low-lying plain with a generally arid climate and occasional large lakes or swamps. The constantly fluctuating sea levels caused environmental conditions at the coasts to change. Rising seas favored the formation of large lagoons behind beaches, but these may have been unstable with lower populations of animals and plants than more productive environments lying farther inland. Although such locations may well have been relatively favorable for human exploitation, they were nothing like as bountiful as the relatively stable shorelines of the past 6,000 years.

Though all Australian archaeologists agree that people were living around the coast and on the fringes of the central desert by at least 20,000 years ago, the nature of initial settlement and colonization is still hotly debated. By 10,000 years later, people were living in every major environmental zone. Some researchers argue that, once people arrived in Australia, small groups expanded rapidly over the continent as a result of their highly mobile lifeway, hunting kangaroos and other large marsupials. Anthropologist Joseph Birdsell of the University of California, Los Angeles, argues that a mere doubling of the population every 20 years after first settlement would have resulted in natural population growth to 18th-century AD levels within only 2,000 years. Others argue that these models are too simplistic, that the process of settlement involved first the sea coasts and then colonization of the arid interior. Such scholars believe that the first settlement was a gradual process, in the hands of people who had to adapt not only to marine conditions, but also to the dry, seasonal woodland environments found in the Australian interior, and, presumably, also on the Arafura landbridge linking New Guinea to Australia. Thus, argue archaeologists Peter White of the University of Sydney and James O'Connell of the University of Utah, there was a slow build-up in human populations, a period of adaptation to new environments and to new plant and animal foods, and gradual expansion into highly varied environments, including the cold climes of Tasmania in the extreme south. As we shall see, recent discoveries in Tasmania have cast doubt on this hypothesis.

When was Australia (southern Sahul) first settled? Archaeologist Jim Allen of La Trobe University in Melbourne points out that there is what he calls a "watershed" at about 35,000 years ago. After that date, there are well-attested living sites and indisputable evidence of human settlement. Earlier sites come in two categories. Some are finds of stone implements in river gravels, often found in circumstances where direct dating of the tools is impossible. One such occurrence is the Upper Swan site, on an ancient floodplain of the Swan River in Western Australia. Here, artifacts, and the remains of stone-flaking floors, cover an area of some 2,700 sq. ft (250 sq. m), and are claimed to come from layers dating to 38,000 years ago. There are persistent reports of earlier sites. Thermoluminescence dating of naturally deposited sands containing stone artifacts is a potentially promising way of documenting even earlier settlement, perhaps as early as 60,000 years ago, but details of this research are still largely unpublished.

A second category of early claims consists of indirect evidence for human activity – geomorphological phenomena that cannot easily be explained through natural causes. For example, fossil pollen experts identified a sudden rise in charcoal levels in the deposits of Lake George near Canberra before 60,000 years ago. They suggested that this was a result of human firing of forests. On the Atherton Tableland in northern Queensland, eucalyptus trees spread rapidly at the expense of rainforest and other fire-sensitive species about 40,000 years ago, perhaps, again, as a result of human activity. It is only fair to say that these, and other such claims, do not constitute unimpeachable evidence for early human occupation.

Most archaeologists are reluctant to accept dates earlier than about 40,000 years ago until more sites are discovered. There is, of course, a possibility that there was a long period of what Allen calls "invisible colonization" for thousands of years before that date, a population movement that is not, so far, represented in the archaeological record. In the meantime, traces of human occupation before, and around, 30,000 years ago have accumulated rapidly in recent years. Some 186 miles (300 km) to the southwest of the Upper Swan site, local people visited the Devil's Lair Cave near Perth occasionally as early as 32,500 years ago, perhaps even earlier, and used the site more regularly from 23,000 until the end of the Ice Age. The Purritjarra rockshelter in the arid center of Australia near the Northern Territory's Cleland Hills was occupied from at least 27,000 years ago to about 6,000 years ago.

Far to the east, in the Willandra Lakes region of western New South Wales, early archaeological sites cluster around long dried-up lakes. One group of sites include shell middens located in dune systems dating to around 32,000 years ago, and as early as 37,000–34,000 years ago. The 26,000-year-old Lake Mungo site comes from the same general area. It is a thin scatter of stone artifacts, hearths, fish, and other food remains, and also has a human cremation. Humans were living in the arid zones of Australia, at such places as Koonalda Cave on the Nullabor Plain in South Australia, by 24,000 years ago. They lived there until 15,000 years ago, visiting the site to quarry stone and making patterned lines or "flutings" on the cave walls during their stays. Arnhem Land in the north was certainly occupied well before 20,000 years ago, with radiocarbon-dated occupations of about 22,900 years ago at Malangangerr rockshelter. Several northern sites were occupied during the driest part of the Würm glaciation, and ocher "pencils" with traces of wear, presumably used for painting, date to as early as 19,000 years ago, and, perhaps even to 30,000 years ago. It is possible that some of the oldest Arnhem Land wall paintings depict extinct animals, but the interpretation is much debated. Dates from coatings of "desert varnish" on engravings on dolomite outcrops at Mannahill in South Australia are said to span a period from 31,000 to 16,000 years ago. Although the Mannahill dates are still controversial, it seems possible that prehistoric Australians were painting and engraving as early as Stone Age artists in distant Europe.

Tasmania

Recent research on the island of Tasmania has thrown up fascinating new evidence indicating that this was the most southerly region on earth to be reached by modern humans during the last Ice Age. The island was connected to Australia by a land bridge on at least three occasions before the last glacial maximum. The most recent occasion lasted from around 37,000 to 29,000 years ago, about the time of the earliest securely dated settlement of Sahul. During much of the last glaciation, climatic conditions throughout the island were quite severe, with ice sheets on higher ground in the interior and temperatures at the glacial maximum as much as 10.8 degrees F (6 deg.C) colder than today. Archaeologist Richard Cosgrove of La Trobe University excavated Bluff rockshelter in the Florentine River valley of south-central Tasmania, which was occupied intermittently for nearly 20,000 years during the last glaciation. The lowest levels date to 30,420 ± 690 years ago, while those at another shelter, ORS 7, to the northwest, on the edge of the central Tasmanian highlands, date to 30,840 ± 480 years ago. Both of these nearly 31,000-year-old occupation levels contain emu eggs, showing that the people here were not deterred by the immensely cold temperatures during late winter and early spring, the period when the eggs would have been collected.

Bluff and ORS 7 were occupied before the glacial maximum, but people continued to live in the rugged landscape of southwestern and central Tasmania right through the coldest millennia of the last glaciation. The Kutikina Cave was occupied between 20,000 and 14,000 years ago, a time when the landscape was open tundra and grassland. The people were hunters of red wallabies, as were the inhabitants of at least 20 other occupied caves nearby. Slightly to the east, another rugged rainforest area has yielded more late glacial human occupation, dating, at Bone Cave, to between 17,000 and 13,000 years ago. The groups in these areas appear to have been part of a common social system that ranged over a wide area for many millennia. Some groups used Darwin Glass, a natural glass from a meteorite crater a minimum distance of 28 miles (45 km) from Kutikina and over 62 miles (100 km) in straight-line distance from the Florentine River.

Several limestone caves in southwestern Tasmania contain panels of paintings 66 ft (20 m) or more from the entrance, and thus only to be viewed by artificial light of some kind. Panels of hand stencils and areas with continuous pigment daubings and red blazes appear at the entrance or on prominent walls. These newly discovered sites contain paintings covered with stalagmite and the art is believed to date to the same period as occupation in the general area. These were the southernmost people living on earth during the last glaciation. With the severing of the land bridge after the Ice Age, the survivors remained isolated from the outside world for thousands of years until French explorer Marion du Fresne met some Tasmanians in 1772.

The Story of the First Australians

Let me conclude this tale of the first seafarers by summarizing what we know, and do not know, about the colonization of Australia. In strictly archaeological terms,.the first settlement of Sahul took place at least 40,000 years ago, and perhaps at least 10,000, or even 20,000, years earlier, from mainland Southeast Asia. This settlement may have taken place relatively soon after the first arrival of *Homo sapiens sapiens* in Southeast Asia, even if we as yet have no such fossils of this age to gaze upon. The first settlers of Sahul were the earliest humans to develop watercraft capable of traveling over considerable stretches of open ocean. To design and build such craft may not have needed elaborate technology, but it would have required the ability to develop the idea of a floating raft to carry people safely over an unfamiliar environment – open water. Such intellectual qualities and the abilities to organize small groups of people to fell trees and construct the raft were, to my mind, beyond the capabilities of *Homo erectus* and early *Homo sapiens*. The expertise to cross water out of sight of land, however accidental initially, was a distinctive skill of *Homo sapiens sapiens*.

It is striking that the well-attested dates for first human settlement cluster between 40,000 and about 30,000 years ago. This implies that the initial colonization of Sahul was not as gradual as White and O'Connell suggest, but was quite a rapid process. Within a few millennia, humans adapted not only to coasts, but to a great range of environments and temperatures, everything from arid desert to chilly southern tundra. There was, apparently, no prolonged period of acclimatization to new environments – these were inventive, adaptable people, probably vastly superior in their intellectual and cultural capabilities to the archaic humans who never ventured offshore.

The first settlers used a simple stone technology that included flaked choppers, sharp flake tools, and occasional ground axes, such as the waisted forms found at Huon in New Guinea, dating to 40,000 years ago. If Alan Thorne is correct, these people were anatomically modern, but with some archaic features that serve to link their ultimate ancestry to primeval *Homo erectus* populations on the mainland, which left the "mark of ancient Java" upon them. The skeletons from Lake Mungo and Kow Swamp display basically modern Aboriginal morphology, but their owners were more heavily built, with larger teeth than more modern Australian populations. It is hardly surprising to find some differences over more than 10,000 years, given the size and ecological diversity of Australia, and the effects of gene flow resulting from later, even small-scale, population movements from elsewhere. At first, the population growth may have been tiny, with small bands of hunters distributed very sparsely over a great diversity of environmental zones, including extremely cold landscapes in southwestern Tasmania. But by the end of the Ice Age, the population of what is now Australia was probably close to its pre-European level of about 300,000 people, a hunter-gatherer lifeway that had its ultimate origins in prehistoric Southeast Asia.

The first Tasmanians successfully confronted and adapted to the cruel winters of their Ice Age island. On the opposite side of the world, similar perils faced the early inhabitants of Europe 40,000 years ago. It was their mastery of winter that opened up the great Eurasian steppe to human colonization, an achievement that led ultimately to the conquest of Siberia and the peopling of the Americas.

PART FOUR

MASTERY OF WINTER

"When you have eliminated the impossible, whatever remains, however improbable, must be the truth."

Sherlock Holmes, in *The Sign of Four*

CHAPTER ELEVEN

The Rise of the Cro-Magnons

We have traced the emergence of modern humans in Africa before 100,000 years ago, and their appearance in the Levant by 90,000 years ago. It took another 40,000 or 50,000 years for modern people to reach distant Australia – an immense length of time on any timescale, but nevertheless a more or less comprehensible one bearing in mind the thousands of miles that separate Australia from the Near East, and the no doubt immeasurably small, non-deliberate movements eastward made by hunter-gatherer bands in any one generation. But what happened in the Levant? It is not much more than a few hundred miles from this region of the world to southeastern Europe, and yet, seemingly, it took modern humans a full 50,000 years to traverse this short distance as well. Why did they not venture northward for so long?

The Frozen North

The simplest and most economical explanation for this 50,000-year time lapse must be an environmental one. As we saw in Chapter Seven, between about 100,000 and 50,000 years ago Europe was a frigid, ice-bound continent, a very different environment from the relatively temperate steppes and woodlands of the Near East. Full glacial conditions persisted after about 75,000 years ago until around 40,000 years ago. This was the world of the European Neanderthals, the intense cold occasionally interrupted by brief warmer interludes. A vast continental ice sheet mantled all of Scandinavia and the British Isles as far south as central England. The Alps were the center of another ice sheet that flowed beyond the confines of the mountains to the edge of the undulating country to the north and west.

Such harsh conditions may, initially, have deterred *Homo sapiens sapiens* from leaving the temperate Levant. To adapt successfully to environments with long, chilling winters may have been beyond the capabilities of people who were still unaccustomed, at any rate initially, to seasonal climatic extremes. Significantly, perhaps, the indigenous Neanderthal populations of the north had evolved a successful physical adaptation to extreme conditions, but this adaptation took tens of thousands of years to appear before 100,000 years ago, and the Neanderthals' very success may have blocked movement north of the physically less robust *Homo sapiens sapiens*.

It may be no coincidence that the first people of modern appearance appear on European soil after 50,000 years ago, during a brief period of more temperate climate. Even then, climatic conditions and seasonal contrast may have been severe enough to require new artifacts, and more sophisticated hunting skills. These adaptations were to evolve rapidly, indeed spectacularly, after 30,000 years ago.

The Power of Words

Perhaps, too, the first settlement of Europe by modern humans coincided with dramatic linguistic change. Archaeologist Paul Mellars of the University of Cambridge suggests that the evolution of fully modern language sparked the technological changes of 45,000 years ago in the Near East. He tends to agree with Philip Lieberman, who argues that the Neanderthals were incapable of fully articulate speech (Chapter Seven). Before 45,000, Mellars believes, humans used languages without tenses, and possessed but a small vocabulary of words with very general meanings. Then drastically enhanced language abilities resulted in rapid cultural and technological change. Some of these changes may be detectable in the archaeological record. For example, argues Mellars, sophisticated languages allowed hunters to cooperate more closely in the chase, enabling them to organize game drives that killed large numbers of animals, and also to concentrate on specific species rather than on merely opportunistic prey. He points out that hunting camps occupied after about 40,000 years ago often contain a lesser variety of game species, as if humans were now focusing on a few animals in carefully planned hunts. For thousands of years, too, people had used simple, multipurpose artifacts in the chase. Mellars believes that the more sophisticated hunting artifacts and technology developed after about 45,000 years ago resulted from improved language. It was also no coincidence that art and jewelry, with all the rich symbolism associated with them, appear after 35,000 years ago.

If human language reached a fully evolved state in the Near East about 45,000 years ago, then it may have been a catalyst for the settlement of more northern latitudes by *Homo sapiens sapiens*. Perhaps, too, it sealed the fate of the Neanderthals, their potential competitors, with whom, apparently, modern humans had lived in the Near East for more than 45,000 years.

The Cro-Magnons and the Aurignacian

In the year 1868, laborers building the Les Eyzies railroad station in France's Périgord region uncovered a small group of human burials in the nearby Cro-Magnon rockshelter, several individuals associated with reindeer bones. The

"Cro-Magnons" were not Neanderthals, but modern-looking people with round heads, high foreheads, and large brains, as highly developed and fully capable as our own. Victorian scientists thought of the Cro-Magnons as Ice Age savages until the discovery of magnificent cave paintings at Altamira in northern Spain and in the Périgord. The Abbé Henri Breuil and other early 20th-century prehistorians were profoundly impressed by the Cro-Magnons' artistry and cultural achievements. In the popular imagination the Périgord and northern Spain became a kind of prehistoric Garden of Eden (long before the geneticists' African version), a place where Stone Age *Homo sapiens* achieved supreme cultural heights. Even today, images of late Ice Age life and mass-market novels are colored by such perceptions. In truth, there was no Garden of Eden here, merely a dramatic efflorescence of hunter-gatherer life throughout much of Europe and Eurasia during the last part of the Würm glaciation. The roots of this cultural explosion lie in a primeval Upper Paleolithic culture of Europe and the Near East – the Aurignacian.

The stone blades and knives found with the original Cro-Magnon skeletons were identical to similar artifacts found by French archaeologist Edouard Lartet in the Aurignac rockshelter in the foothills of the Pyrenees in 1860, whence "Aurignacian." Aurignacian tools soon turned up in deposits above Mousterian (Middle Paleolithic) levels in caves and rockshelters throughout southwestern France and northern Spain, then in central and southeastern Europe. During the 1930s, Dorothy Garrod found Aurignacian deposits in the upper levels at Mount Carmel in the Near East, above the Mousterian there. She was the first to argue that the Aurignacian originated in the Near East, and spread from there into Europe in the hands of the Cro-Magnons.

In Europe, the Aurignacian people enjoyed a much more diverse culture than their Neanderthal predecessors. They were expert hunters and pursued a wide range of large and small periglacial animals, using bone-pointed spears and a distinctive stone toolkit that included sharpened and notched blades and highly characteristic steep-edged scrapers. Unlike the Neanderthals, the European Aurignacians were artists, who adorned themselves with perforated carnivore teeth and seashells. They were people with what must have been an intricate symbolic life. But what was the process by which these people came from the Near East?

The Levantine Aurignacian

At least two cultural traditions flourished in the Near East between 40,000 and 20,000 years ago, identified by stone tools from large numbers of open-air sites in the Levant. The "Ahmarian" emphasizes blade production, and the people used large numbers of long, narrow blades in their toolkits. This local tradition is still poorly defined. The better known "Aurignacian" used many flakes and a simpler blade production technology that resulted in much heavier, larger blades, also small, twisted-profile bladelets that formed part of a technology that relied heavily on steep-edged artifacts such as scrapers. The people used bone tools like tanged points, awls to work hide or leather, antler and horn core polishers, and, rarely, bone points with split bases. The Aurignacians also ground red ocher into fine powder and smeared it on artifacts and stone slabs, adorned themselves with bone pendants and incised bones. From what we know of Aurignacian material culture, it was more elaborate and used a wider range of raw materials than did earlier Near Eastern cultures.

We know little of the lifeway of these people. There are hints that local bands were more mobile than their forebears, exploiting sources of food over very large areas. It is possible that many of the coastal caves and rockshelters were used on a seasonal basis, but so far open-air sites are rare. Everywhere, the Aurignacians may have concentrated more regularly on animals in their prime, for the change to blade technology permitted the use of lighter weapons, allowing hunters to attack prey selectively from a distance.

Israeli archaeologists Ofer Bar-Yosef and Anna Belfer-Cohen believe that the Levantine Aurignacian represents the archaeological remains of a large hunter-gatherer band, a "macro-band" in technical parlance, which exploited a large region from the flanks of the Taurus Mountains in the north to the Judean Hills in the south. It is important to realize that hunter-gatherer populations were sparse at the very beginning of the Upper Paleolithic. If the coastal Levant was indeed occupied by just a wide-ranging macro-band, then one might logically expect hunter-gatherer populations to be just as thin on the ground in Turkey and in other regions to the north.

A small, widely ranging Upper Paleolithic hunter-gatherer population in the Near East, adapted to circumstances that required great mobility, and with fleeting contacts with just as sparse neighboring groups at the outer limits of group territory – these might well be circumstances under which new ideas and adaptations might be diffused over large areas at the hands of Aurignacian peoples, or their immediate predecessors. Judging from radio-carbon dates from Boker Tachtit in Israel's Negev Desert (Chapter Eight), this process may have begun as early as about 45,000 years ago. At the time of writing, the earliest radiocarbon date for the Levantine Aurignacian is at about 32,000 years ago, with a few sites dating to as late as 17,000 years ago. However, extrapolations from dated levels at K'sar Akil rockshelter in Lebanon imply that earlier Aurignacian occupations may date to at least 38,000 years ago, with the transition from Middle to Upper Paleolithic technology dating to an estimated 43,000 years ago, a date that agrees well with the Boker Tachtit chronology. Further afield, both Shanidar and Yafteh caves in the Zagros Mountains of Iran have yielded traces of distinctive Upper Paleolithic occupation of non-Aurignacian type dating to about 38,000 years ago and underlain by Mousterian levels. The same general technological transition between Middle and Upper Paleolithic may have taken place elsewhere in the Near East at about the same time.

Southeastern and Central Europe

Replacement or indigenous origin – the debates we touched on in Chapter Seven about the origins of anatomically modern Europeans are still waged fiercely, no more intensely than in southeastern Europe, with its close links to the Near East. There are abundant traces of Neanderthal occupation along the Danube and in the Balkans, not only thick cave deposits crammed with artifacts and bones, but a scatter of fossil remains as well. These have generated considerable debate, with some physical anthropologists claiming the fossils show evidence of evolution toward modern humans, while others consider the local Neanderthals identical to the robust, squat populations to the west. Fred Smith of the University of Tennessee argues that there were two groups of Neanderthals in central Europe. The earlier were virtually indistinguishable from western populations, while the later group "approaches the modern *Homo sapiens* condition to a consistently greater extent than the early group does." Smith believes there was a "distinct morphological continuum" between his late group and the earliest anatomically modern people in central Europe. Few of the Neanderthals in his sample are securely dated, certainly not with the precision needed to trace gradual evolutionary change over a period of 10,000 to 20,000 years.

The selective anatomical features that Smith uses to argue for continuity include the form of the supraorbital region (the area above the eyes), and the shape of the back of the skull. His critics point out that these traits cannot necessarily be selected out as criteria for continuity, when there are others that should be taken into account. Most Neanderthal experts believe that the central European fossils share many robust features, and that, despite some variability, they are to all intents and purposes identical to "classic" Neanderthal populations in western Europe. They argue for some form of population replacement on both anatomical and cultural grounds.

The cultural evidence for population replacement is much more striking than the anatomical grounds, for there is a marked technological break between Mousterian and Upper Paleolithic levels. Sometimes the earliest Upper Paleolithic occupation consists of little more than a scatter of blades and crude artifacts, soon replaced by well-formed Aurignacian artifacts, as if the new blade technology was still ill-formed as it came into use throughout the region. Thick Aurignacian occupations follow, sometimes associated with modern humans anatomically close to the Cro-Magnons.

Aurignacians or their immediate predecessors were living at Bacho Kiro cave in Bulgaria as early as 43,000 years ago, during a period of warmer climate. They continued to visit the cave until as late as 29,000 years ago.

Unlike their Neanderthal predecessors, they used not local stone but fine-quality flint imported from elsewhere. More Aurignacians visited Istallösko Cave in Hungary's Bukk Mountains at least as early as 40,000 years ago, and continued to flourish in the vicinity for at least 9,000 years. In many places, the newcomers lived alongside Neanderthal groups, who were visiting caves only a few miles away. The occupation levels of some sites like Szeleta Cave in the Bukk Mountains contain mixtures of Middle and Upper Paleolithic tools, perhaps evidence for sporadic cultural contact, or for Neanderthal experimentation with new technologies. Between 36,000 and 32,000 years ago, however, the Upper Danube Valley became wholly Aurignacian territory, and other groups moved onto the plains to the north at about the same time.

The radiocarbon dates for the Aurignacian and its possible, as yet undifferentiated, immediate predecessor, range from before 43,000 to about 22,600 years ago. This is a wider range of dates than that of the Aurignacian in western Europe, which spans a period from about 40,000 to 24,540 years ago. While the Aurignacian reached its climax in both areas at about the same time, this distinctive culture associated with anatomically modern people appears somewhat earlier in the east. The chronological gradient from east to west is striking, perhaps in the order of 5,000 to 10,000 years, maybe less if recent northern Spanish dates in the 40,000-year range are verified elsewhere. On anatomical, stratigraphic, and cultural grounds, there is certainly a strong case to be made for population replacement in the east, and for the movement of anatomically modern people into the west. Quite what form this population replacement took remains an enigma. There may have been interbreeding between the two populations. The resulting gene flow would have produced mosaic-like changes, which may be reflected in what appears to be a degree of variability in some early Cro-Magnon populations. Or the Neanderthals may have been forced into territories on the periphery, where they lived alongside more modern neighbors for some millennia.

We can envisage, then, a long process not only of gene flow and small-scale population movement, but a gradual flow of cultural innovations as well – of new technologies, new strategies for the hunt. Such a flow of ideas would be fostered in situations where hunter-gatherers exploit large territories and are careful in their selection of toolmaking stone, for fine-grained rocks are far from evenly distributed and may have been exchanged with more fortunate neighbors. And, under such circumstances, technological innovation may have preceded gene flow and population replacement, resulting in Neanderthals experimenting with more sophisticated artifacts.

Châtelperronian and Aurignacian in Western Europe

It was Abbé Henri Breuil who first identified the earliest Upper Paleolithic occupation levels in western Europe. They were thin, inconspicuous horizons, often little more than a scatter of stone artifacts by a hearth. The tools and blades were crude, the most characteristic a backed flake-knife which Breuil called the Châtelperron point, after the rockshelter where it was first identified. This Châtelperronian phase or culture, as it is commonly called, is still rather a shadowy entity – just like the earliest Upper Paleolithic occupation of southeastern Europe.

Châtelperronian occupations occur from the French Pyrenees through southwestern into central and north-central France, a tiny area by prehistoric standards. Since the 1960s, more scientifically conducted stratigraphic researches have shown that the Châtelperronian and Aurignacian occupations alternate with one another at several sites, and that they are almost certainly at least partially contemporary. How, then, is one to interpret them? Do they represent two distinct cultural traditions associated with ethnically distinct groups? Or do they chronicle quite different activities, that used different artifacts at various seasons of the year?

The earliest dated occurrences of both Châtelperronian and Aurignacian occupation are before 34,000 years ago, perhaps as early as 40,000 years ago, somewhat later than equivalent dates from southeastern Europe. The period of overlap between Châtelperronian and Aurignacian persists until sometime after 33,000 years ago, after which only Aurignacian occupations are found. Using pollen analyses and sediment analyses from cave deposits, French scholar Henri Laville has been able to correlate climatic changes between 40,000 and 30,000 years ago with both radiocarbon dates and human occupations. Before 37,000, the climate was cold, with Neanderthal groups throughout the region. Then cool, more temperate conditions prevailed, at a time when the first Châtelperronian occupations appear abruptly. Most Châtelperronian occupation dates to the long period of fluctuating climate from 37,000 to 33,000 years ago. Now Mousterian sites were on the periphery, in Cantabrian Spain, while early Aurignacian occupations occurred to the south and in the center of the region, with some overlapping of the two traditions in the Châtelperronian sphere. Then the climate cooled again, and the Aurignacian alone is found.

The caves of Arcy-sur-Cure lie between Auxerre and Avallon, southeast of Paris. Famous for their immense galleries adorned with stalactites, they have attracted tourists for centuries. The caves were formed in impressive limestone cliffs, close to excellent flint sources. Here, in the 1950s and 1960s, prehistorian André Leroi-Gourhan uncovered several well-defined levels of Châtelperronian occupation in the Grotte du Renne, the cave of reindeer.

Neanderthals were the first to use the Grotte du Renne, the last of them at a time when conditions were somewhat more temperate than in earlier millennia. These "Final Mousterians" were making not only the usual points and side scrapers made with Levallois core techniques, but also numerous backed knives and notched and saw-edged forms fabricated on more elongated blanks that are almost blade-like, resembling later Châtelperronian technology.

The Châtelperronian levels were between 16 and 30 in (40–75 cm) thick. They contained many flakes made on Levallois cores, Middle Paleolithic side scrapers and triangular points, also notched and saw-edged flakes. But, at the same time, new elements appeared, including classic Châtelperron points, Upper Paleolithic end scrapers and rare burins (a type of engraving tool). However, these new artifacts are far from standardized and display considerable variation and none of the economy of retouch and sureness of standardized manufacture so characteristic of the Aurignacian and later Upper Paleolithic cultures.

The same levels contained not only flint artifacts but granite grinding stones, hammers, and pounders, and pallets used for producing red ocher. Unlike their predecessors, the newcomers were accomplished boneworkers, who grooved and split both antler and ivory to obtain long slivers of raw material for making awls, points, and other tools. They sawed bird bones into tubes and used horse, bison, and mammoth rib picks to dig postholes for the huts they built in the entrance to the cave. Since wood was rare at the time, and fragments of about 15 mammoth tusks were found in the same level, Leroi-Gourhan believed that a skin superstructure was supported by tusks and bones from these large beasts, an architectural device used far to the east on the west Russian plains.

The often crude and far-from-standardized artifacts of the Châtelperronian levels in the Grotte du Renne contrast sharply with those from the overlying Aurignacian horizons, radiocarbon-dated to about 30,400 years ago. Here, the Mousterian elements in the toolkit vanish abruptly and completely. Aurignacian technology is sophisticated and economical, an industrial tradition that cannot be related to the Châtelperronian or the Mousterian.

The Arcy-sur-Cure finds raised the real possibility that Châtelperronian artifacts were the work of Neanderthal stoneworkers, especially as three human teeth found in the Châtelperronian levels bear enormous, archaic-looking cusps, which are more characteristic of Neanderthals than *Homo sapiens sapiens*. Then, in 1979, François Lévêque and Bernard Vandermeersch unearthed a Châtelperronian level in the Saint Césaire rockshelter in southwestern France, associated with two Neanderthal skeletons. The same level was radiocarbon-dated to about 32,000 years ago. These are the latest known Neanderthals in Europe, for all human remains more recent than 32,000 years ago are of anatomically modern form.

The Saint Césaire discoveries imply that at least some elements of Upper Paleolithic technology were adopted by Neanderthals living alongside anatomically modern people. Perhaps the Châtelperronian, like the occupations at Szeleta Cave in Hungary, was a Neanderthal response to the more advanced culture of puzzling newcomers.

Continuity or Replacement?

What, then, is the story of the first settlement of Europe by modern humans? Almost certainly, complex processes of biological replacement brought anatomically modern people into Europe some time during the brief climatic amelioration between 50,000 and 40,000 years ago. This process of biological replacement was far more complex than mere population movements, and probably involved slow assimilation and hybridization of Neanderthal populations. We are on fairly solid ground with the replacement hypothesis in Europe, for there are none of the highly varied *Homo sapiens* populations found in the Near East and in Africa before 50,000 years ago.

Archaeologist Ezra Zubrow of the State University of New York at Buffalo has produced a theoretical demographic model that is based on the assumption that contemporary Neanderthal and *Homo sapiens sapiens* populations interacted with one another, as we are almost certain they did in central and western Europe. He believes that only a small demographic advantage was necessary for the newcomers to grow rapidly, and for the indigenous population of Neanderthals to become extinct. With a difference of mortality rate of only 1 percent, the Neanderthals might have become extinct within 30 generations, within a mere millennium.

In strictly technological terms, the transition is far more complex than this, for Saint Césaire and Arcy-sur-Cure, and several central and southeastern European locations, show that Mousterian technology was already foreshadowing Upper Paleolithic artifices, among them blades, thousands of years before the Cro-Magnons appeared. But there are revealing differences. The Neanderthals tended to use relatively few types of toolmaking stone, while the Cro-Magnons brought in good-quality flint from considerable distances. The same general tool forms appear over large areas of Neanderthal Europe, whereas there is considerable local variation from early in Upper Paleolithic times, and tool forms, from Aurignacian times onward, are much more standardized than ever before. Neither the Mousterians nor the Châtelperronians made many bone tools, although, judging from Arcy-sur-Cure, the latter had mastered the art of making long grooves in reindeer antler, the preliminary to fabricating points, awls, and other delicate tools – artifacts that were critical to survival in the arctic. It is not until the appearance of the Aurignacian that fully developed Upper Paleolithic culture appears in Europe. And once the Aurignacian was well established, between 34,000 and 32,000 years ago, the Cro-Magnons became the sole masters of Europe.

CHAPTER TWELVE

A Cultural Apogee

By 25,000 years ago, climatic conditions in northern latitudes were deteriorating, as Europe and northern Asia were gripped by fierce winters during the last cold cycle of the Würm glaciation. It was during these millennia that *Homo sapiens sapiens* finally mastered winter. Not that the entire globe was wrapped in bitter cold. Outside northern latitudes, temperatures were cooler and changing rainfall patterns brought drier conditions to much of Africa, southern Asia, and to Sunda and Sahul. But it was in Europe and northern Asia that human ingenuity and endurance were tested to the full. The successful conquest of these environments was one of the final chapters in humanity's peopling of the globe. How did *Homo sapiens sapiens* master Ice Age winters? And why do we have such a rich legacy of art and artistic achievement from this cruelly severe epoch?

Winters that Killed

The late Ice Age Europeans were denizens of a desolate, almost treeless landscape swept by bitterly cold winds. Vast tracts of open steppe and scrub-covered steppe-tundra dominated much of Europe and Eurasia from the North Sea to the Urals. Yet, away from the open plains, in the Périgord, northern Spain, and southeastern Europe, sheltered valleys could support both periglacial vegetation and temperate warmer-loving trees, an ever-changing mix of steppe and forest. Over the period 35,000–11,000 years ago, there were centuries when temperatures were extremely cold, then cycles when near-temperate conditions prevailed in sheltered locations. Both animals and humans adjusted to each cycle of warmer and colder weather. In general terms, the vegetation of the Périgord, for example, was closer to that which flourishes some 3,000 ft (1,000 m) up in the Massif Central today. Harvard University archaeologist Hallam Movius recovered pollen grains from birch, pine, oak, alder, juniper, hazel, and willow trees from the long-occupied Abri Pataud rockshelter near Les Eyzies. The hunters were constantly on the move – in open country during the short summer months, concentrated in more sheltered river valleys during the winter, in such places as the Périgord or the Danube Basin.

The Cro-Magnons were experts at selecting habitation sites, often rockshelters that were occupied again and again at irregular intervals on a seasonal basis over thousands of years. The occupation deposits at some large, and obviously much favored, sites reach 16 ft (5 m) or more. By no means all locations were rockshelters, for many were in the open, often with commanding views of the surrounding landscape. Within the Périgord valleys, the people tended to live on the south-facing slopes, where the sun provided natural warming. Almost every Cro-Magnon site was located near water, either by a spring or close to a river. The Cro-Magnons probably spent much of their time in open encampments, where they erected square or rectangular dwellings of skins and hides, thrown over frameworks of wood or animal bones. The floors sometimes consist of carefully laid down pavements of river pebbles, the stones almost invariably burned before they were placed in position. By heating the stones in a fire first, then placing them on frozen ground, the builders could create a secure platform that prevented domestic activities from melting the underlying, and consequently muddy, ground.

In the final analysis, it was not the extremes of cold weather that killed Stone Age hunters, it was probably the cumulative effects of months of subzero temperatures and often scarce, unpredictable food supplies. To accumulate and store food for lean months was vital for survival. So was a highly effective way of keeping warm outside when the wind chill factor was −50 degrees F (−45 deg. C) and temperatures could change by 30 degrees F (17 deg. C) in minutes as winds rose or died down. All technology had to be highly portable, extremely efficient, and easily replaced if broken. Above all, anyone living in late Ice Age Europe had to be adaptable, capable of cooperating regularly with others, and to be opportunistic but also cautious.

The Reindeer Hunters

Europe's diverse late Ice Age environment supported a remarkably varied cold-tolerant fauna of both open-landscape and forest animals. Reindeer, red deer, bison, elk, aurochs (wild ox), horse, boar, and mountain goat were commonplace, while woolly rhinoceros and mammoth flourished. Not that the Cro-Magnons relied solely on big game, for they took many species of smaller animals, among them arctic fox, wolf, beaver, and rabbits, for their skins and fur as well as for meat. They snared partridge, grouse, mallard, duck, and pigeons, and many other bird species. After about 16,000 years ago, the Cro-Magnons also fished for salmon, trout, perch, and eels from rivers and streams.

With such a great diversity of animals, one can hardly be blamed for assuming that food was always abundant for the late Ice Age Europeans. In reality, survival depended on diversification, on never concentrating on just one or two species of animal to the exclusion of all others. Even so, archaeologists have always been struck by the abundance of reindeer bones at Cro-Magnon sites. Judging from the bones at the Abri Pataud rockshelter, reindeer provided up to 30 percent of all prey there over a period of more than 10,000 years. Reindeer are eclectic feeders, consuming lichens and other foods in delicate plant communities. Constant movement is adaptive for them, since it minimizes the effects of fluctuations in food supplies. The hunters located their camps near shallow crossings or fords where they knew migrating animals were likely to pass. The enormous Laugerie Haute site on the Vézère River in the Périgord is one such location. Excavators found nearly complete reindeer skeletons between the rockshelter and the river ford. On a nearby rise were pits dug about 3 ft (1 m) into the ground, filled with bones and stone tools. Perhaps these were storage pits, or traps into which reindeer were driven, or conceivably blinds in which hunters waited for their approaching prey.

Canadian scholar Bryan Gordon has studied the complex group movements of Magdalenian hunters in southwestern France during the late Ice Age using an ingenious technique. (The Magdalenian culture, named after the La Madeleine rockshelter on the Vézère River, flourished in central and western Europe between about 18,000 and 10,000 years ago.) He measured the growth increments on individual reindeer and caribou teeth, which are thick and clear for warm-season growth, dark and thin for winter growth. The principle is somewhat similar to that used to date trees through annual growth rings in their trunks. The increments on the teeth, when compared with modern control samples, gave an indication of the age of reindeer slain at different Cro-Magnon sites.

Gordon compared the tooth increments of 2-year-old reindeer from two Magdalenian sites, La Madeleine and Canecaude (in the Pyrenees), which are some 124 miles (200 km) apart. All the teeth had two winter increments, but those from La Madeleine had thin spring ones, whereas those from Canecaude had half-grown summer increments. Reindeer teeth near each of these sites had the same characteristics, whereas those near Canecaude had moderate to full outer, transparent increments, characteristic of late spring to fall growth. The two groups of sites are a sufficient distance apart to represent the normal positions of winter and summer ranges of moving reindeer herds. Gordon believes there was a rapid spring and fall migration that had the reindeer herds traveling between 186 and 250 miles (200–400 km) in a few weeks, a roughly equivalent distance to that traveled by Canadian Barren-lands caribou. He also believes that the hunting groups followed the herds, which accounts for the close similarities in trade goods, art traditions, and other artifacts over long distances.

Bryan Gordon's research hints at very complex group movements, at a rhythm of reindeer hunting that persisted over many millennia. By the time the Magdalenians occupied the Périgord, there were eight reindeer ranges in

Reindeer hunters at Pincevent – an artist's impression of the scene at this Upper Paleolithic camp in southern France.

the west that we can identify, three in southwestern France, others to the north and east. The tradition of following these ranges may go back far into Upper Paleolithic times. Was, in fact, herd-following introduced as an innovation by the incoming Cro-Magnons, or did the Neanderthals also track migrating reindeer? If the Neanderthals were pursuing a different hunting pattern, then the Cro-Magnons may have introduced a new and dynamic way of exploiting large numbers of animals. Their hunting strategies may have been made even more lethal and effective by close cooperation, perhaps enhanced speaking abilities, and by a versatile, specialized technology, whose potential was not recognized by their predecessors.

For most of the year, Cro-Magnons lived in small groups, subsisting off a variety of game and stored foods. In summer, they would range widely over the uplands and open country outside the sheltered valleys. The times of aggregation may have been in spring, summer, or early fall, when they knew that reindeer (and, in later times, salmon) were abundant. This period of coming together would have been an important annual occasion, when social life was at its most intense, and people arranged marriages, conducted initiation ceremonies and bartered raw materials, artifacts, and other commodities with one another. Then, as the winter closed in, the groups would disperse through the sheltered river valleys, returning to their stored foods and the small herds of game animals that also took refuge from the arctic winds.

This basic way of life survived for thousands of years, from at least 32,000 years ago right up to the end of the Ice Age some 10,000 years ago, when the glaciers finally melted and dense forest spread over the open plains and deep valleys of western Europe. Not that life remained the same throughout these millennia, for climatic conditions changed constantly. What was important was that the Cro-Magnons had such a wide choice of food resources available to them, and such an effective toolkit to exploit them, that they could readily adjust to altered circumstances.

The Swiss Army Knife Effect

What was the technological basis for the Cro-Magnons' successful, long-term adaptation to the challenges of such harsh environments? Their technological success, foreshadowed in the Châtelperronian, depended on four interrelated factors – careful selection of fine-grained rock for blade cores, the production of relatively standardized, parallel-sided artifact blanks, the refinement of the burin, and the use of the "groove and splinter" technique for fabricating antler tools. These technological innovations have a far wider significance to human prehistory outside the narrow confines of the European world, for they were the material means by which humans adapted to the climatic extremes of Ice Age Eurasia and Siberia as well.

Cro-Magnon stoneworkers, whether in central Europe or the Périgord, were highly selective in their use of flint and other stone. Their primary objective was to produce long, parallel-sided artifact blanks that could then be turned into a very wide range of specialized artifacts with specific uses right across the spectrum of their daily life. These tools were used for hunting, butchery, processing other foods and critical game byproducts, for woodworking and clothing manufacture – and for the production of the raw materials needed to create specialized antler tools in an often treeless environment. With such concern for fine-quality raw materials, there can be no doubt that the Magdalenians, and their predecessors as far back as the Aurignacians and Châtelperronians, bartered and had regular contacts with other groups living at considerable distances. These contacts were also expanded by the large distances that the hunters apparently traveled during the year.

Once procured, the precious raw materials were turned into the cylindrical cores that were the basis for the entire Cro-Magnon toolkit. La Ferrassie and other rockshelters contain densely packed layers of intermittent occupation, living surfaces where stoneworkers once fabricated blades by the hundreds, examining them carefully, and sometimes abandoning blanks that were not suitable for the task at hand. One should think of the cores as forms of savings accounts, a fine-grained rock that may have been carried over considerable distances, perhaps in pouches. Then the rock was brought out to produce a few blanks that were turned into finished tools appropriate for butchering, woodworking, or whatever activity was on the agenda for that moment. In a real sense, blade technology like this is truly opportunistic, for stoneworkers carried around their raw material, able to respond at a moment's notice to an opportunity to cut up an animal, or to cut deep grooves into fresh reindeer antler, without having to carry a heavy span back to base. Light, cylindrical cores and parallel-sided blades were extremely portable, much more so than the heavier disc and Levallois cores favored by the Neanderthals. The closest analogy in our own technology is, perhaps, the familiar Swiss Army Knife, a surprisingly effective multipurpose artifact built on a strong chassis with a special spring system that enables the user to call on a wide variety of different tools – everything from a pair of scissors to a corkscrew. The Cro-Magnons' chassis and spring system were the cores and the blades that came from them. By having such an effective technological base at hand, they were able to envisage specialized tasks and applications that were far beyond the capabilities of their predecessors.

Of all the stone artifacts fashioned by the Cro-Magnons, much the most important was the burin. In modern times, the burin is the tool used to engrave copper plates. It is a delicate implement for carving fine lines. The Cro-Magnons' graving tool was also a delicate tool, used for a myriad day-to-day tasks – in woodworking, for cutting grooves in hides, for engraving designs on bone and antler, and on rock walls. But the burin was all-important to the

Cro-Magnons as a catalyst for a new, and previously unexploited avenue of tool technology – the systematic use of reindeer antler and, to a lesser degree, ivory and bone for making specialized tools.

Grooves and Splinters

The Cro-Magnons relied on animals not only as sources of food, but as vital providers of hides, sinews, and other essentials. Once the hunters had learned how to process them economically, fresh reindeer and red deer antler, to say nothing of elk, was as invaluable a source of raw material for tool manufacture as fine-grained flint cores and blades. But it was the new stone technology that enabled the hunters to exploit the full potential of fresh antler.

Reindeer antler is soft and easy to work when it is fresh from the beast, or collected when recently shed in the wild. The Cro-Magnons were able to rely on regular supplies of fresh antler, but the large beams and tines were of somewhat limited use as tools. They could serve as crude picks or levers for digging up plants, for excavating soil for semi-subterranean dwellings, or could be used for levering out lumps of red ocher. It was not until the burin and the sharp-edged blade came along that antler as a material for tools came into its own, being ideal for fashioning lightweight spearheads and barbed harpoons for hunting all manner of game, and many other fine artifacts.

The blade and burin made possible the so-called "groove and splinter technique" that produced the necessary blanks. Armed with a sharp burin or blade, the hunter would work two deep, longitudinal grooves into the beam of a fresh antler, grooving carefully until the burin penetrated the soft, spongy tissue that formed the antler core. The grooves formed a V-shape through the tough outer layer of antler, and the long splinter could be undermined, then levered out of the beam, thereby providing a rough blank that could be cut and shaped very readily into any number of specialized artifacts. Even a moderate-sized beam would produce several blanks, which could readily be removed from a kill while the carcass was being butchered, thereby saving the energy needed to carry a heavy antler span back to camp. In a real sense, the blade and burin gave the Cro-Magnons access to a raw material that was to transform not only their hunting, but their culture and society as well.

Antler and bone tools, and the groove and splinter technique, appear with the Aurignacians throughout Europe, but the new technology did not assume a really important role in Cro-Magnon society until after some 25,000 years ago, when people seem to have grasped the full potential of bone and antler. The basic stone tool technology of the Cro-Magnons – scrapers, awls, burins, and backed knives – underwent many local variations, with a general tendency toward smaller and more delicate artifacts, many of which may have been mounted in bone or wood shafts or handles. The real advance was in lightweight technology, especially for the chase. Furthermore, the same

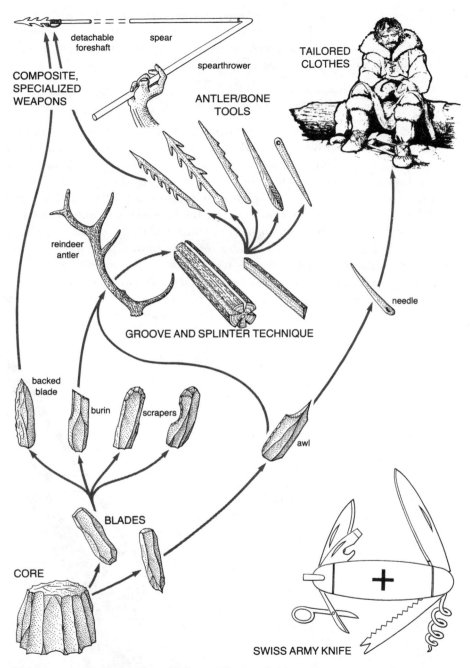

COMPOSITE,
SPECIALIZED
WEAPONS

detachable
foreshaft   spear

spearthrower

TAILORED
CLOTHES

ANTLER/BONE
TOOLS

reindeer
antler

GROOVE AND SPLINTER TECHNIQUE

needle

backed
blade

burin   scrapers

awl

BLADES

CORE

SWISS ARMY KNIFE

*The Swiss Army Knife effect: like its modern multipurpose counterpart, the core
and blade technique was a flexible artifact system, allowing Upper Paleolithic
stoneworkers to develop a variety of subsidiary crafts, notably bone- and antler-
working, which likewise gave rise to new weapons systems and tailored clothing.*

hunting weapons, with minimal modification, could be used for spearing running salmon, for dispatching rabbits, even for developing rudimentary bows and arrows. The new technology was versatile and lethal, far more lethal than any earlier hunting technology known on earth.

Points, Harpoons, and Spearthrowers

Henri Breuil classified much of the Upper Paleolithic of the Périgord on the basis of changes in bone and antler projectile points. The Aurignacians of 30,000 years ago fashioned rather flat-based bone points with split ends, and conical-based points were in common use for thousands of years. But it was the Magdalenians who developed the finest antler points, using not only delicate forked-based and conical forms, but barbed points and harpoons as well. Some of the latter have small protuberances at the base, to which a sinew or fiber line was once attached. Almost certainly, most of them were mounted in foreshafts. This simple device was a major step forward in hunting technology. The spear point was not mounted directly into the main shaft, but to a short wooden or antler link-piece, or foreshaft, that in turn was bound to the shaft. When the point hit its quarry, the foreshaft would break off from the shaft, allowing the hunter to recover it. Within a few moments, he could

The spearthrower: (right) a modern Australian Aborigine using one; (left) an elaborate Upper Paleolithic example from Le Mas d'Azil, France, carved in the shape of a defecating mountain goat.

simply mount a new point and foreshaft assembly to his spear. This form of weaponry was ideal for hunter-gatherers who were on the move, and especially in situations where the Cro-Magnons were involved in ambushing large numbers of migrating animals such as reindeer. It was obviously advantageous to be able to rearm rapidly, without having to carry around large numbers of heavy spear shafts.

The blade and burin also opened up endless possibilities for fabricating other useful, specialized artifacts. One was the spearthrower, or throwing stick, a simple and ingenious device that increased the range, the velocity, and the accuracy of a hurled spear. In its simplest form, still used by Australian Aborigines, the throwing stick is little more than a hooked stick or light board. The spear is hooked onto the thrower, then propelled with a deft flick that sends the light spear toward its target with lightning speed. The Cro-Magnons undoubtedly used such simple devices, made from large antler fragments, but they also fashioned some of them into magnificent art objects. The artist would fashion the spearthrower from a segment of antler beam with the palm still attached, carving, smoothing and engraving the hook end into a naturalistic depiction of the hunter's prey – a bison, a wild horse, or, in a fine example of prehistoric humor, a mountain goat perched on an imaginary peak looking back as it relieves itself, a bird perched on the emerging feces serving as the hook. We cannot tell whether these magnificent spearthrowers were ever used in the chase, but the artistry on them is both intricate and astoundingly naturalistic.

Pioneers of Tailored Clothing

Some of the most important artifacts, such as the humble perforated needle, might seem insignificant to us. Yet they played a vital role in the peoples' ability to survive the extremes of late Ice Age winters. The needle first appears in archaeological sites some 20,000–18,000 years ago, at the height of the last glaciation. Perhaps this was no coincidence, for the needle, made from bone or ivory blanks cut out with stone burins and perforated with sharp, pointed flint awls, revolutionized human clothing.

The Eskimo of the far north knew of the advantages of layered, tailored clothing long before Europeans did. And it was no coincidence that the first arctic explorers to adopt Eskimo clothing practices were the most successful. For example, one reason that the Norwegian explorer Raold Amundsen reached the South Pole before Englishman Robert Scott in 1912 was because he knew of the advantages of layered clothing, whereas the British relied on more traditional European designs that were less effective in extreme cold. The secrets of Eskimo garments are threefold – careful selection of raw materials for different clothes such as underclothing, parkas, and boots; the use of multiple layers that can be donned or shed as conditions change; and custom tailoring of each item to fit the individual user. All of these factors prevent heat loss, especially from the extremities. Until the invention of the needle – an innovation requiring blades and burins to prepare bone and antler blanks and to bore fine holes – custom-tailored clothing was an impossibility. The needle was a highly adaptive invention, especially for hunters living in an environment where hides and skins from all manner of fur-bearing animals were available for every form of clothing imaginable. Anthropologist Richard Nelson, an expert on Alaskan peoples, records how the Eskimo use sealskin for boot uppers as it resists water well, while wolf fur is best for parka fringes, as it prevents one's breath from freezing. Knowledge as specific as this may well have been part of Cro-Magnon culture. Now the invention of the needle enabled them not only to tailor clothing, but also to join reindeer hides and other skins to make summer tents, to create screens for rockshelters in winter, to fabricate finely tailored skin bags and leather pouches for carrying spear points and foreshafts, ornaments and other precious possessions.

There are only occasional clues to Cro-Magnon clothing that come from occasional burials and cave paintings and engravings that depict human figures. At the Gabillou cave in the Isle Valley in Vienne, a human is shown wearing what appears to be a parka, while a nearby hunter or possible sorcerer perhaps wears a bison skin with the head still attached. Bone and shell beads cover some Cro-Magnon burials. Possibly they were ornaments once sewn to their clothing.

The "Swiss Army Knife" analogy can be carried even further, for the blade technology of the Cro-Magnons enabled them not only to cut fine grooves, to engrave and adorn antler, but also to drill fine holes in raw materials soft and sometimes surprisingly hard. Pointed flint awls allowed people to perforate leather clothing, to sew garments with needles, and, in another expansion of human activity, to create pendants and other body ornaments fashioned not only in bone and antler, but in ivory as well. The Neanderthals perforated animal teeth and made grooved ornaments, but the Cro-Magnons with their superior technology achieved much greater ornamental sophistication, which played a central role in their social and ritual life.

The Shape of Society

The Cro-Magnons were in contact with neighbors near and far throughout the year, at seasonal gatherings as well as on a more individual basis. We know this because of the considerable quantities of exotic objects found in Cro-Magnon sites. As we have seen, the Cro-Magnons were highly selective in their use of fine-grained rock. Originally, barter networks may have developed to handle the regular exchange of this stone and the finished artifacts between different individuals and widely separated bands. In time, these networks handled other exotic objects, too, many of them ornaments or

26 **Art of the Sacred** Two bison, modeled in clay at one-sixth life size by an Upper Paleolithic artist, lie deep within the French cave of Le Tuc d'Audoubert.

27–31 **The Mysteries of Cave Art** The magnificent cave paintings and sculptures of western Europe represent the first rich flowering of the fully developed human imagination. The cave artists of southwest France and northern Spain delighted in sketching or carving primarily horse (*above*) and bison (*right, center* and *right, above*), but also mammoth (*below*), deer (*right, below*) and other animals. The precise meaning of the art still eludes us. Yet the strange image of a prostrate man (*right, above*) and other scenes hint at shamanistic rituals held in remote cave chambers.

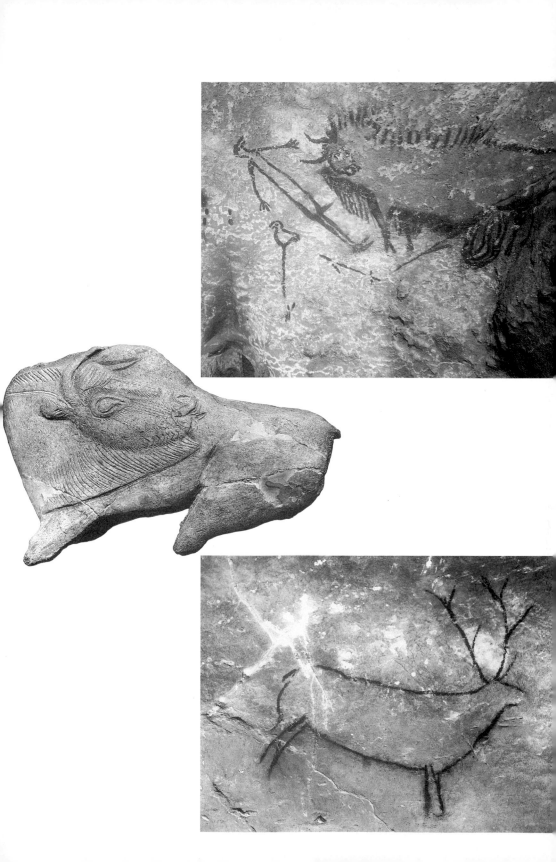

32–35 **A Clothing Revolution** The introduction of stone blade tools, such as sharp-pointed burins (gravers), enabled Cro-Magnon people to develop an elaborate bone and antler technology. They incised reindeer antler to produce fine works of art (*above*). More significantly, they created the humble bone needle, which made it possible to sew the world's first fully tailored clothing. A Cro-Magnon believed to be wearing a parka (*above right*, wall engraving in the French cave of Gabillou) can be compared with Eskimo of historical times (*left* and *right*), with their highly advanced multi-layered garments that successfully combat arctic cold.

36–39 **Mammoth Hunters of the Plains** In order to survive the bitter winters of the west Eurasian plains at the height of the last Ice Age, modern humans cooperated in the construction of substantial base camps. The 18,000-year-old Mezhirich site, on the Dnepr River, has yielded the remarkably complete remains of oval dwellings built out of mammoth bones (*opposite page*). Partially dug into the ground for insulation, these structures would have had a final roof covering of hides and sod.

Camp dwellers on the plains had the same capacity for art and ritual as their counterparts to the west. At the site of Dolní Věstonice, in modern Czechoslovakia, they created this "Venus" figurine (*right*) from a mixture of clay and bone powder some 24,000 years ago. At about the same time, hunters at Sungir, near Moscow, buried an elderly man (*below*) and two children fully dressed in their sewn clothing, ornamented with mammoth ivory beads.

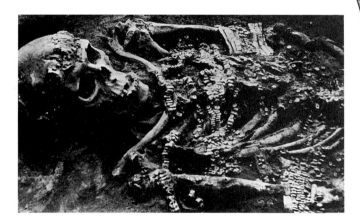

40 Plains Life A hunter carves a figurine while his companions cook meat in front of a mammoth-bone dwelling – an artist's impression of the scene at the site of Ostrava Petrkovice, in modern Czechoslovakia, during the late Ice Age.

materials with probable ritual associations. Judging from modern analogies, these acts of exchange were far from random, and were based on symbolic acts of giving and receiving that fostered long-term obligations between generations of individuals. Along with these obligations went social bonds connecting different families living dozens, if not hundreds, of miles apart.

Some groups used flint from sources long distances away. Baltic amber, a yellow-brown fossil resin that when rubbed seems "electric," has been found in Cro-Magnon settlements in southern Europe. Seashells from the shores of the Mediterranean, the Atlantic Ocean, and the English Channel were valued as ornaments in dozens of sites, as were shells from fossil shell beds hundreds of miles away. Sharks' teeth and marine shells may have had important magical properties for people living a hundred miles (160 km) or more inland, and may have assumed major social significance in societies where social ranking was an important factor in daily life.

There is a tendency to think of simple hunter-gatherer societies as ones where everyone was of similar rank. In fact individual age and experience, to say nothing of gender, have always played important roles in differentiating people's status in small-scale societies. In the case of the Cro-Magnons, with their complicated annual round, social rankings may have been more complex, in other words, more stratified. About the only way in which archaeologists can discern such rankings is through excavated burials.

Cro-Magnon burials display great variation, but many individuals wore ornaments, which, presumably, reflected their daily adornment, and, perhaps, their social ranking. The skeletons from the Cro-Magnon site wore shell necklaces, as did a young girl found at La Madeleine. Her limbs were adorned with strings and bracelets of shell beads, and she wore a band on her head. Pierced bear and lion teeth sometimes lie around the necks of young and adult males. Perhaps these adornments were a barometer of social status and age in life, perpetuated in death. And it is with the Cro-Magnons that we find the first traces of such concerns in European society.

The Symbolic World

There is no doubt that the Cro-Magnons, like some of their contemporaries in Africa and Australia, lived in a complex, intensely symbolic world, a world defined philosophically and creatively in ways that were unimagined among earlier humans. We know this because the appearance of these people in Europe coincides with a new concern with the abstract, with artistic expression and body ornament. In all probability, the symbolic and ceremonial life of the Cro-Magnons was little different from that of their contemporaries living throughout the Old World. The difference is simply one of preservation, for the Cro-Magnon artists used cave walls as their canvas, durable antler and ivory, not wood and skins, as palettes.

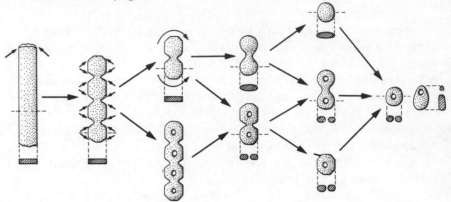

Part of Marcel Otte's analysis of Upper Paleolithic bead manufacture, starting from a pencil-like rod of ivory.

New York University archaeologist Randall White, building on the work of French scholars Marcel Otte and Yvette Taborin, has recently studied the earliest Upper Paleolithic body ornaments, those made by the Aurignacians. These early Cro-Magnons made ornaments from exotic materials, such as perforated carnivore teeth, perhaps, as Randall White suggests, attempting to evoke some of the qualities of their prey. The Aurignacians gouged small holes in tooth roots and seashells, then pushed a sharp object through to the other side. It was not until after about 20,000 years ago that fine stone drills came into use. They made ivory beads from blanks removed from the outer layer of mammoth tusk, whittling them down into pencil-like rods, then segmenting them so that they could snap off roughs to make into finished beads for necklaces, sewing onto clothing, or for use in other ways.

This sudden explosion in body ornamentation defies easy analysis. White believes that it coincides with a realization that body ornaments could define and communicate social identity – gender, group affiliation, even social roles. Perhaps it is significant that body ornaments are most common at those very sites where engraved and painted limestone slabs, mammoth ivory sculptures, and decorated antler and bone appear for the first time. The same abstract images such as crosses, notches, incisions, and punctuations occur at site after site. White believes that the Aurignacians had mastered the ability to think in specific visual images that also served as a medium of communication. They may have been some of the first humans to think visually, using the linguistic abilities that they now had to share and communicate images and ideas. These manipulated images may have been an important, indeed revolutionary, catalyst in the millennia of dramatic social, technological, and economic change that followed the emergence of anatomically modern humans. They resulted in complex and diverse art traditions that lasted for more than 20,000 years, with the greatest efflorescence between about 21,000 and 11,000 years ago.

The surviving Ice Age art of Europe and Eurasia is but a minor fraction of the Cro-Magnons' artistic endeavor, for the artists almost certainly used many perishable materials – clay, wood, fiber, bark, perhaps even ice, snow, hides and bird feathers. Without question, they also used red ocher and other pigments as body paint, for decoration and as a way of maintaining body heat. Upper Paleolithic art occurs over an enormous area of Europe and Eurasia, from North Africa to Siberia, with major concentrations in northern Spain, southwestern France, and also central and eastern Europe. On cave walls, the artists engraved and painted animals and occasional humans, also schematic motifs: single lines, elaborate panels, and complex shapes. The artists engraved antler, bone, and ivory with consummate skill. They created animals in the round, engraved bison with strokes so sure that you can see the tear duct in an eye, the long hairs of mane and coat. There are figurines of animals and humans in ivory, soft stone, and baked clay, such as the celebrated "Venus" figurines that depict women of all ages.

In western Europe, both portable art objects and cave art tend to concentrate at relatively few sites, at such famous locations as Lascaux in the Périgord, Trois Frères in the Pyrenees, and Altamira in northern Spain. No less than 60 percent of all Périgord portable art comes from four sites. In the Ariège region of the Pyrenees, four caves account for nearly 84 percent of all the wall art.

Upper Paleolithic art is full of compelling images, many of them concentrated in what we must assume to be places of unusual significance and importance. Such places as the great Mâs d'Azil cave in Ariège in the French Pyrenees were centers of artistic endeavor as well as living sites. British cave art expert Paul Bahn speculates that "they must have served as storehouses, meeting-places, ritual foci, and socio-economic centers, not only for local groups, but for a far wider area, as is confirmed by their artefactual links with far-flung sites and with one another."

Some painted caves were occupied over long periods of time, but some of the most important painted and engraved caves were sacred places used occasionally for important ceremonies. Nowhere is this more dramatically illustrated than at Le Tuc d'Audoubert, also in Ariège, where two carefully modeled clay bison lie in a remote, low-ceilinged chamber, placed against a rock. The bison are about one-sixth full size, shaped with the artist's fingers, also with a spatula, while a pointed object was used to insert the eyes, nostrils, and other features. There are ancient heel marks around the figures in this remote chamber, as if this was the site of intensely sacred rituals in deep darkness. In many other caves, paintings and engravings are far from daylight, and there are several instances in which footprints of both Magdalenian adults and children are preserved in damp clay. Some caves may also have been chosen for their resonant qualities, for their natural sound effects.

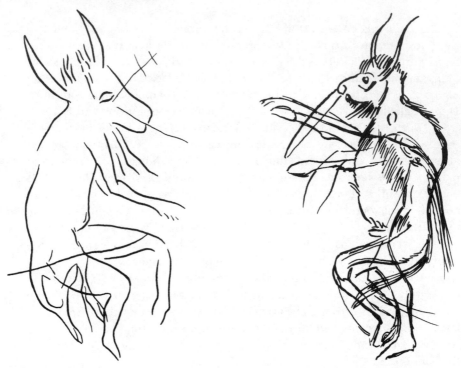

Possible shamans or sorcerers depicted on the cave walls at Gabillou (left) and Les Trois Frères (right), both in southern France.

Upper Paleolithic art defies easy interpretation, for it communicates symbolic messages from a world utterly remote from our own. Yet, there is an immediacy and a vividness about it that makes one realize how very powerful a communication device it was. I will always remember the sight of animal engravings deep inside Les Combarelles cave near Les Eyzies. The guide used an acetylene lamp that flickered in the intense blackness. The lamp made the animals seem larger, as if they moved in the uncertain light, an illusion that heightened the feeling of mystery, of magic. What, then, did the art mean? Did Cro-Magnon artists paint art for art's sake, or were they engaging in "sympathetic hunting magic," in which they symbolically killed their prey before setting out on the chase? These explanations are simplistic. We can be sure that the motivations for the art extended far beyond just environmental and subsistence concerns. For instance, the artists at Lascaux drew but one definite reindeer, yet this animal represented over 90 percent of the animal bones found there!

Shamans were always important people in hunter-gatherer societies, being intermediaries between the living and the revered ancestors. They were gifted individuals who cured illnesses, mediated between the forces of nature and mere humans. Perhaps, argue some experts, the cave art was intimately involved with shamanistic rituals, being images of spirit animals. Or perhaps the animal figures were a source of life-force for the shamans, who used this force to serve the people – which might account for the lines that sometimes emanate from the mouths of animals on the cave walls. Such hypotheses are hard to support if one simply studies the often stylized human figures that appear on the cave walls themselves.

Fortunately Stone Age artists continued to paint and engrave in Australia and southern Africa until modern times. These art traditions, perhaps as old as those of the Cro-Magnons, give us revealing insights into the kinds of complex symbolism that lay behind the art. The southern African San drew running hunters, people fishing from boats, and scenes of honey-gathering and foraging for plant foods. Men and women in skin cloaks sit around camp fires and dance. The hunters stalk game in disguise, run helter-skelter across cave walls, hotly pursue wounded quarry, raid the cattle herds of their agricultural neighbors in later centuries. A few surviving San artists, hounded by European settlers and soldiers, even depicted British troops and their horses in the valleys beneath their mountain caves.

Archaeologist David Lewis-Williams of the University of Witwatersrand in Johannesburg has studied oral traditions of San life collected in the 19th

Art of the San, southern Africa: a wounded eland staggers under an assault by spear-carrying hunters and dogs.

Enigmatic painted pebbles (above and opposite page) from Le Mas d'Azil, southern France.

century and shown how many of the paintings depict complex metaphors in the symbolic world of the hunters. Some of the paintings show eland with dancers cavorting around them. Lewis-Williams believes the dancers were acquiring the potency released by the death of the eland. The dancers go into trances so powerful they become eland themselves. This vivid symbolism survived into the 19th century. When Victorian anthropologist George Stow showed some rock paintings to an elderly San couple, the women began to sing and dance. The man begged her to desist because the old songs made him sad. But eventually he joined in, and Stow watched the old couple reliving the symbolism of past days. By then, however, the old Stone Age lifeways were virtually extinct. What survives of San painting lore makes one realize just how rich the symbolism behind Cro-Magnon art must have been.

Other theories about the European art are based on detailed, site-by-site studies that have focused not only on the art itself but also on the placement of individual works and friezes on cave walls. Under this approach, the gaps on the walls are as important as the paintings and engravings themselves. With a more complete and objective database, it may be possible to identify regional styles, even to define styles that were in fashion for short periods of time. It is almost certain that the art was a way of storing and transmitting information, everything from directions within caves to much more elaborate constructions. There were public and private rituals associated with the art. Alexander Marshack, who has worked with Harvard University's Peabody Museum, has spent many years studying the visual forms of Cro-Magnon art. He believes that many patterns of dots, notches, lines, and other marks are sequential notations of events and other phenomena, predecessors of calendars and part of an advanced record-keeping system. Marshack's ideas are controversial, but few archaeologists would disagree with him that the art played an important role in communicating information between individuals and different generations.

Most authorities agree that much of the art in dark caves was associated with initiation rites, with the journey through dark passages being part of the disorienting ordeal that went with the ceremonies. The paintings were often positioned in remote chambers and niches, in locations where they could be used to maximum sensory and emotional effect. Almost certainly, the art was a way of transmitting information from one generation to the next. Australian Aborigines, for example, commit to memory vast quantities of information about their territory, and this is closely tied to the mythical and symbolic world of their ancestors and of the Dreamtime. Much of this data is vital to survival, constantly imparted to the young in ceremonies and rituals.

The masterpieces of Altamira and Lascaux, of Niaux and Trois Frères, tempt us to think of the Cro-Magnon societies of southwestern France and northern Spain as exceptionally rich and unusual. But, judging from clear signs of anatomical stress in a few Cro-Magnon burials, life was not always easy, and the threat of starvation was never far away. The Cro-Magnons enjoyed a richly symbolic social and ceremonial life during those special weeks of the year when shamans sang and danced, when age-old rituals sanctified human and animal fertility, the close relationship that always existed between Ice Age peoples and their environments. Then, like hunter-gatherers everywhere, they moved on, some to follow migrating herds on familiar routes, others to venture into unknown territories to the east – the harsh steppe-tundra of the north Eurasian plains.

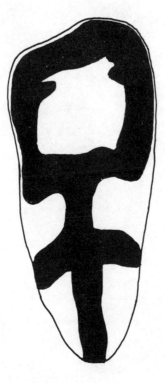

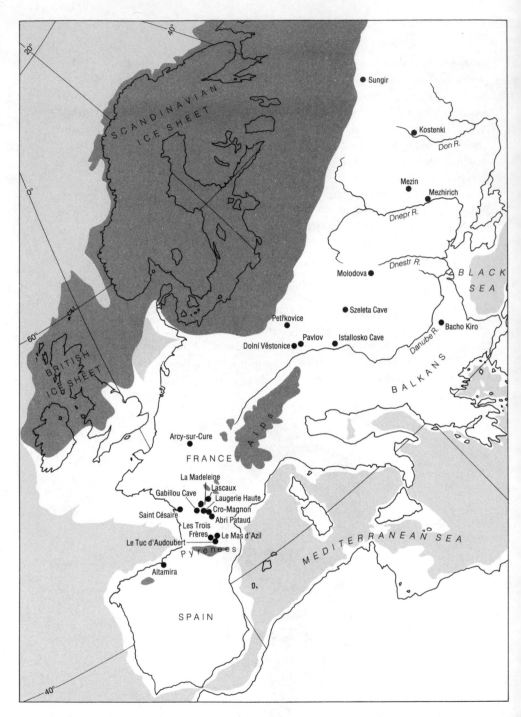

Sites in western Europe and Eurasia referred to in Chapters Twelve and Thirteen.

CHAPTER THIRTEEN

The Plains Dwellers

During much of the later part of the Ice Age, a vast belt of rolling, virtually treeless landscape extended across northern Europe, from the North Sea in the west into the depths of Siberia in the east. These open plains were an inhospitable environment for human beings, bitterly cold and dry, besieged for days on end by cutting arctic winds that brought clouds of fine glacial dust from the ice sheets to the north. Winters lasted 9 months, subzero temperatures were the norm. The summers were warm, often humid, with a short, intense growing season in late spring and early summer. These were the northern lands of the Ice Age world.

The human beings who eventually settled this undulating landscape were scattered in small numbers over thousands of square miles of the tundra, extending from central Europe deep into the Soviet Union. We know something of their way of life from excavations in once game-rich valleys in Czechoslovakia, near the Danube River, and from the Dnestr, Dnepr, and Don river valleys of the Central Russian Plain. Most of these sites date to later than 25,000 years ago, to the height of the last cold cycle of the Würm (known to Soviet scholars as the Valdai) glaciation, long after *Homo sapiens sapiens* had appeared on the open tundra. But some Neanderthal groups lived in the same valleys much earlier. We know most about these early hunting peoples from Soviet excavations on the Central Russian Plain.

Neanderthals on the Central Russian Plain

Conditions in this open country were not always as harsh as they were during the height of the last glaciation. During the last interglacial, the northern half of the Central Russian Plain was covered by broadleaf forest, while southern areas saw more open country, a mix of deciduous woodland and meadow steppe. The oldest Neanderthal occupations on the Central Russian Plain and in the Crimea date to the very end of the interglacial, before 90,000–80,000 years ago. The early millennia of the last glaciation itself saw few, if any, permanent human settlers on the Plain. A scatter of finds show that the Neanderthals penetrated temperate, subarctic, and dry, arctic steppe-tundra

177

at least as far north as 52 degrees N in central Europe, and 49 degrees N in the eastern Soviet Union between 60,000 and 40,000 years ago. Near the Don River, they hunted mammoth, bison, wild horse, and the saiga antelope, a species that flourishes on dry continental steppe. Here, as elsewhere, Neanderthals camped near permanent water, in places sheltered from strong winds, where gallery forests grew, but close to the open plains. Later Neanderthal communities lived in a period of deteriorating climate, until as late as about 38,000 years ago. In areas such as the narrow, canyon-like middle section of the Dnestr Valley, where different elevations provided a more complex mix of food resources, human occupation was continuous, even during periods when winter temperatures were between 18 and 27 degrees F (10–15 deg.C) lower than today. For example, the Molodova V site contains no less than 12 major archaeological horizons, of which the lower three contain Mousterian (Middle Paleolithic) tools, presumably the work of Neanderthals, with minimum ages between about 45,600 and 40,300 years ago, putting them in a somewhat warmer climatic interval, the one that saw anatomically modern humans appear in southeastern Europe.

Neanderthal groups adapted successfully to the Central Russian Plain, but population densities were low, and settlement usually transitory. The more easterly parts of the Plain were sporadically exploited, during a long period when constant climatic change depleted plains environments. It was left to *Homo sapiens sapiens* to maximize the potential of this inhospitable landscape.

A Frozen Land

As elsewhere in the Ice Age world, the final cycle of the last glaciation reached its peak about 20,000 to 18,000 years ago, with extreme arctic conditions. The northern ice sheet extended as far south as 53 degrees N, lying within 93–124 miles (150–200 km) of concentrations of Stone Age sites in the Don and Dnepr valleys. Great glacial lakes lay at the edges of the ice sheet, which overflowed during warmer cycles into the river valleys. To the south, a much smaller Black Sea was, in fact, a glacial lake, isolated from the Mediterranean at the Bosphorus, and fed with glacial meltwater from the Dnepr and its tributaries. The overloaded rivers may, at times, have been chains of glacial lakes or deep channels, overlooked by the small camps of hunter-gatherers surviving in this harsh land. Between about 18,000 and 10,000 years ago, the ice sheets retreated irregularly, but the glacial lakes and associated drainage system persisted until at least 15,000–14,000 years ago.

In the second half of the glaciation, this area was dry and very cold, with permafrost underfoot. Cooler ocean temperatures and the close proximity of the Scandinavian ice sheet profoundly affected atmospheric circulation. The ice sheet to the north effectively blocked off moisture-bearing Atlantic and oceanic air masses, lowering temperatures and reducing snowfall. Most rain fell in the warmer months of the short summer. Snow cover in winter was light.

Such, then, were climatic conditions during much of the late last glaciation with occasional warmer oscillations that brought higher rainfall and greater forest cover in more sheltered areas. These changes affected animal numbers and distributions. Food resources for human predators fluctuated constantly as a result, much more so than in, say, the savanna environment of sub-Saharan Africa.

The Plains Bestiary

The seeming wilderness of the plains was inhabited by a surprising variety of animals, many of them now extinct. Much of their homeland was arid, periglacial tundra, giving way in many more southerly locations to steppe-tundra. The distinction between tundra and steppe-tundra is important, for the former has but sparse vegetational cover, while steppe-tundra carries more grass and scrub. These diverse environments were home to more than 40 species of large mammals, ranging from the mammoth and woolly rhinoceros to reindeer, marmot, and arctic foxes. Actual animal densities may have been low overall, but game concentrations may have been higher in frontier zones where the forests and grasslands of river valleys intersected with the open steppe-tundra. Stone Age hunters may have timed their movements out of such valleys to coincide with regular migrations of mammoth, reindeer, and other species.

Of all the animals hunted by Stone Age people, the mammoth is the most famous. Mammoths were not quite the gigantic beasts of legend, but they still stood about 11 ft (3.4 m) tall at the shoulder – a formidable quarry for any hunter. They had broad feet, adapted to support their heavy bodies in swampy terrain. Thick hair covered every part of the body except the soles of the feet. Their underwool was up to 6 in (15.2 cm) thick. Olga Soffer of the University of Illinois has summarized the available, but sketchy, data, arguing that mammoth populations fluctuated considerably during the late last glaciation, decreasing during warmer centuries. The overall mammoth population was probably fairly small, with maximal densities of no more than about 0.13–0.5 mammoth per square kilometer even during the most favorable times. Human predation and climatic stress may have led to periodic population crashes.

The mammoth may have been the giant of the Upper Paleolithic fauna, but steppe bison were large animals, too, and were hunted regularly, especially in the more grassy country close to the Crimea. They were heavily built, with large heads and massive horns, and a coat as much as 30 in (76 cm) thick to protect them against arctic cold. The musk ox was another gregarious animal

The Plains bestiary as depicted in Upper Paleolithic cave art: reindeer (top), bison and horse (middle row), and mammoth (bottom).

of the steppe-tundra, capable of surviving extreme subzero temperatures and of obtaining food from beneath snow up to 8 in (20 cm) deep without trouble. There were saiga antelope, a plains animal capable of speeds of 40 mph (64 kph), with large hooves for digging under snow and running over it. Other staples included the ubiquitous reindeer and wild horse. The populations of these various species may have fluctuated greatly, with horses decreasing in numbers when forests spread in warmer cycles, and reindeer perhaps becoming more common in times when there was more open country.

Adapting to Open Country

On the scrub-covered steppe-tundra, there were no deep river valleys with high cliffs, where *Homo sapiens sapiens* hunters could take refuge during winter, as in the Périgord region of France. Even in the wide valleys they preferred, modern humans had to survive in the open, creating their own winter dwellings and protective clothing that prevented frostbite and hypothermia in the extreme cold.

It may have taken the plains hunters some time to realize the full potential of their complex environment. As with the Cro-Magnons to the southwest, there may have been a "Swiss Army Knife" effect, a technological catalyst that opened up new possibilities to inventive minds. As in the Périgord, this may have been the cylindrical core and the long, parallel-sided blades punched off it. Sharp-edged blades and burins were especially effective for cutting into hard ivory from mammoth tusks, for grooving bone and ivory to produce the slender blanks that were then perforated and turned into fine needles. And these needles enabled *Homo sapiens sapiens* to abandon ill-formed skins and to sew form-fitting arctic clothing, everything from underclothes to parkas, fur-lined hoods, and special footwear for hunting and trapping in subzero temperatures.

The hunters also needed winter dwellings that were both durable and energy efficient in months of subzero weather. Away from forested areas, on the open plains, they had to rely on their prey for winter housing materials. Such dwellings were a far cry from the simple hide tents and brush shelters that probably sufficed in the warmer season, for they had to be energy efficient, offer little resistance to the wind, and be large enough to house an entire family, or even a band. To construct such houses required not only hunting efficiency, but an intellectual ability to conceptualize houses made of mammoth bone or other available materials, and the expertise to organize house construction by several families – demanding a higher level of cooperation than in earlier times.

To settle on the steppe-tundra thus required well-developed social institutions. For months on end, families and sometimes larger groups were concentrated in small, artificial dwellings, without the luxury in more benign climates of being able to settle quarrels and disputes by individuals simply moving away. There were other important ways in which plains hunters had to cooperate for survival. Ambushes needed to be organized during spring or fall migrations. After such hunts, cooperation was required to butcher and cut up the carcasses, to dig large storage pits into the permafrost, and to stack dressed meat in them. Survival on the steppe-tundra must have depended on cautious behavior, constant cooperation, and careful leadership, perhaps in the hands of shamans or spirit mediums, who gauged the tone of the band as they defused quarrels, transmitted group lore, and reinforced the ties between people and their prey.

What is the archaeological evidence for this complex adaptation to the plains by modern humans?

The Arrival of Modern Humans

Here, as elsewhere in Eurasia, *Homo sapiens sapiens* replaced earlier Neanderthal populations, bringing characteristic Upper Paleolithic techno- logy with them. The site of Molodova V on the Dnepr River provides critical stratigraphic evidence for early Upper Paleolithic occupation with an estimated age of between 38,000 and 36,000 years ago, while Kostenki XVII, one of the famous Kostenki sites in the Don River valley to the east-northeast, was occupied by Upper Paleolithic hunters by 36,500 years ago. Somewhat similar dates come from at least one other Kostenki site. It is likely that some other known early Upper Paleolithic settlements may prove to be even earlier, perhaps dating to before 40,000 years ago.

Such artifacts as have been recovered from Upper Paleolithic sites dating to between 40,000 and 25,000 years ago in the Dnestr and Don valleys are somewhat amorphous and include both Mousterian-like bifacial points and occasional blades, burins, and retouched flakes. Here, as further west, the break between Middle and Upper Paleolithic occupation seems pronounced, making a case for population replacement quite compelling, even if there was interbreeding between archaic and modern populations.

The appearance of Upper Paleolithic occupation in the Kostenki–Borshevo area of the Don Valley marks a recolonization of the Central Russian Plain between about 36,000 and 32,000 years ago. The colonization expanded over the millennia, with increasing numbers of sites on the eastern, central, and southern parts of the Plain. The artifact forms found in the Dnestr and Don valleys are sufficiently different to cause Olga Soffer – one of the few archaeologists from the West to have studied Soviet sites and artifacts at first hand – to believe that they may have been colonized by groups from different areas.

As in western Europe, initial Upper Paleolithic settlement is scattered and ill-defined, but by no means confined to the south of the plains region. There are traces of such occupation as far north as the Pechora Basin, at about latitude 65 degrees N, before 25,000 years ago. Subsequently, the area was abandoned as the Scandinavian ice sheet advanced, creating vast glacial lakes in the region.

Some burials have been reported from early Upper Paleolithic sites in the Don Valley lowlands. Three come from Kostenki sites, but the most significant were discovered far to the north, at Sungir, northeast of Moscow. Here, three graves lay among Upper Paleolithic settlement debris. One contained the bodies of two young children laid head to head. Straightened mammoth ivory spears lay by their sides, also some stone tools, ivory rods, and pierced antler rods, and a carving of a horse outlined on an ivory sliver. Both these skeletons, and that of an adult male nearby, were covered with thousands of shell beads. It was as if the beads had been sewn on clothes and head coverings. The dead had worn anoraks and long trousers, perhaps sewn directly to leather footwear, a practice that was commonplace among later Siberian groups. Some other upper garments had also been thrown over the bodies. The Sungir discoveries are especially important, for they show that the scattered *Homo sapiens sapiens* populations of the plains had achieved technological mastery of an extremely cold environment early in their occupation of the region.

Olga Soffer believes that there was a significant change in hunting strategies between Middle and Upper Paleolithic groups. Middle Paleolithic hunters were opportunistic, exploiting whatever food resources came to hand. In contrast, Upper Paleolithic newcomers "mapped on" to food resources over a wide area as a deliberate strategy. In areas with considerable seasonal fluctuations in food supplies, the people would focus on two or three important species, relying heavily on group planning and the storage of food for lean months. In regions with more dispersed, diverse food resources scattered over large areas, the hunters would consume a wider range of products, while still storing food for the winter months. Since exotic stone is much more widely used by Upper Paleolithic peoples, Soffer believes they exploited more extensive territories, with regular seasonal movements.

The Mammoth Hunters

According to Olga Soffer, there were two major periods of later Upper Paleolithic occupation in western Russia. The first was between about 26,000 and 20,000 years ago. Then there was a brief interregnum during the height of the last glaciation, with renewed occupation after about 18,000 years ago for another 6,000 years. Only a handful of sites belong to the early period, but there are many more after 18,000 years ago. During both periods, the peoples of the Central Russian Plain exploited the same gregarious herbivores, organizing their procurement of animals in much the same way for thousands of years. However, the exploitation of their quarry intensified over the

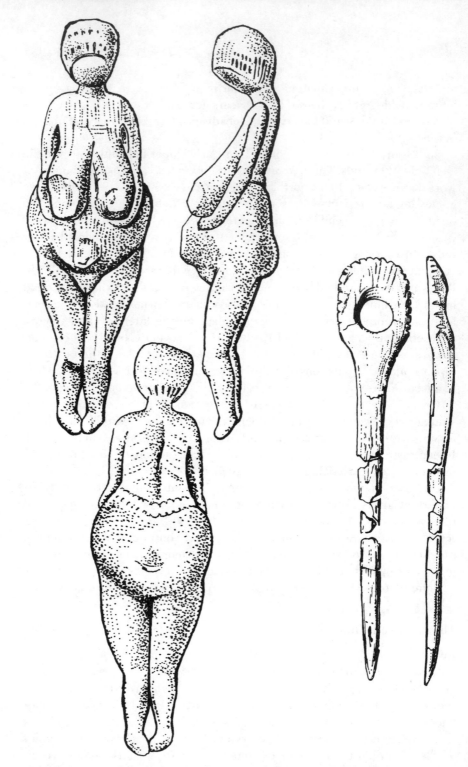

Art of the mammoth hunters: ivory figurine and dress ornament from the site of Kostenki.

millennia, probably, as Olga Soffer convincingly argues, because of periodic stress brought on by the constant climatic fluctuations after 18,000 years ago. Under these circumstances, food resources became less predictable, and sometimes less abundant as, say, mammoth and bison, reacted to warmer conditions by altering their migration patterns. One key to survival was to concentrate along the margins of river valleys, a process that created a linear settlement pattern. This, in turn, may have caused additional stress by circumscribing the hunting territories available to each band, in an environment where the carrying capacities of the land were extremely low, even under ideal conditions. Two sets of stresses, then, some environmental, the others demographic, led to major changes in human society in these broad river valleys during the late Ice Age.

Archaeologically, Olga Soffer makes a distinction between base camps with their storage pits, presumably occupied for some time, and more temporary encampments without such structures, sometimes even without traces of dwellings. Elaborate dwellings made of mammoth bones mark the more complex base camps. The Mezhirich site, on the Dnepr River, occupied about 18,000 years ago, has yielded remarkably complete mammoth bone dwellings. These structures have outer retaining walls made of patterned mammoth skulls, jaws, or long bones. In one house, the jawbones formed a herringbone pattern. In another, the builders used mirror imagery and repetition to duplicate bone patterns in the walls. The completed oval dwellings, each measuring about 16 ft (5 m) across, were dome-like houses, partially excavated into the ground and roofed with hides and sod. Nearby lay large storage pits filled with mammoth and other bones. To collect the dozens of heavy mammoth bones required for these houses and to erect them needed the cooperation of considerable numbers of people if the job was to be completed within a reasonable time. Significantly, great numbers of decorated ivory objects, perforated teeth, and other ornaments come from complex base camps like Mezhirich, all of which would have required substantial labor to manufacture. Some of the Mezhirich bones show considerable signs of weathering, as if they were scavenged from mammoth carcasses that had lain on the open steppe for some time. Perhaps the house frameworks were collected from mammoth kills as well as from beasts that had died of natural causes. Soffer has calculated that it would have taken 14 or 15 workers 10 days to construct Mezhirich, and about 16 days for some mammoth bone structures at Mezin upstream on the Desna River, a tributary of the Dnepr. Three times as much labor went into the construction of the complex base camp with its mammoth bone dwellings than was the case with simpler base camps.

The Mezhirich site and other large base camps such as Mezin tend to contain higher proportions of the bones of beavers and other fur-bearing species, also about twice the variety of game animals when compared with more transitory seasonal camps, hunting stands, or sites where people collected and processed flint from nearby outcrops. Furthermore, the complex base camps yield higher proportions of art and jewelry, commonly agreed to be marks of individual status, as well as considerable quantities of exotic materials such as amber and Black Sea shells.

The base camps would have been the places where ritual and ceremonial activities were especially important. At Kostenki, N.D. Praslov of the Academy of Sciences in Leningrad has recently excavated a series of 23,000-year-old mammoth bone dwellings separated one from another by low walls. This particular Kostenki location has yielded many signs of ritual activities. One collapsed dwelling house once bore two musk-ox skulls, which Praslov thinks may have served as totem symbols. This particular Kostenki location has yielded four burials, female figurines in stone and ivory, also necklaces of arctic fox teeth and four delicate mammoth ivory headbands. It was abandoned about 20,000 years ago, perhaps when the inhabitants moved southward away from deteriorating climatic conditions.

The pattern of seasonal movement is still little understood, but there are reasons to believe that some groups also occupied summer base camps, perhaps living in the open, or under large tents made of mammoth hide. After careful analysis of such data as estimated weights of mammoth meat from discarded bones and settlement size, Olga Soffer has argued that winter base camps were occupied for about 6 months, summer settlements for about a month or a month-and-a-half. This pattern is somewhat equivalent to that of modern groups in the Bering Strait region far to the northeast, who live in distinct summer and winter settlements, even if they are only a short distance apart. The hunters of the Central Russian Plain would have formed groups of between 30 and 60 people in winter floodplain-based camps, with mammoth bone dwellings being occupied by two or three families at the most. Here, the people lived off stored food, except for occasional forays in search of ptarmigan or hare, when they would use cold-weather satellite camps. Come the warm season, co-resident groups moved into their temporary summer base camps close by. During these months, too, smaller groups of hunters, stoneworkers, and others would probably move away for short periods of time, to take advantage of game migrations, plant foods, and other such opportunities. This seasonal pattern was to persist for many thousands of years.

For all their relatively limited mobility, the plains people exchanged exotic artifacts and materials over very long distances, just like the Cro-Magnons far to the west. Mountain crystals were brought to Mezhirich and other sites from southern locations between 62 and 93 miles (100–150 km) away. In some places, the hunters collected flint from at least 37 miles (60 km) away. Amber, fashioned into beads and also, perhaps, prized for its magical properties, came from deposits near the modern city of Kiev. Amber is more common at locations closer to Kiev, and its frequency drops off, as if it was handed "down the line" from one community to the next, with each group retaining a proportion of the exotic material for its own use.

Fossil marine shells from the lower Dnepr Valley, close to the Sea of Azov and Black Sea, passed far into the interior, as far north as Timonovka on the upper Desna River, more than 403 miles (650 km) from source. Interestingly, most shells come from northern sites rather than from more southerly locations. Soffer argues that the peoples of the far interior may have organized special expeditions to procure the shells, which were then worked into finished ornaments at northern base sites.

The items that moved along these exchange networks were predominantly non-utilitarian, luxury goods, items that were vital social and political indicators. Much of the long-distance trade may, indeed, have been ceremonial, with strong ritual undertones, a means of validating important ideologies, of ensuring exchange of information and cooperation in daily life – just as it was elsewhere in Europe at the time (Chapter Twelve).

Big Game Hunting to the Northeast

We can guess that very scattered populations of *Homo sapiens sapiens* were hunting over the northeastern tundra by 35,000–30,000 years ago, following pockets of arctic animals through sheltered river valleys, by glacial lakes, and in other favored locations, moving over enormous distances in relatively short times. But how did they arrive there – from western Russia or from the south, from China? We turn now to the intricate story of the first modern humans in northeastern Asia.

CHAPTER FOURTEEN

Northeast Asians

How did people first colonize the vast expanses of northern and eastern Asia? Did they journey inexorably eastward across the Russian plains, or did they instead venture north out of China? In order to understand the first settlement of these inhospitable lands, we need to take a plunge backward in time – to the remote world of *Homo erectus* more than 200,000 years ago. In this enormous region of the Old World, unlike the Central Russian Plain, controversy again surrounds the appearance of anatomically modern humans. As before, there are passionate advocates for regional evolution of *Homo sapiens sapiens* in these varied landscapes, quite independent of evolutionary events in distant Africa. And with equal vehemence, other scholars argue for a replacement of more archaic forms by fully modern people who originated elsewhere.

The Fossil Evidence

Homo erectus flourished in China for a very long time indeed, from before 700,000 years ago until at least 200,000 years ago. As we saw in Chapters Nine and Ten, some physical anthropologists, many Chinese scholars among them, believe that anatomically modern humans evolved within Asia from ancient *Homo erectus* roots. They argue forcefully for regional evolution, basing their arguments on the Zhoukoudian fossils, and on scattered archaic *Homo sapiens* finds of about 200,000 years ago from Dali, Maba, and Dingcun. There are other archaic *Homo sapiens* fragments, too, like those from the Xujiayao site in northeastern Shanxi, which is said to date to later than 200,000 years ago. Paleoanthropologist Wu Xinzhi of the Institute of Vertebrate Paleontology and Paleoanthropology of the Academia Sinica is a firm believer in the Candelabra hypothesis. "In *Homo erectus* in China you have already a clear Chinese type of person," he says. He points to the flat face and the anatomy of the area between the cheekbone and the upper jaw. Chinese *Homo erectus* fossils have shovel-shaped incisors, a dental feature that is of vital importance when tracing the origins of the first native Americans (Chapter Fifteen).

The actual fossil evidence for these claims is, however, so incomplete that anatomists find it hard even to agree on what long-term traits are evidence of evolutionary continuity. There is, however, some agreement that there was a gradual increase in brain size among Asian *Homo erectus* and archaic *Homo sapiens* populations after 200,000 years ago. Dali and other presently known fossils in this time range are simply too incomplete to provide definitive answers. Certainly the case for regional evolution rests on weak anatomical ground, leaving one with the replacement argument as the best alternative.

Much the same genetic and anatomical arguments can be applied to the Chinese fossils as has been applied to those from Southeast Asia. There, a replacement hypothesis has *Homo sapiens sapiens* appearing perhaps as early as 70,000 to 60,000 years ago, but, as in China, we lack the fossils to document the biological change, except for the 67,000-year-old Linjiang skull, said to be an archaic-looking *Homo sapiens sapiens*. In China, the changeover may well date to much later, as it does in Europe and on the Russian plains, perhaps to as late as 40,000 to 35,000 years ago. Here, as in Southeast Asia, there is a yawning gap in the fossil record, between about 200,000 years ago, and some fragments of human bone from Salawasu in Mongolia that have been uranium-dated to between 50,000 and 37,000 years ago and are said by Chinese experts to be from *Homo sapiens sapiens*.

The Microblade Phenomenon

There is an unspoken, and probably correct, assumption that *Homo erectus*, originally an Africa-bred, tropical and subtropical animal, settled in the warmer southern part of China first, then radiated northward into more extreme environments. But how much farther north? Only the Zhoukoudian caves near Beijing provide a sketchy chronicle of ancient life in northern China before about 200,000 years ago. It is not until much later, some time before 35,000 years ago, that there are a few signs of human settlement to the north in Mongolia – and by now the settlers were probably anatomically modern people. Here, in Mongolia, the Huang He River flows through arid grasslands attracting tributary river valleys that were once the focus of hunter-gatherer settlement. These so-called "Ordosian" peoples are known from such sites as Salawasu, with its loosely dated modern human remains, already mentioned. The Ordosians were hunters with spears and bolas (hunting slings made of thongs or fibers weighted with stone balls), who used a technology that combined Middle Paleolithic Levallois and disc-core techniques with smaller blades struck from prismatic cores. There are a handful of sites in the 36,000-to-25,000-year range in northern China that have yielded evidence of a similar longterm trend to that in Mongolia – a significant reduction in artifact size in every category from knives to projectile points and scrapers.

Chinese archaeologist Chen Chun believes that these sites may reflect a primitive "microblade" cultural tradition that emerged in Asia quite soon after the appearance of anatomically modern humans in the region. In time, microblade technologies were to dominate Stone Age cultures throughout northern China, Korea, Japan, and far to the north and east in Siberia, and possibly extreme northwestern North America as well.

The microlith (a term derived from the Greek *micros*: small, *lithos*: stone) is a highly distinctive artifact, fabricated throughout much of the Stone Age world after the Ice Age and, in places such as China and India, many thousands of years earlier. These diminutive blades required considerable skill to manufacture, and were struck off carefully prepared wedge-shaped, conical, and cylindrical cores that may represent different technological artifices, or simply the demands of different fine-grained rocks. By their very size, microliths were designed to be mounted in antler, bone, or wooden hafts – to serve as spear barbs, arrowpoints, or as small knife or scraper blades.

The long-lived microblade cultures of northern Asia appear at least 30,000 years ago. So far, the earliest dates come from China rather than Siberia, as if the trend toward technological diminution emerged first somewhere in temperate Asia, then spread into the arctic north and northeast. Northern Asian microblade cultures represent as distinctive a tradition as that of the Cro-Magnons in central and western Europe, or of the plains hunters of the Ukraine. In more favored areas, these groups may have settled astride game migration routes, or along lakes and rivers where seasonal foods were abundant, and, perhaps, they could exploit fish and other year-round resources. But in more arid areas, like the Gobi Desert and Mongolia, the people were highly mobile, dependent on a stone technology that was economical, easy to carry and manufacture, and yet capable of arming spears and, perhaps very late in the Ice Age, arrows with sharp, lethal points for taking game on the run in open country. This same technology was so effective that it proved advantageous not only in more temperate and arid regions, but in far harsher periglacial environments to the north. In a real sense, microblade technology is *the* material innovation that can safely be tied to *Homo sapiens sapiens* in northern Asia. And it may have formed part of the toolkit that accompanied the first human colonizers of the Americas into their new homeland (Chapter Fifteen).

One of the manufacturing techniques used in the Upper Paleolithic microblade technology of northern China.

Japan

Microblade technology spread over an enormous area of northeastern Asia, being used not only in continental environments but offshore in Japan as well. Japan has not been an island for very long. During peak periods of glaciation, like that of 20,000 years ago, the Japanese Archipelago was an appendage of the Asian mainland. The Japan Sea was an enormous bay with only a narrow entrance to the Pacific in the north. When, then, did modern humans first settle the Japanese Archipelago?

The date of first settlement has long been controversial. *Homo erectus* may have hunted in Japan, but the few stone tools claimed to document these archaic people are unconvincing. The earliest well-documented artifacts date to at least 50,000 years ago, mainly heavy choppers and crude flakes, and occupation levels in the 40,000-year range occur in the lowest levels of several Japanese caves. Some form of toolmaking tradition based on simple flakes lasted until about 20,000 years ago in some parts of Japan.

Here, as in Southeast Asia, the archaeologist must confront the issue of early seafaring. About 30,000 years ago, sea levels were high enough to sever Japan from the mainland. Yet it is at about this time that new blade and edge-grinding technologies appear in the islands. Such technologies presumably arrived by sea. A young *Homo sapiens sapiens* skeleton found in Yamashita-cho Cave on the long-isolated island of Okinawa to the south dates before 32,000 years ago, convincing evidence of seafaring in Japanese waters by the time other modern humans were colonizing the Solomon Islands in Sahulian waters (Chapter Ten). As in Southeast Asia, seafaring may have been stimulated by trading activities. By at least 21,000 years ago, hunters living on Honshu, the main island of Japan, were obtaining obsidian from Kozushima Island, 31 miles (50 km) offshore. It may be that the first appearance of *Homo sapiens sapiens* in any numbers coincided with the beginnings of seafaring in these temperate waters.

Blade technology was adopted slowly in Japan, and the human population of the archipelago did not increase significantly until after about 20,000 years ago. Tool forms became more varied, and more standardized, and sizes diminished, as they did on the mainland, with microblades becoming common during the remainder of the last glaciation, as they did elsewhere in northeastern Asia.

There is evidence, then, in China, Mongolia, and Japan for a diminution in stone blade size and the evolution of microblades after 30,000 years ago. But what of the much harsher lands to the north, in Siberia? When did human pioneers first colonize this remote region of the world? Do stone tools and other evidence hint at an origin for these people in China, or far to the west, in central Asia?

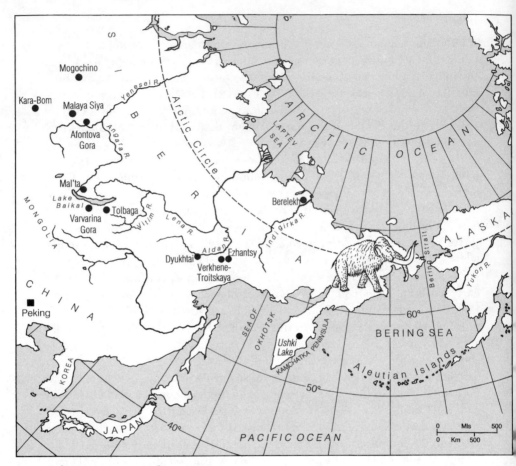

Relevant sites in northeast Asia.

Central Asia and Southern Siberia

By some 35,000 years ago, we know that anatomically modern big-game
hunters flourished in some river valleys of the rolling steppe-tundra that
extended from central Europe to the Ukraine and beyond, even if we do not
know their precise distribution over this enormous region. To the north and
east lies an archaeological vacuum extending hundreds of miles into western
Siberia. We can assume that somewhat similar periglacial hunting cultures
inhabited these bitterly cold regions, but we know nothing of them.

Middle Paleolithic peoples lived in the Altai region, but Upper Paleolithic
peoples were the first to settle farther north in the open country west of Lake
Baikal, in southern Siberia. The recently discovered Malaya Siya site on the
White Iyus River west of Lake Baikal lies on the slope of a ravine above the

river, in an area of low mountains. Malaya Siya is said to date to about 34,500–33,000 years ago, and lay in the midst of a hilly steppe. The inhabitants hunted mammoth, horse, reindeer, bison, and other arctic mammals large and small, just like their contemporaries in the Ukraine. The stone tools include large and medium-sized blades, some microcores, also large pebble scrapers known throughout Siberia as *skreblos*, as well as bone artifacts and small sculptures, bas-reliefs, and engravings of animals, birds, and other animals that are as old as, if not older than, the earliest European art.

This elaborate early Upper Paleolithic site contains artifacts that are similar to those from contemporary settlements east of Lake Baikal, Varvarina Gora and Tolbaga, which date to about 34,900 years ago. South of Malaya Siya, in the Altai, the Kara-Bom site has yielded not only the bones of elephant, horse, and bison, but also blade tools that may resemble those from Malaya Siya. There are also said to be both Levallois and blade cores, as well as projectile points and *skreblos*, in the same level, estimated to be between 30,000 and 40,000 years old.

Malaya Siya and related early Upper Paleolithic sites in the 40,000-to-30,000-year range contain a developed blade technology, with, however, a persistence of earlier stoneworking methods. The stone artifacts are far from diminutive, however, and there is less variation in stone tool inventories than is the case within a few millennia, at the height of the late last glaciation.

By 25,000 years ago, two very different technological traditions flourished in western Siberia – the Mal'ta and the Afontova Gora-Oshurkovo traditions. The Mal'ta tradition is known from clusters of sites west of Lake Baikal, many of them located in places sheltered from the prevailing northerly winds. The Mal'ta settlement itself, one of semi-subterranean houses, covers more than 6,458 sq. ft (600 sq. m) and may have been occupied many times. Mal'ta was

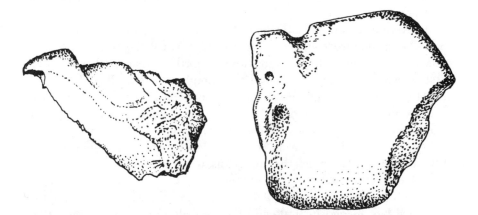

Schematic carvings of an eagle (left) and a mammoth (right) from Malaya Siya, southern Siberia.

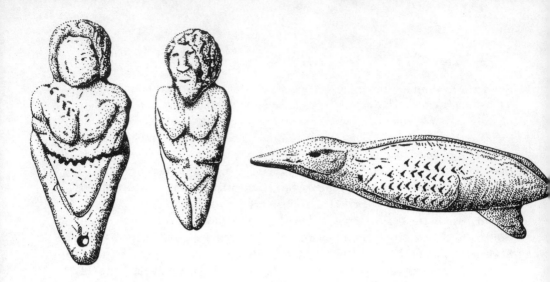

Ivory carvings from Mal'ta on the Angara River in Siberia include these two female figurines and an arctic waterbird.

probably a winter base camp of houses built of large animal bones with a lattice of interlaced reindeer antler to support the skin or sod covering. The hunters pursued mammoth, woolly rhinoceros, and reindeer, also smaller animals. Mal'ta is famous for its ivory carvings that include depictions not only of mammoth, but of women and wildfowl as well. Recent excavations give a strong impression of a big-game hunting society that was remarkably similar to that of the Ukraine peoples far to the west. But Soviet archaeologist Vitaliy Larichev, who excavated Malaya Siya, believes that the cultural roots of the Mal'ta tradition lie in the early Upper Paleolithic of the region, and that it achieved its greatest elaboration between 18,000 and 12,000 years ago. In many respects, the widespread Mal'ta tradition resembles Upper Paleolithic cultures to the west, but there seems little question that it developed from indigenous cultural roots.

The Afontova Gora-Oshurkovo tradition was once thought to be a purely local Siberian culture, confined to the Yenesei River Valley, but now appears to have flourished over an enormous area of northern Asia, perhaps from the Altai to the Amur River. The oldest sites, Afontova Gora itself on the Yenesei and Mogochino on the Ob' River, date to between 21,000 and 20,000 years ago. The inhabitants hunted the usual arctic mammals, making large tools fashioned on pebbles, blade artifacts, *skréblos*, and, in the Afontova sites of the Yenesei, microblades as well. To the south, later sites on the upper reaches of the Yenesei contain much the same tools, with considerable elaboration of microblade technology.

There are many general similarities between the Mal'ta and Afontova traditions, which tend to transcend the local differences between artifact collections. Soviet archaeologist Yuri Mochanov believes that together they form a widespread Upper Paleolithic tradition that reflects a varied adaptation by *Homo sapiens sapiens* to an enormous area of central Asia and southern Siberia from well west of Lake Baikal to the Pacific coast. North and east of the Yenesei and Lena watersheds flourished yet another Upper Paleolithic tradition, the Dyukhtai.

For years, western scholars have thought that anatomically modern humans, and the big-game hunting culture associated with them, spread into central Asia and Siberia from western Eurasia. One can hardly blame them, for the rich archaeological record of the Altai and Lake Baikal regions was little known outside the confines of Soviet archaeological literature. Now, Malaya Siya and other discoveries have redefined the antecedents of Mal'ta and other similar sites. Here, as elsewhere in Asia, Upper Paleolithic cultures developed between 40,000 and 30,000 years ago, with a significant local flavor. It remains to be seen whether these new cultures resulted from population replacement movements of archaic by modern *Homo sapiens*. Was there a sharp technological break at the beginning of the Upper Paleolithic, with, perhaps, some thin transitional layers where archaic *Homo sapiens* groups experimented with the new technology, as happened, for example, with the Châtelperronian in the Périgord?

Dyukhtai and the Settlement of Northeast Asia

The earliest traces of human occupation in eastern Siberia come from excavations in the Middle Aldan Valley. In 1967, Soviet archaeologist Yuri Mochanov excavated Dyukhtai Cave, close to the river floodplain. There he found mammoth and musk-ox remains associated with bifacially flaked spear points, burins, blades, and other Upper Paleolithic-like tools, as well as large stone choppers. The cave deposits were disturbed by freezing, thawing, and other natural perturbations, so Mochanov was unable to date the occupation levels any more closely than to between 14,000 and 12,000 years ago.

Mochanov made a distinction between the Afontova Gora site with its choppers and Dyukhtai, with its fine bifacial points. He soon found more Dyukhtai-like sites on the banks of the Aldan, this time open-air locations with deposits he had radiocarbon-dated to about 35,000 years ago. Thus was born the Dyukhtai culture, a far-flung late Ice Age hunter-gatherer tradition, whose hallmarks – small microblades and characteristic wedge-shaped cores and bifaces – have been found over wide areas of northeastern Asia, across the Bering Strait in Alaska, and as far south as British Columbia.

Since Mochanov's excavations, however, the chronology of the Dyukhtai tradition has been thrown in doubt. Mochanov's radiocarbon dates from the Middle Aldan come from river terrace deposits that contain concentrations of animal bones and artifacts much disturbed by violent seasonal freezing and thawing cycles, such as are common in extreme arctic climates. Furthermore, the radiocarbon samples come from wood fragments, which are often much older than the deposits in which they are found. Preservation conditions are so good in the cold that wood can survive for centuries, if not for millennia, in permafrost.

The earliest securely dated Dyukhtai site is Verkhene-Troitskaya, also on the Aldan, which has been radiocarbon-dated to about 18,000 years ago. Here well-made, characteristic artifacts of the Dyukhtai tradition were found. Many American scholars believe that this is indeed the earliest manifestation of Dyukhtai, considerably later than Mochanov claims. Certainly, micro-blades and characteristic wedge-shaped cores are widespread throughout northeastern Siberia after 14,000 years ago. The Berelekh site at 71 degrees N near the mouth of the Indigirka River is the northernmost Dyukhtai location known. Berelekh is celebrated for its "mammoth cemetery," where more than 140 well-preserved mammoths drowned during spring floods. The archaeological site contained the remains of two mammoths and dozens of arctic hares, together with a small assemblage of microblades and small bone and ivory tools.

With its microblades and wedge-shaped cores, the Dyukhtai tradition has plausible cultural links with widespread microblade cultures to the south, in China. Since microblade industries were well developed in northern China earlier than they were in northeast Asia, a case can be made for originating the Dyukhtai tradition in the south. And since Dyukhtai was, apparently, culturally linked with the earliest human societies of the Americas, this potential connection is of great importance.

Sinodonts and Sundadonts

We know enough about the Upper Paleolithic cultures of Asia to realize that this was not a backward, peripheral region of a world of *Homo sapiens sapiens* centered far to the west. Nor can we invoke simplistic hypotheses of first settlement by modern humans that had mammoth hunters moving inexorably northeast from the Ukraine into hitherto uninhabited territory. Rather, the spread of anatomically modern humans into central Asia, northern China, and Siberia was a complex process that began at least 35,000 years ago.

Culturally speaking, the initial Upper Paleolithic traditions may have reflected lingering earlier technologies and subsistence practices. But there seems little doubt that it was anatomically modern people who were the first to settle in the heart of Siberia and in the far northeast. As in the west, it may have been the superior intellectual capabilities of *Homo sapiens sapiens* that enabled people to develop specialized technologies to master climatic extremes at the fringes of the Ice Age world, to grasp the unique opportunities of harsh steppe-tundra environments. Biologically, the ultimate ancestry of the Upper Paleolithic northern Asians and Siberians remains somewhat of a mystery. But recent dental researches are revealing close connections

UPPER JAW

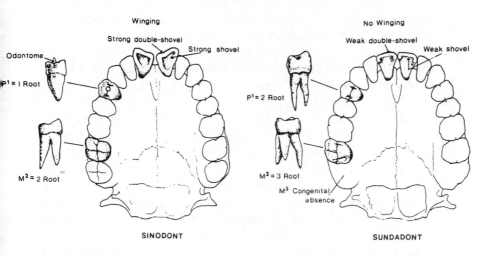

LOWER JAW

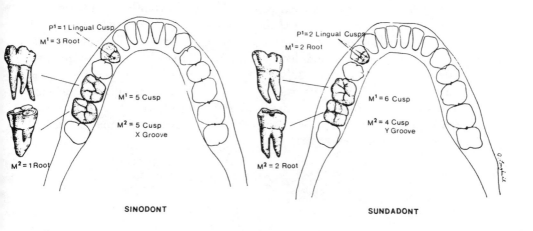

Some of Christy Turner's theories about the peopling of America are based on differences between the teeth of so-called Sinodonts (northern Asians and all native Americans) and Sundadonts (eastern Asians). Sinodonts display among other features strong incisor shoveling (scooping out on one or both surfaces of the tooth), single-rooted upper first premolars, and triple-rooted lower first molars.

between northeastern Asia and regions to the south rather than to the west.

Christy Turner of Arizona State University is an expert on the changing physical characteristics of human teeth. He has shown that tooth features of the crowns and roots give clues to the degrees of relationship between prehistoric populations. These tooth features are more stable than most evolutionary traits, with a high genetic component that minimizes the effects of environmental differences, sexual dimorphism, and age variations. In particular, he has focused on a pattern of specialized tooth features he calls "sinodonty." Sinodont hallmarks include incisor shoveling (the scooped-out shape on the inside of the tooth), double-shoveling (scooping out on both sides), single-rooted upper first premolars, and three-rooted lower first molars. Turner has recorded sinodonty in northern Chinese skeletons at least 20,000 years old, and believes sinodont traits evolved much earlier.

Assuming a common origin for all *Homo sapiens sapiens* populations, the dentally more specialized northern Chinese would have had to have originated from more generalized eastern Asian populations. The few Upper Paleolithic skeletons from the Lake Baikal area do not display sinodonty, nor do teeth from burials at Kostenki and other sites in European Russia. The morphological differences are so striking that Europeans and Southeast Asians (Turner calls the latter group "sundadonts") are seen to have nothing to do with the peopling of northeastern Asia and, ultimately, the Americas.

Christy Turner's research is really a study of evolutionary divergence, using statistical calculations that allow one to date the approximate moments at which sinodont populations split off from ancestral Chinese groups. The first of these divergences led ultimately, Turner believes, to the first settlement of the Americas through eastern Mongolia and the Upper Lena Basin, across eastern Siberia, and from there across the Bering Strait along the now-submerged continental shelf to Alaska. And with that momentous development, *Homo sapiens sapiens* expanded beyond the limits of the Old World for the first time.

CHAPTER FIFTEEN

The Settlement of the Americas

North and east of Lake Baikal in Siberia, the late Ice Age steppe-tundra stretched on for mile after mile. It extended to the shores of the Arctic Ocean in the north and right into Alaska in the east, for the Bering strait was dry land. Despite an initial impression of monotony, the traveler would have found a broken landscape of rugged plains, hills, mountains, and deeply indented coastlines. This was the harsh, periglacial terrain that was the springboard for the first settlement of the Americas. What do we know of the mysterious, now-submerged Bering land bridge? And when exactly did people first cross it?

The Bering Land Bridge

The low-lying, windy shelf that was the Bering land bridge formed the heart of a now-vanished Ice Age continent called Beringia that extended from Siberia across the Bering Strait into the unglaciated parts of Alaska. The land bridge extended far into the Chukchi and Bering Seas, and there were wide shelves off the Siberian and Alaskan coasts. The Siberian shore is relatively steep and rugged, while the Alaskan side is bounded by low-lying coastal plains. Despite these topographical differences, both sides of the strait formed part of an arid system of huge, interconnected, and unglaciated plains and lowlands that extended all the way to eastern Europe.

The Bering Strait separated the Old and the New Worlds until the onset of the last glaciation about 100,000 years ago, when seas fell far below modern levels and the land bridge was formed. As was the case with Sahul (Chapter Ten), the land bridge was only at its maximum extent at the intense climaxes of the glaciation, about 50,000 years ago, and again around 20,000 years ago. But in the interim, shorelines still lay on average about 131 ft (40 m) below modern contours, enough to join Siberia and Alaska with an ice-free shelf dissected by north-facing estuaries that were no obstacle to the foot traveler. The land bridge did not finally vanish under rising seas until about 12,000 years ago. Theoretically at any rate, it would have been possible for Ice Age hunter-gatherers to traverse central Beringia any time after about 100,000

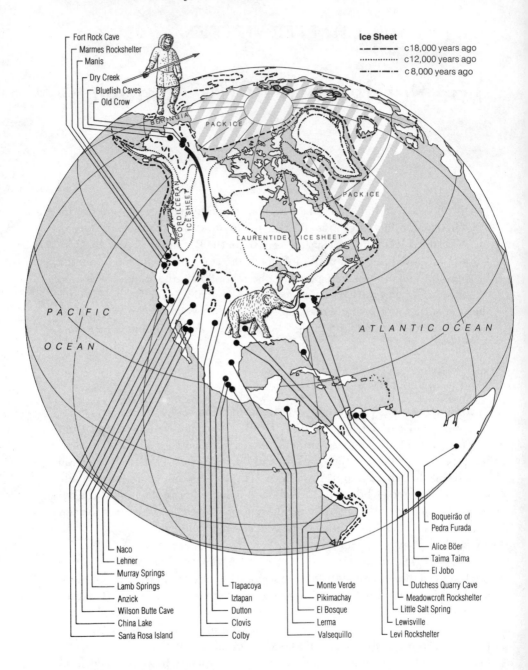

Fort Rock Cave
Marmes Rockshelter
Manis
Dry Creek
Bluefish Caves
Old Crow

Ice Sheet
--------- c18,000 years ago
·········· c12,000 years ago
-·-·-·- c8,000 years ago

BERINGIA
PACK ICE
PACK ICE
CORDILLERAN ICE SHEET
LAURENTIDE ICE SHEET

PACIFIC

OCEAN

ATLANTIC OCEAN

Boqueirão of
Pedra Furada

Naco
Lehner
Murray Springs
Lamb Springs
Anzick
Wilson Butte Cave
China Lake
Santa Rosa Island

Tlapacoya
Iztapan
Dutton
Clovis
Colby

Monte Verde
Pikimachay
El Bosque
Lerma
Valsequillo

Alice Böer
Taima Taima
El Jobo
Dutchess Quarry Cave
Meadowcroft Rockshelter
Little Salt Spring
Lewisville
Levi Rockshelter

The Americas during the last stages of the Ice Age, when first settlement took place. The routes that humans used to move south are still uncertain.

years ago without using watercraft. The actual date when this occurred is a matter of controversy.

Not that central Beringia was a hospitable environment, even in the warmest millennia of the last glaciation. Like the great plains of eastern Asia during the late Ice Age, it was arid steppe-tundra, covered with a patchwork of very different kinds of vegetation – grasses, sedges, and clumps of wormwood – and many marshes and shallow ponds. These conditions favored grass-dominated wetlands, where mammoth, bison, and other large mammals would find summer fodder. The large rivers that crossed the lowlands traversed floodplains, where willow brush and other ideal fodder for herbivores grew.

Central Beringia differed considerably from modern tundra. This was a largely treeless environment, but one that may have been more productive than modern tundra and capable of supporting scattered herds of arctic animals, members of the "Upper Paleolithic fauna" found throughout the northern reaches of the late Ice Age world. It was the vegetational diversity of central Beringia that was vital, for it enabled small communities of mammals to succeed one another, utilizing patches of the bare, treeless environment in an endless succession of grazing patterns that persisted as long as the continental ecosystem remained intact.

The ever-shifting sea coasts of central Beringia may have offered completely different environmental conditions, perhaps the prospect of relatively productive marine food resources such as fish and sea mammals, but we know nothing of their ecology, and little of their configuration.

When Did Humans Cross into the Americas?

Few subjects in American archaeology have generated such controversy as the thorny question of first settlement. While scientists agree that the Beringian route was the only one by which humans could have entered the Americas, the timing and very nature of the crossing are passionately debated. The broad consensus is that anatomically modern humans were the first settlers, that neither *Homo erectus* nor archaic *Homo sapiens* set foot in the New World. Claims for human settlement before 40,000 years ago are totally unsubstantiated, not only because no archaeological sites of this age come from the Americas, but also because there are, to date, no signs of such early occupation in northeastern Siberia.

This leaves us with two competing chronologies for first settlement, both with their advocates. The first argues for late Ice Age occupation perhaps as early as 30,000 years ago, on the basis of a handful of sites, mainly in South America. The second hypothesizes that humans first crossed into Alaska at the very end of the Ice Age, perhaps as central Beringia flooded, after 15,000 years ago.

The Case for Settlement before 25,000 years ago

Despite the most diligent of searches for more than a century, only a handful of stratified archaeological sites contain what has been claimed as evidence for human settlement earlier than about 15,000 years ago. Most of these claims come from Central and South America.

Supporters of a settlement before 15,000 years ago reserve their greatest enthusiasm for several possible early occupation sites from South America. The earliest of these is a large rockshelter named Boqueirão de Pedra Furada in an area of northeastern Brazil famous for its prehistoric rock paintings. Here, Nième Guidon of the Centre National de Recherche Scientifique has excavated deep into occupation deposits that go back at least 10,000 years. There are deeper gravel and sand levels that are said to contain ash-filled "hearths," stone implements of various forms, even fragments of what are claimed to be painted rock spalls from the walls. The excavator claims radiocarbon dates of 32,000 years or more for the lowermost of these levels. But others raise serious questions about how these early levels and the stone artifacts in them were formed. The archaeological jury is still out on the Boqueirão site.

Veteran American archaeologist Richard MacNeish of the Foundation for American Archaeology excavated the Pikimachay Cave in the Peruvian highlands, where he unearthed stone artifacts associated with giant sloth bones that may date to as early as 14,000 years ago. Two radiocarbon dates from animal bones found lower in the cave date to around 20,000 years ago and are said to be associated with crude, humanly made cores, but the stratigraphy is jumbled, and the human origin of the artifacts remains in doubt.

Much further south, in northern Chile, Tom Dillehay of the University of Kentucky has uncovered a remarkable Paleo-Indian settlement on the edge of a small stream. Monte Verde has two occupation levels; one dates to between 12,000 and 14,000 years ago, the other is claimed to be much earlier, in the 33,000-year range. Dillehay has excavated the upper levels of Monte Verde with great care, but has so far only probed the lower horizons. The later Monte Verde people were living along a stretch of stream bank 1,312 ft (400 m) long, in a settlement of simple wood dwellings furnished with clay-lined braziers. They were hunting big game and foraging for the abundant plant foods in the area with but the simplest of stone and wooden artifacts, including crude choppers. The still largely unexcavated lower levels have yielded a split basalt pebble, wood fragments, and some modified stones, but most experts await large-scale excavations before accepting the validity of the early dating.

With serious doubts surrounding the claims of pre-25,000-year-old settlement in Central and South America, what about the United States and

Canada? Again, there have been many claims over the years, almost all of them failing to stand up to detailed scrutiny. The best documented is Meadowcroft, 30 miles (48.2 km) southwest of Pittsburgh, excavated by James Adovasio of the University of Pittsburgh with meticulous care. He found evidence for human settlement that extended back from about AD 1250 to 12,000 years ago, and perhaps even earlier. The lowermost levels of the rockshelter contain small humanly-struck flakes and blades, a projectile point and some delicately flaked bifaces, and have yielded radiocarbon dates between 16,000 and 11,000 years ago. A possible basketry fragment dated to 19,600 ± 2,400 years ago associated with stone flaking debris comes from even lower in the site. But there are serious technical doubts about the validity of the early radiocarbon dates which remain unresolved. Meadowcroft must therefore remain a tantalizing question mark.

There is no reason why *Homo sapiens sapiens* could not have moved south from Beringia well before 25,000 years ago, but we lack credible proof of such early human settlement. Whether this is because the Americas were still uninhabited, or because the human population was so mobile and so tiny that little or nothing survived continues to be a matter of intense debate. Most American archaeologists tend to believe that the New World was uninhabited until after 15,000 years ago. This theory agrees well with what we know from genetics, dental morphology, linguistics, and Beringian archaeology.

The First Americans

Conventional scientific wisdom has long held that the first Americans were big-game hunters, whose remote ancestors could be glimpsed in the Ukraine and among other late Ice Age hunting cultures in distant Europe. While it is true that Beringia was part of a vast, interconnected periglacial plains landscape that extended right across the northern Old World, this same landscape has always been open to cultural influences not only from the west, but also from the south along its frontier with more temperate climatic zones (Chapter Fourteen). If recent Soviet radiocarbon dates are reliable, what appear to be Upper Paleolithic populations were exploiting the Altai and living in open country around Lake Baikal by at least 35,000 years ago. By about 10,000 years later, the Mal'ta and Afontova Gora people were part of a hunter-gatherer tradition that extended from Mongolia and Lake Baikal all the way to the Pacific Ocean. Microblade technologies, perhaps first developed in northern China and more southern areas, later came into widespread use over this large area, and in northeastern Siberia as well. These cultures, adapted to both terrestrial hunting and to coastal environments, were closely related to the ill-defined Dyukhtai tradition that flourished over most of northeastern Asia during the closing millennia of the last glaciation.

These, in general terms, were the people who also inhabited central Beringia, and perhaps Alaska as well. They were Asians, not Europeans, but people whose periglacial adaptations, given the nature of their harsh environment, may have shared features in common with late Ice Age cultures far to the west. It would be naive to think of them as mere big-game hunters, however, for their varied toolkit displays considerable regional variation and hints at specialized economic tasks. In later postglacial times, fishing and especially sea mammal hunting were important economic staples on both shores of the Bering Strait, and it may be that maritime subsistence assumed ever greater importance during the late Ice Age, even to the point that Alaska was first settled by sea mammal hunters, as some scholars have argued. It is possible that late Ice Age hunters had mastered the art of navigating cold northern waters in skin boats, with all its attendant risks of hypothermia and ice floes.

If on archaeological grounds, then, the Beringians – the first Americans – are linked decisively with northern Asia, what of the biological evidence: does this tell the same story?

The Ancestry of the Native Americans

How much do we know of the biological ancestry of the native Americans? Ever since the 19th century, scientists have recognized that there are general biological similarities between Siberians and native Americans. Genetic family trees are unanimous in splitting off the native Americans from northeastern Asians, although their chronological estimates for the bifurcation are clouded by the high probability of enhanced rates of genetic change in tiny, isolated arctic populations. In recent years, a team of physical anthropologists from all over the United States has collaborated on a study of the variants (called Gm allotypes) of one particular protein found in the fluid portion of the blood, the serum. All proteins "drift," or produce variants, over the generations, and members of an interbreeding human population will share a set of such variants. Thus by comparing the Gm allotypes of two different populations one can work out their genetic "distance," which itself can be calibrated to give an indication of the length of time since these populations last interbred. The research team sampled thousands of Indians from four cultural groups in western North America, and found their Gm types divided into two groups, with the Aleuts and Eskimos of the far north forming a third one. One group is thought to relate to the first Americans (usually called "Paleo-Indians"). More than 14,000 Central and South American Indians shared the same grouping as well. The geneticists believe their data point to a single, early migration, followed by two later movements that brought interior hunters like the Athabaskans of Alaska and sub-arctic Canada and coast-adapted Eskimo-Aleuts to North America.

Some biological data come from studies of dental morphology among Asian and native American populations, including prehistoric burials. As we saw in Chapter Fourteen, Christy Turner of Arizona State University believes that tooth crowns and roots are more stable than most evolutionary traits. His studies of thousands of prehistoric and recent teeth highlight the basic homogeneity of native American dental morphology compared with that of eastern Asians. As we have seen, sinodonty only occurs in northern Asia and the Americas. Turner is certain that it evolved perhaps as early as 40,000 years ago. Sinodonty tends to add bulk to the tooth crown, an adaptation that Turner believes to be an adjustment to the dentally demanding conditions of periglacial northeastern Asia. The morphological differences are so striking that Turner argues that the New World was settled by sinodonts from northern Asia.

Christy Turner produced what he calls "dentochronological" separation estimates of when native Americans split off from Asian populations. He moves his sinodonts into eastern Mongolia about 20,000 years ago, and dates the first native Americans to about 14,000–13,000 years ago.

Linguist Joseph Greenberg of Stanford University has classified native American languages into three basic linguistic groups: Amerind, Na-Dene, and Aleut-Eskimo. The earliest and largest of these groups was, he believes, the Amerinds, for Amerind languages occur throughout the Americas and show deeper internal divisions than Na-Dene or Aleut-Eskimo, both of which are more homogenous, and therefore much more recent arrivals. Greenberg believes the Amerinds arrived before 11,000 years ago, a conclusion that agrees well with the dental chronology, even if it is challenged by many linguists.

The Process of Colonization

No one doubts that the primeval Americans were simply a tiny scatter of late Ice Age bands, probably no more than a few families. The most plausible model assumes that the late Ice Age population of northeastern Asia was very thin on the ground, widely dispersed, and highly mobile. Given the lack of geographical barriers, the existence of a land bridge of some kind throughout the late last glaciation, and the generally uniform climate throughout the area, we can reasonably assume, too, that central Beringia, and perhaps Alaska, were settled within a few thousand years of the first human settlement of extreme northeastern Asia as a whole. The major barrier to the colonization of the Americas may not have been the Bering Strait, but the great ice sheets that covered the northern latitudes of North America east and south of the unglaciated portions of Alaska.

The earliest known human inhabitants of northeastern Asia were the bearers of the Dyukhtai tradition. Although a date of 35,000 years for them is possible, most American observers are more comfortable with dates in the 18,000-to-12,000-year range. We can envisage, then, a tiny population of Dyukhtai-like people living throughout Beringia, even in Alaska, any time after about 18,000 years ago. Perhaps the first human populations moved into these inhospitable lands after the last glacial maximum of 20,000–18,000 years ago.

There are no securely dated archaeological sites in Alaska earlier than Bluefish Caves in the western Yukon Territory, which date to between 15,000 and 12,000 years ago. The earliest Alaskan sites, including Bluefish, contain highly varied stone toolkits, some of which include microblades, while others do not. Without question, the cultural ties of these exiguous assemblages lie in northeastern Asia.

In the final analysis, the first settlement of the Americas was the culminating development in a slow expansion of anatomically modern humans from Africa into other tropical and temperate latitudes, then into periglacial environments across the north of the Ice Age world. Like their distant relatives elsewhere, these people were ingenious and inventive, as they had to be to survive in their inhospitable surroundings.

Ice-Free Corridors, Coastal Shelves, and Ice Sheets

For much of the last, "Wisconsin" glaciation (the North American equivalent of the Würm), two great ice sheets mantled most of northern North America, from the Atlantic coast along the southern shores of the Great Lakes west to the Pacific. The Laurentide ice sheet was centered on Labrador and the Keewatin area of Canada, while the Cordilleran ice sheet lay in the mountainous west. From about 50,000 to some 25,000 years ago, there was a prolonged glacial retreat, when most of the glaciated areas were ice-free. It would have been possible for human groups – had any existed in North America – to move southward during these millennia. Then, for at least 10,000 years during the height of the late Wisconsin glaciation, icy barriers would again have blocked access to the south, except perhaps for the low-lying Pacific continental shelf and some other low-altitude land routes, and through what was once believed to be an "ice-free corridor," a narrow defile between the Laurentide and Cordilleran ice sheets.

Neither of the main routes would have been easy at the height of the late Wisconsin. The ice-free corridor, if it ever existed, may have extended from the Yukon in the north to the Medicine Hat area of Alberta in the south, a barren, perhaps biologically sterile glacial defile that can never have been attractive for human settlers. The western continental shelf is also narrow, and was by no means the only way between the mountains to the south. Most likely, any movement south took place after the final retreat of the ice sheets began about 15,000 years ago.

Clovis and the Paleo-Indians

The earliest indisputable evidence for human occupation in the Americas dates to between 14,000 and 12,000 years ago. In North America, Bluefish Caves in the Yukon Territory, Meadowcroft, and Fort Rock Cave, Oregon, all date to this time bracket. So do a scatter of sites from Central and South America, among them Valsequillo in Mexico, Taima Taima in Venezuela, perhaps some Brazilian sites, Pikimachay in Peru, and Monte Verde in Chile. All these sites have yielded small scatters of stone artifacts, occasionally a projectile point – precious little documentation of human presence, but undoubtedly human for all that. What is striking is the immediate appearance of isolated traces of human settlement throughout the Americas directly at the end of the last glaciation. None of these locations is without its problems, but they may well represent the predecessors of the numerous Paleo-Indian sites that date to about 11,500 years ago and later. At about that time, the archaeological record mushrooms from virtually nothing into a well-documented scatter of locations not only throughout North America, but in Central America and as far south as southern Chile, where Fell's Cave was occupied before 11,000 years ago. If first settlement south of the ice sheets was around 14,000 years ago, with most early sites clustering between 12,000 and 11,000 years ago, then a tiny population of newcomers expanded rapidly into all corners of the New World, adapting to a great diversity of local environments in the process.

As elsewhere, the archaeological signature of these highly mobile peoples is confined in the main to stone tools, mostly undated scatters of flakes, cores, and blades, with occasional distinctive projectile points that sometimes serve to distinguish the earliest Paleo-Indians from the later hunter-gatherer cultures that evolved from them. We are fortunate that much of the earliest Paleo-Indian occupation is associated with characteristic stone projectile heads, especially the Clovis point.

The Clovis tradition once flourished over much of the Americas, including deep into South America. Clovis is best, and perhaps misleadingly, known from occasional mammoth kills on the North American Plains. These open grasslands expanded at the end of the Wisconsin glaciation, their short grasses providing nutrients for mammoth, bison, and other ruminants. Clovis bands preyed on these and smaller animals. They were always on the move, often camping along rivers and streams and close to waterholes. Here they killed mammoth and other animals, butchering their prey where it fell. Some groups may have wintered in caves and rockshelters in the Rocky Mountain foothills.

Nowhere were Clovis populations large, and nowhere were their encampments of any size. As befitted people constantly on the move, these people used a lightweight toolkit, based on an expert stone technology that created fine, fluted-based points. The hunters mounted these on wooden

North American Paleo-Indians enjoy the rich pickings of a successful caribou hunt.

foreshafts, propelling their spears with atlatls (throwing sticks) for increased power, accuracy, and range – just as Magdalenian hunters did in distant western Europe. The Clovis people butchered animals with large bifaces flaked from fine-grained rock such as chert or chalcedony that they obtained from considerable distances. These same bifaces served as cores for making projectile points and other small artifacts, so that economic use was made of toolmaking stone. So far, it has proved impossible to trace Clovis roots in earlier, or contemporary, Beringian traditions.

Our picture of early Paleo-Indian life is heavily biased toward big-game hunting, largely because the Plains sites are the best known, and they are almost invariably kill or butchery locations. While there can be little doubt that the ultimate ancestry of Clovis people was among terrestrial hunting societies of the late Ice Age in the far north, it would be a mistake to assume that every Clovis society focused on big-game animals. Scatters of Clovis settlements and occasional camp sites occur as far northeast as Nova Scotia, where the people probably hunted caribou, throughout eastern North America, and on the shores of long dried-up western desert lakes. In Central and South America, early Paleo-Indian sites lie in locations where big game must have been scarce and where people would have relied heavily on foraging for plant foods, or perhaps fishing and shellfish collecting. The Monte Verde site in northern Chile with its evidence of forest adaptations is a reminder that early Paleo-Indian society was far from homogeneous, and as opportunistic and flexible as any of the many late Ice Age societies of the Old World that were its remote progenitors.

By 11,000 years ago, Stone Age hunter-gatherers occupied every corner of the Americas. The overall population probably numbered no more than a few tens of thousands, and they had adapted to every form of local environment imaginable. As the Wisconsin glaciers retreated and the post-Ice Age climate warmed up, environmental conditions changed constantly and many species of Ice Age big game vanished. The descendants of the first Americans adapted to these new conditions in highly diverse ways, along trajectories of cultural change that led to the brilliant array of American Indian societies that Europeans encountered in the 15th century AD.

PART FIVE

LEGACY

"The Crumpet smiled indulgently.
'Ingenious,' he said . . . 'Quite ingenious. But a
little far-fetched. No, I prefer to think the
whole thing . . . has something to do with the
Fourth Dimension. I am convinced that this is
the true explanation, if our minds could
only grasp it.'
'Absolutely,' said the Bean.'"

P.G. Wodehouse, *Young Men in Spats*

CHAPTER SIXTEEN

After the Ice Age

It is a remarkable fact that the great period of initial colonization of the globe by modern humans coincided with the long epoch of the last Ice Age – when winters at extreme latitudes were immeasurably harsher than they are today. By 12,000 years ago, *Homo sapiens sapiens* had conquered arid steppe-tundras with 9-month winters in Alaska and Siberia, endured freezingly cold glacial landscapes in Tasmania, and hunted big game on the plains bordering the ice sheets in Eurasia and North America. But then the glaciers began to melt, and a whole way of life developed over thousands of years came under threat. How did people adapt 10,000 years ago to global warming? And why did it take them so long to colonize the last great unpeopled region on earth – the farflung islands of the Pacific Ocean?

The World Warms Up

By scientific convention we live in postglacial times, known as the Holocene, the 12,000 or so years that have followed upon the last glaciation. In fact the glaciers have not gone for good; we are only enjoying a brief warmer interlude before the ice sheets advance again. Some statistical projections place the peak of the next cold snap about 23,000 years into the future, provided the humanly caused greenhouse effect does not cause global meltdown before then. The term Holocene is an arbitrary one, defined with reference to key stages in the retreat of northern ice sheets, a useful convenience for geologists and others focusing on recent climate change.

The warming trend began worldwide about 15,000 years ago. Whereas the onset of the last glaciation had been gradual, over some 20,000 years of increasing cold, the thaw was swifter, lasting no more than between 5,000 and 7,000 years. During these brief millennia, the great ice sheets of northern latitudes retreated dramatically, and world sea levels rose to near-modern heights, isolating the Americas, Japan, the offshore islands of Southeast Asia, and flooding continental shelves everywhere. There were considerable changes in rainfall patterns and vegetation, especially in Europe, North America, and some parts of the tropics. In both the Old and New Worlds,

Homo sapiens sapiens had to adapt to radically new ecological conditions, to high sea levels, to rapidly spreading forest landscapes, and to ever more diverse local environments. It is safe to say that people living on earth after about 12,000 years ago confronted global warming on a scale which we have not even remotely begun to experience in our own times.

The Challenge of the Holocene

During the early Holocene, *Homo sapiens sapiens* once again demonstrated a brilliant ability at adjusting to new challenges, fresh environmental circumstances. One of the most catastrophic effects of global warming was a radical impoverishment of mammalian faunas all over the world around 10,000 years ago. Dozens of familiar Ice Age mammals vanished from Europe, Asia, and the Americas, many of them, like the woolly rhinoceros, mammoth, mastodon, and steppe bison, favored prey for human hunters for tens of thousands of years. Only the African savanna still supported much of its Ice Age faunal diversity. Even there, many large animal species vanished. The larger and more specialized game animals may have vanished fastest, perhaps as a result not only of climatic change, but also of overhunting by human predators. The issue of overhunting and big-game extinctions is much debated, and is still unresolved, although many archaeologists believe that humans played a role in faunal decimation, especially in the Americas, where Paleo-Indian settlement occurred very fast indeed, and where big-game animals vanished rapidly at the end of the Clovis culture in North America, about 11,000 years ago. In Australia, too, human hunters may have accelerated the extinction of larger Ice Age marsupials – but, again, the issue is controversial.

How did people adapt to the loss of so many big-game species? All over the world, similar responses evolved: people everywhere broadened their diet to include a greater range of small animals, more plant foods, and sea mammals and shellfish as well as fish. Interestingly, many of these changes can be traced back into the late Ice Age, when the warming trend began around 15,000 years ago. In southern Africa, for example, Richard Klein of the University of Chicago has documented alterations in diet at the Klasies River Caves and also at Nelson's Bay Cave. In the period after about 15,000 years ago, the inhabitants of Nelson's Bay began to adopt a far more varied diet than their predecessors. As well as larger animals such as eland, and hartebeest, they went after fish, sea mammals, cormorant and other flying birds. When the larger animals began to diminish before 9,000 years ago, the Nelson's Bay hunters switched to medium- and small-sized animals, along with more intensive foraging for plant foods.

Similarly, the successors of the Clovis people in North America diversified their food quest, by concentrating on small prey, even rabbits, by foraging for

A lakeside camp in Britain shortly after the end of the Ice Age, when people everywhere turned increasingly to a wider range of foods, including fish.

plant foods, and by taking birds and fish. The peoples of the Eastern Woodlands, east of the Mississippi, lived in widely scattered bands, hunting deer and subsisting off seeds and nuts. Only on the Great Plains, west of the Mississippi, did a big-game hunting way of life continue to flourish right into historical times, thanks to the survival of the North American bison.

In faraway Europe, as the glaciers retreated and the forests advanced, red and roe deer and other forest ungulates replaced the migratory reindeer that had been so significant in late Ice Age times. Plant foods such as nuts assumed great importance. Coasts, estuaries, and lakes were now highly productive, as they were in North America, especially when taking into account such seasonal resources as salmon, waterbirds, and sea mammals, many of them relying on increased seasonal production of plankton in the now warmer oceans.

The glacial retreat and warming up of the world thus yielded gains as well as losses for human populations. On the debit side were the drowning of coastal plains and the demise of so many large animal species. On the plus side were the increased fertility of the oceans and the greater abundance of smaller animal species and of plant foods. As people adapted successfully to these worldwide changes, human populations grew. At the same time, the increasing complexity of obtaining adequate food supplies from a greater variety of plant and animal resources led to increasing complexity in human social organization. Both phenomena – population increase and greater social complexity – laid the foundations for the single most important human adaptation to the Holocene world: the development of farming.

The Rise of Complex Societies

"Complexity" is somewhat of a buzzword in archaeological circles, for it has long been considered a hallmark of farming societies and early civilizations, which indeed it is. This should not, however, blind us to the fact that social complexity had begun to evolve among many hunter-gatherer societies long before the introduction of agriculture. Complexity implies sedentary or semi-sedentary settlement, sizeable settlements that might almost be called villages, and sometimes dwellings, like the mammoth bone structures at Mezhirich in western Russia, that were used over many generations. Complex hunter-gatherer societies like these stored food and probably even manipulated their environments in ways that altered the availability or abundance of food – for instance by constraining the ranges of wild animals. Some archaeologists believe that the later Cro-Magnons of southwestern France enjoyed a measure of social complexity, with, perhaps, some degree of social differentiation between different individuals.

In Holocene times there were complex hunter-gatherer societies along the Pacific Northwest and California coasts of North America, and along Peru's shoreline. Some southern Australian societies may also have achieved a degree of cultural complexity based on fishing economies. Here, as everywhere else, increased social complexity evolved from simpler cultural mechanisms as an adaptive way of providing leadership, maintaining territorial boundaries, of settling disputes, and of redistributing food and other goods. And such complexity became even more important when humans first became farmers and herders some 10,000 years ago.

Nearly everywhere, early Holocene societies intensified their exploitation of game and plant foods, of fish, shellfish, birds, and marine mammals. As populations rose, they paid more attention to less obvious foods, and to those like shellfish or acorns that require more labor-intensive processing methods than game and other such resources. In some areas, like the Near East, labor-intensive methods included the harvesting of wild cereals such as wheat and rye, and in time these proved to be crops that people could successfully propagate themselves – just as they could successfully domesticate wild goats and sheep, the animals they had been hunting intensively for millennia.

Some 11,000 years ago, the first inhabitants of Abu Hureyra near the Euphrates in Syria exploited seasonal migrations of desert gazelle from the south each spring. They lived on the margins of desert, floodplain, and woodland, so they also hunted across the local wooded steppe where game was abundant and harvested stands of wild rye, einkorn, and barley nearby.

41   The Discoverers   A historic meeting in China in 1931: the Abbé Breuil (*right*), cave art expert extraordinary, joins Pei and Wong, Chinese discoverers of Peking Man, at Zhoukoudian, findspot for the *Homo erectus* fossils.

42–44 The First Americans Despite numerous claims to the contrary, so far the most reliable evidence indicates first human settlement of the Americas after 15,000 years ago. The oldest distinctive Paleo-Indian tradition, characterized by Clovis projectile points (*above*), flourished some 11,500–11,000 years ago, particularly on the Great Plains. Even after many big-game species, including mammoth, died out at the end of the Ice Age, the survival of bison on the plains ensured the continuance of a big-game hunting way of life here into historical times (*above left*, a 10,000-year-old bison kill at the Casper site, Wyoming; *left*, Assiniboin hunting on snow shoes, 1833).

45 After the Ice Age When the world warmed up and sea levels rose at the end of the Ice Age, people everywhere turned increasingly to oceans and rivers for

their food supplies. These hunter-fishers at the site of Lepenski Vir, in modern
Yugoslavia, built their huts on the banks of the Danube some 8,000 years ago.

46–48 Colonizers of the Pacific The settlement of the far-flung islands of Melanesia and Polynesia marks the final chapter in the first peopling of the globe.

Native New Guineans at Kuk Swamp (*opposite page*) helped in the study of some of the world's oldest gardens, dug by their forebears over a period stretching back at least 8,000 years. East of New Guinea, early settlers voyaged from island to island in double-hulled or outrigger canoes (*left*, a small-scale modern version), by AD 500 reaching remote Easter Island, famous for its statues (*above*).

49 Journey's End The colonization of New Zealand 1,000 years ago by the ancestors of these modern Maoris signals the end of humanity's initial peopling of the world.

The population of this pit-house village rose rapidly to between 200 and 300 people. Then, about 10,000 years ago, drought and perhaps deforestation resulting from heavy consumption of firewood caused the hunters to leave. Only a few centuries later, a small farming village of rectangular mudbrick houses occupied the same site. The changeover to cereal cultivation was rapid, since the new economy proved highly effective, but millennia-old hunting and foraging techniques remained in use until the exhaustion of the gazelle population around 8,500 years ago, when these untameable animals were replaced at the site by domesticated sheep and goat.

The same dramatic shift in human subsistence patterns took hold in the Nile Valley at about the same time, in the Indus Valley, Southeast Asia, northern China and Europe by 8,000–6,000 years ago, and in Central America after 7,000 years ago. Agriculture came late to the game-rich savannas of East and southern Africa, only between 3,000 years ago and the time of Christ – and never to arid, isolated Australia. Agriculture was no revolutionary invention, for even the simplest hunter-gatherer society knows full well that seeds germinate when planted. To cultivate the soil, however, requires a loss of mobility, or at minimum a careful scheduling of the annual round to care for, and to harvest, the precious crop. People had probably exercised some degree of control over their food supplies very much earlier. Perhaps Upper Paleolithic peoples who depended heavily on reindeer or mountain goats made some attempt to manage the prey herds. Conceivably, too, some hunter-gatherer groups living on the fringes of tropical rainforests may have engaged in intermittent horticulture, planting yams and other food plants for future use. In a sense, food production was a logical survival strategy for people faced with the age-old need to feed growing populations. And, as such, it is merely another example of the brilliant opportunism that marks, and has always marked, *Homo sapiens sapiens* from the earliest times.

The long-term consequences of agriculture and animal domestication were far more momentous than their mere adoption. There were dramatic increases in population, much-enhanced and sometimes catastrophic manipulation of the natural environment, and ultimately the emergence of cities and civilizations. The rapidly accelerating tempo of cultural evolution since 10,000 years ago can be directly attributed to the new economies. They also led to the final chapter in the peopling of the globe by modern humans: the settlement of the offshore islands of the Pacific.

The Settlement of Melanesia and Polynesia

The vast open waters of the Pacific offered an entirely new environment for humanity, an enormous trackless ocean dotted with countless tropical islands. The Pacific belies its peaceful name, for it can be a stormy and pitiless enemy, especially for those voyaging in small craft. Even short inter-island passages could end in sudden disaster, as hurricane-force squalls overwhelmed open canoes, or wrecked them on hazardous coral reefs. The settlement of the Pacific was as much a challenge for humanity as the first colonization of the steppe-tundra of the north. And it was not until very late in prehistoric times, perhaps starting some 6,000 years ago, that *Homo sapiens sapiens* mastered the arts of deep-water voyaging and navigated canoes hundreds of miles across open water.

Modern humans were capable of at least short passages across open water at least 40,000 years ago, for, as we saw in Chapter Ten, voyages of at least 50 miles (80 km) were needed to cross from Sunda to Sahul. We know, too, that people were living on the Solomon Islands by at least 28,000 years ago. The myriad archipelagos of Sunda and Sahul with their usually predictable weather were an ideal nursery for people adapting to a life dependent on simple watercraft and rudimentary navigational skills. But once the southern end of the Solomons was reached, the sea distances became much larger, with distances of more than 186 miles (300 km) out to the Santa Cruz Islands, which were a much smaller target area even for expert navigators. Perhaps even more significant, the marine technology may have been up to the task, but the longer voyages would also have taken the hunters over a biogeographical boundary at the end of the main Solomons. The islands to the south and east lie within a region with no indigenous terrestrial mammals except bats, and a progressively impoverished flora and fauna. Perhaps such remote oceanic environments were insufficient to support hunter-gatherers, even if they had canoes suitable for voyaging in open water. Even if hunters and gatherers had undertaken such journeys, they would have had to have developed larger offshore canoes, sophisticated deep-water navigational skills, and to have grown the easily storable food to feed them on their voyages and at the other end until newly introduced crops matured.

Short journeys of a couple of days would have been possible without large water storage containers, especially if there were frequent tropical showers. Some early Sahulians could probably manipulate wild root plants and grow them deliberately in sufficient numbers to acquire small surpluses for taking on short offshore passages. Longer voyages would have depended on root crops such as bananas, taro, and yams that could sustain mariners and island settlers for months on end. Chickens, dogs, and pigs were also valued as canoe food. It was not until between 6,000 and 4,000 years ago that expert sailors, voyaging with domesticated crops and animals aboard, crossed what may have been the ultimate navigational barrier for Stone Age hunter-gatherers in the Pacific. They began voyaging out of sight of land for days on end.

Domesticated plants were an essential prerequisite for settling offshore islands. The peoples of New Guinea were clearing forest gardens by at least 8,000 years ago, and perhaps much earlier. It is probably no coincidence that within a few millennia, and certainly by 6,000 years ago, canoes were

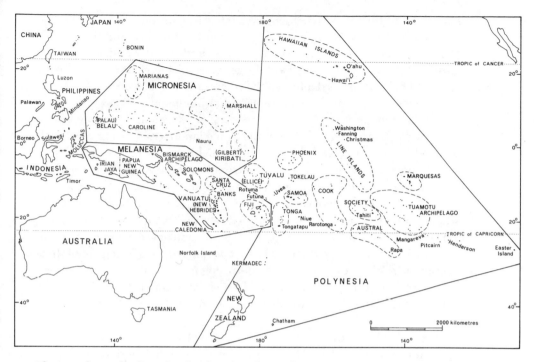

The complex web of Pacific island groups that make up Micronesia, Melanesia, and Polynesia.

venturing much further offshore, trading foodstuffs, shells, and other valued commodities from one island to the next. Such trading systems, like the celebrated *kula* ring of the Trobriand Islands, have existed for many centuries, linking New Guinea and much of Melanesia with lasting social and economic ties. The constant maritime activity, and good access to easily worked woods and fibers for canoe building, probably stimulated innovations in watercraft design, refined in sheltered coral lagoons, then tested in offshore fisheries and on short inter-island passages. In time, the trade networks of the southwestern Pacific became highly organized, maintained with efficient twin-hulled canoes over distances up to nearly 400 miles (643 km).

For years, scholars speculated about the motives that sent prehistoric sailors offshore in search of new islands over the horizon. Were Melanesia and Polynesia colonized as a result of accidental voyages when canoes were blown offshore? Or did skilled mariners set off on deliberate voyages of discovery and colonization, driven, perhaps, by political or social turmoil in their homelands, or by overpopulation and the need for new land? Until the 1960s, almost nothing was known of the indigenous navigational skills of the Pacific islanders. Then amateur anthropologist and yachtsman David Lewis and others learned how to navigate using traditional methods. They apprenticed themselves to the few surviving master navigators in the islands, used star paths and zeniths in the tropical sky, gauged the distance and direction of landfalls by observing swells, wind waves, and clouds, and learned the centuries-old navigational lore that one generation of navigators passed on to the next. There can be no doubt that the colonization of the Pacific Islands was a deliberate process in the hands of expert seamen and navigators.

Many of the voyages were of relatively short duration, for many islands present a far larger target than just their own landmasses. Great coral reefs surround their shores, and those of their neighbors, giving the navigator a broader mark to aim for. All the way out from New Guinea to Polynesia, there were few open-water passages longer than 300 miles (482 km). The process of island hopping continued for thousands of years, probably as a result of entirely natural human motives such as a desire to expand trading contacts, to find new farming land, or to relieve over-population or escape social tensions at home. At times, too, we can be sure that people went exploring out of sheer curiosity or restlessness, just as a modern Polynesian will sail a canoe for a week against the trade winds to a neighboring island simply to buy a packet of cigarettes. It is the experience that counts rather than the purpose of the voyage.

Archaeological sites on even remote islands tell a remarkable tale of exploration and voyaging. The characteristic "Lapita" pottery associated with the earlier voyages appears in island Melanesia at least 6,000 years ago and in New Caledonia by 4,000 years ago. From Melanesia, canoes voyaged to Polynesia, taking the plants and domesticated animals of their home islands with them. The Marquesas, the Society Islands, and Tahiti were all probably settled sometime before AD 500. Then *Homo sapiens sapiens* undertook the ultimate challenge – long-distance voyages over the empty horizon in search of more, invisible islands beyond the confines of the known Polynesian world. It is as if humanity was at a threshold of confidence in itself, a confidence that allowed explorers to set off knowing that they could return if they wished, because they had sufficient mastery of their environment to do so. The first canoes arrived on Easter Island by AD 500 and in Hawaii by AD 600. Finally, sometime between AD 1000 and 1200, some Polynesians sailed southward into more temperate waters and colonized New Zealand. A slow, but inexorable, process of global prehistoric settlement, begun more than 100,000 years earlier, finally ended.

CHAPTER SEVENTEEN

The Journey from Eden

Are we indeed descended from an ancestral African population, whose successors ultimately peopled the world? If the geneticists are to be believed, the reconstruction of our family tree, not only its roots, but its branches and the chronology of their sprouting, may be within our grasp. Stephen Jay Gould, always an eloquent advocate of evolution, calls this emerging genealogy the "basic datum of history." Using genetics, paleoanthropology, archaeology, and many other academic disciplines, we can weave at least a tentative outline of our ancestry, perhaps, even, the vestiges of a family tree.

Again and again in these pages, we have touched on the two competing hypotheses of our origins, hypotheses that agree on little except a general statement that the first human tool-users originally evolved in Africa. The real argument revolves around when and where *Homo sapiens sapiens* emerged. Was it relatively recently, in one place – Africa – or all over the world, after *Homo erectus* had radiated out of Africa hundreds of thousands of years earlier? Did modern Africans originate in Africa, modern Europeans in Europe, and so on? The debate cannot be decided on the basis of fossils alone, any more than it can by genetic analyses either. At present, all we can do is to evaluate evidence from many scientific disciplines, and try to create from it a tentative scenario for our ancestry.

The first toolmaking hominids evolved in sub-Saharan Africa around 2.5 million years ago. For about a million years, human biological and cultural evolution was infinitesimally slow. Then, about 1.6 million years ago, early *Homo* became *Homo erectus*, a still primitive but much more advanced human. It was *Homo erectus* who tamed fire, who developed slightly more sophisticated hunting and gathering cultures. But *Homo erectus* may not have been capable of anything but the most rudimentary speech. Between about 1 million and 700,000 years ago *Homo erectus* radiated out of Africa not only into the Near East, Europe, and parts of northern Asia, but also into tropical southern and southeastern Asia. In the Asian forests, bamboo and other woods were used to fashion sharp-pointed spears and hunting weapons. The human world was a tiny place by the standards of later prehistory, inhabited perhaps by a few tens of thousands of people. Entire continents – the

Americas and Australia – were still uninhabited. No one had the technology or intellectual capacity to live in extremely cold environments. In the archaic world of 200,000 years ago, much of Eurasia and northern Europe was offlimits for human settlement.

Despite the seemingly homogeneous nature of *Homo erectus* populations in Europe and Asia, there are signs of gradual biological evolution in many parts of the world toward an archaic form of *Homo sapiens*. In Eurasia, *Homo erectus* evolved into the Neanderthals, who, if Philip Lieberman is correct, were incapable of fully articulate speech. African *Homo erectus* fossils display greater anatomical variation than their relatives elsewhere, and it is here, south of the Sahara', that the earliest anatomically modern humans appear in the archaeological record.

Both genetics and paleoanthropology point increasingly strongly toward sub-Saharan Africa as the cradle of *Homo sapiens sapiens*, with but a single and discrete origin for anatomically modern humans, perhaps as early as 200,000 years ago. Mitochondrial DNA tracks primeval, anatomically modern populations back at least to 150,000 years. The Cavalli-Sforza table of genetic distance and separation is still but a crude formulation, but one that separates Africans from all other *Homo sapiens sapiens* populations earlier than any others. Quite apart from the separation date itself, the genetic data support an African origin. So too does the archaeological and fossil record, incomplete as it is, especially the meticulously excavated Klasies River sites in southern Africa.

If anatomically modern humans did evolve in Africa, how and when did they radiate out of Africa? The Sahara and the Nile Valley must have played vital roles in this process, as they did over 700,000 years ago. The desert may have been like a vast pump, highly sensitive to constant climatic change, acting alternately as a barrier and as an open doorway to the Nile Valley and the Mediterranean world.

The Qafzeh thermoluminescence dates place *Homo sapiens sapiens* in the Near East at least 90,000 years ago. It is here in the Near East that Neanderthal populations display the greatest variation, where modern anatomy is well documented relatively early in the Würm glaciation. It is here, too, that Arthur Jelinek, Anthony Marks, and others have traced the profound technological changes that evolved slowly before 50,000 years ago, and that presaged the development of sophisticated, blade-based toolkits during the late Ice Age.

The genetic blueprint chronicles another basic split in modern humanity, between Asians and Europeans, a split that took place at least 40,000 years ago, probably earlier. Therein lie two major unanswered questions: Why did it take *Homo sapiens sapiens* as long as 40,000–50,000 years to move northward into the colder, more challenging environments of Europe? And how did anatomically modern humans spread into southeastern Asia?

We have argued that harsh environmental conditions were an initial deterrent to the colonization of Europe by *Homo sapiens sapiens*. Perhaps it was modern humans' capacity for articulate speech, for much enhanced intellectual conceptualization that enabled them, ultimately, to develop the technological devices, hunting strategies, and deftness at cooperation to move north into more extreme climates after about 45,000 years ago. Indeed, modern humans' vastly superior linguistic abilities may have given them the longterm edge over all other human forms, and the potential for such dramatic innovations as seafaring and artistic self-expression.

Spreading eastward into southern and southeastern Asia involved no drastic adjustments to harsher climates. The Noah's Ark model has *Homo sapiens sapiens* radiating out of Africa through the Levant, and coming in contact with archaic *Homo sapiens* populations in the Near East, Mesopotamia, and India. If this was the case, did the same cultural trends develop in southern Asia as in the Near East more than 50,000 years ago? There are no fossils to document such a transition, but there are scattered archaeological hints of a gradual technological change that began, as it did in the Levant, long before 50,000 years ago. One would like to believe that stratified sites similar to those on Mount Carmel will come to light in India, where both human fossils and rich artifact assemblages will chronicle a complex transition from archaic to fully modern, from Levallois and disc-cores to sophisticated blade technology.

Beyond India lies the so-called Movius Line, forested, tropical lands where bamboo may have replaced stone, where conservative *Homo erectus* populations flourished in relative isolation for hundreds of thousands of years. Virtually no human fossils fill an enormous prehistoric void from perhaps as early as 200,000 years ago up to about 30,000 years ago, when anatomically modern people are known to have lived in what is now Australia. Herein lies one of the great controversies of paleoanthropology. Did *Homo sapiens sapiens* evolve independently in this region, as Milford Wolpoff and others claim – on the basis of archaic features perceived to be in common between Javanese *Homo erectus* and much later anatomically modern skeletons from Australia? Or are these features retained in both forms from a long-distant shared ancestor? If the second hypothesis is correct, did *Homo sapiens sapiens* settle in this area some time after, say, 70,000–60,000 years ago, a few thousand years after modern people appeared in the Near East, as the "Noah's Ark" theory might suggest? There was certainly some anatomical continuity in Southeast Asia, but many experts now favor the replacement theory, even if we still lack the fossils to document it.

Most scholars also believe that anatomically modern people were the first seafarers. They crossed open water and settled the continent of Sahul, now New Guinea and Australia, at least 40,000 years ago, perhaps 10,000 or even 20,000 years earlier. By 28,000 years ago, their descendants were capable of navigating relatively long distances, from New Guinea to the Solomon Islands, and had settled in all corners of Australia and Tasmania. Further offshore lay the outer limits of the late Ice Age world, for *Homo sapiens sapiens* still lacked the seafaring and navigating skills, and the easily stored cultivated foods, to sustain canoe crews at sea, and in the ecologically impoverished islands at the other end.

Some 50,000 years ago, anatomically modern people were still largely confined to temperate and tropical regions of the Old World, in the Near East, in southern Asia, and in the vast tracts of archaeologically unknown landscape that stretch south and east from Turkey and the Caspian Sea. To the north lay much colder landscapes – the rolling plains and broken topography of central and western Europe, and the open emptiness of the periglacial tundra that stretched from the Ukraine to the Urals and far beyond. *Homo sapiens sapiens* appears to have moved into these regions after 50,000 years ago, perhaps during a brief warmer interlude in the Würm glaciation. We can trace the spread of new Upper Paleolithic technologies, and of the Cro-Magnons from southeastern Europe into the far west, where Aurignacian peoples were well established by 30,000 years ago. By this time, the indigenous Neanderthals were extinct, perhaps assimilated or replaced by the new population. Anatomically modern people had settled in the Dnepr and Don river valleys of the Ukraine by 35,000 years ago, well before the last intense climax of the Würm glaciation some 20,000 to 18,000 years ago. Then began the efflorescence of late Ice Age hunting cultures in the north and west. These societies are famous for their magnificent artistic traditions, for their elaborate and sophisticated arctic adaptations based on the hunting of mammoth, bison, horse, and reindeer, and for the commemoration of Ice Age beasts in antler, bone, and on cave walls for thousands of years. These were cultures based on new technological artifices and intellectual frontiers, on the needle, tailored clothing, and all manner of specialized tools, and also a deep, abiding symbolism commemorated with mysterious rituals.

These populations were never large, with the greatest densities in sheltered areas with relatively predictable food resources, in such regions as northern Spain, the Périgord, and central European and Ukrainian river valleys. But the vastly enhanced intellectual and technological capacities of *Homo sapiens sapiens* enabled our remote ancestors to survive permanently in areas of extreme cold, and to settle the open plains that stretched from western Europe to Siberia, and beyond.

We do not know when modern humans first settled in the varied landscapes of Kazakhstan and the Altai, or how they replaced the Neanderthal populations of these regions. What Soviet archaeologists call "Upper Paleolithic blade technology" appeared in the rolling steppe-tundra landscape north and west of Lake Baikal in central Siberia by 35,000 years ago. According to dental expert Christy Turner, the few *Homo sapiens*

sapiens skeletons from the Lake Baikal region display sundadonty, whereas those from eastern Siberia and northeastern Asia are sinodont, with biological roots in northern China and further south. It may be that the biological and cultural frontier between the big-game hunting societies of the Russian plains and those of northeastern Asia lies somewhere west of Lake Baikal. Again, we must patiently await more excavations, and more human fossils.

The human fossils from Zhoukoudian in China have made it fashionable to espouse theories of evolutionary continuity, to argue for an independent origin of modern humans in eastern Asia. Dali and other archaic *Homo sapiens* fossils are, however, simply too incomplete to support this hypothesis. There are some finds that display more modern anatomical features than those of earlier *Homo erectus* populations, including the fossil fragments from Salawasu in Mongolia, said to be more than 37,000 years old. Salawasu and other such sites lie in open, arid country, in unforested environments where widely moving populations were unlikely to be as isolated as those dwelling in dense tropical forest or even temperate woodland. The chances of regular gene flow, of regular, small-scale population movements are higher here than in southeastern Asia, just as they would have been in the more open country of southern Asia. There are no theoretical grounds why one cannot argue for population replacement in this large northern area as early as, or only slightly later than, that in India, or even the Near East. Judging from Christy Turner's dental researches, the path of biological evolution in Asia involved diverse populations and the perpetuation of some ancient anatomical traits right into modern times. But, again, without more fossils and sites to work with, one is arguing in an archaeological and paleoanthropological vacuum.

By 25,000 years ago, *Homo sapiens sapiens* flourished throughout northern Asia, with scattered populations living not only in Mongolia and northern China, but over a broad belt of periglacial territory from Lake Baikal in the west to the Amur River and the Pacific in the east. By 20,000 years ago, and perhaps earlier, many of these bands were using stone technologies based on the production of small microblades, ideal for use as insets in hunting weapons. This technology may have developed in northern China, and spread subsequently to Japan, deep into Mongolia, and into northeastern Asia.

There is uncertainty about when human beings first settled the inhospitable landscape of northeastern Siberia, the lands closest to the Americas. Some Soviet archaeologists believe that *Homo sapiens sapiens* had colonized northeast Asian river valleys and coasts as early as 35,000 years ago, but it is not until about 18,000 years ago that the somewhat vaguely defined Dyukhtai tradition is on firmer chronological ground. It was somewhere in this enormous area of archaeologically little-explored country that the first settlers of the Americas may have originated.

Genetically and dentally, the first Americans were northeast Asians, perhaps with an ultimate ancestry in northern China. They were big-game

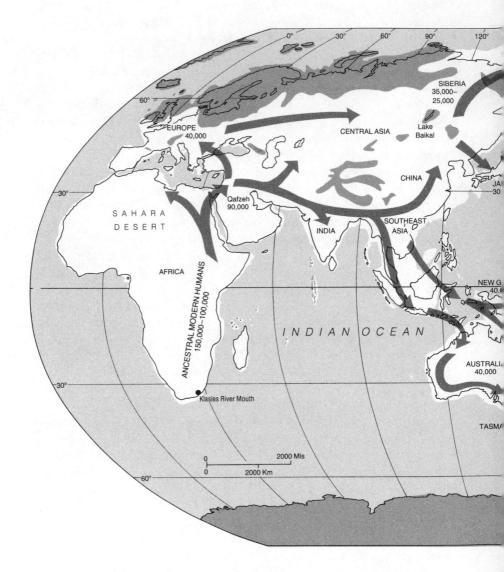

The long journey from Eden. Very approximate dates of first settlement by anatomically modern humans are indicated (in years before the present) for those regions where there is sufficient evidence.

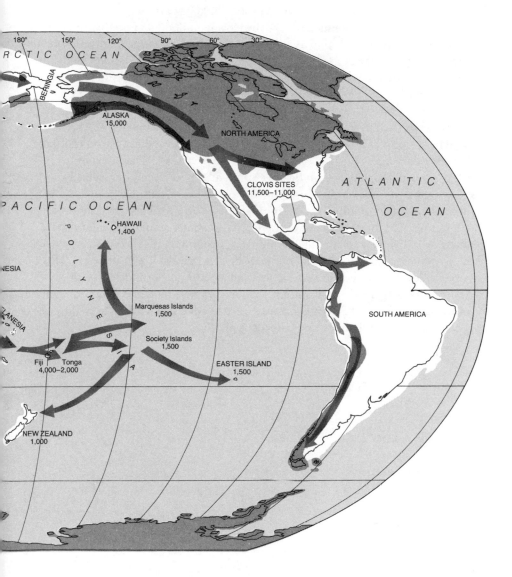

hunters, just like Stone Age groups right across the northern Old World. Perhaps some of them hunted sea mammals and fished as well, exploiting late Ice Age coasts, now deep below modern seas. They could have crossed central Beringia, the Bering land bridge, before 25,000 years ago, but it seems unlikely that they did so much before the closing millennia of the Ice Age, for both genetic data and the available archaeological clues point to first settlement no earlier than about 15,000 years ago. Despite constant claims to the contrary, there are no unimpeachable archaeological sites dating to much earlier than 13,000–12,000 years ago between Alaska and Tierra del Fuego.

With the first settlement of the Americas, the great radiation of *Homo sapiens sapiens*, the wise person, was nearly complete. This was the second great radiation of humanity, one that followed a primeval diaspora more than 700,000 years ago. But this one, what we have called "The Journey from Eden," was perhaps the catalytic development of early human history. From it stemmed not only the brilliant biological and cultural diversity of humankind, but agriculture and animal domestication, village life and urban civilization, and the settlement of the Pacific offshore islands – the very roots of our own diverse and complex world. It is astounding just how recently we have evolved, and how shallow our genetic roots go back into the past. This very shallowness serves to remind us that we are all "products of a recent African twig." And such reminders of our common biological and cultural heritage, of our recent common ancestry, are needed in a world where racism is commonplace and altruism in short supply.

Acknowledgments

Writing *The Journey from Eden* has been a memorable and extraordinary intellectual experience, both on account of the scholars I have met, and on account of the archaeological and anthropological trail our forebears left behind them. Who can forget the first time one handles an original Neanderthal skull, views a Magdalenian wall engraving by flickering candlelight, or gazes on an arctic landscape where our remote ancestors once hunted? My greatest debt is to colleagues and friends in every part of the world, who have introduced me to sites, taken me on excavations, and discussed academic issues large and small with me at all hours of the day and night, everywhere from above the Arctic Circle, to a British Airways jet far above the African Rift, or seated in a small bistro in southwestern France. I hope that this synthesis of their collective work represents at least a reasonable consensus on a complex issue. Their tolerance of my inquisitive questions is much appreciated.

I am very grateful to Professor Richard Scott of the University of Alaska at Fairbanks, who critiqued the manuscript meticulously, and set me straight on many points of biological anthropology. He made the revising of the book an intellectual adventure. I am also indebted to many colleagues and friends, too numerous to mention, who reviewed portions of the text during its three years of complex gestation.

Victoria Pryor suggested this book, and encouraged me along what at times was a difficult and harrowing path. Her friendship and support are much valued. As always, Thames and Hudson's editorial department has been immensely helpful. Lastly, my deepest appreciation to Shelly Lowenkopf, writer of vast experience and good friend. He was always ready with an encouraging word, with sound advice when the project bogged down in writer's block. The least I can do is dedicate *The Journey from Eden* to him, to remind him of the innumerable cups of coffee we have shared together at Xanadu Coffee Shop in Santa Barbara.

Financial support for this project came from the Academic Senate Research Fund, University of California, Santa Barbara, also from the Catticus and Lindbriar Corporations.

List of Illustrations

Plates

bone house. Giovanni Caselli.

41 Breuil, Pei and Wong at Zhoukoudian, 1931. Musée de l'Homme, Paris.

42 Casper site. Photo George Frison.

43 Peter Rindisbacher, Assiniboin hunting on snowshoes (detail), 1833. Amon Carter Museum, Fort Worth, Texas.

44 Clovis points from Naco site, Arizona. Arizona State Museum, University of Arizona. Photo E.B. Sayles.

45 Reconstruction painting of Lepenski Vir. Giovanni Caselli.

46 Two New Guineans, Ul and Korowa, display paddle-shaped spades of wood recovered from a drainage trench at Kuk Swamp.

Photo P.J. Hughes, courtesy of Professor Jack Golson.

47 Re-erected statues of Ahu Akivi, Easter Island. Photo P. Bellwood.

48 Outrigger canoe. Photo Garuda Indonesia.

49 Wakatoa (war canoe) paddlers with traditional painted masks. New Zealand Tourist and Publicity Office.

Further Reading

The Journey from Eden is far from a library work, for it is based on years of site visits, museum laboratory sessions, and conversations with colleagues, to say nothing of fieldwork experiences in many corners of the world. The references cited here are but a fraction of what came together as part of the research. This guide to further reading is presented chapter by chapter, with an annotated list of major sources followed by further, more technical references. The reference lists are cumulative, make no claim to be comprehensive, and a reference given in one chapter is not repeated for another. It can be assumed, however, that the more major papers quoted here contain comprehensive bibliographies, and the reader should consult these for more detailed reading. For brevity's sake, I have grouped some of the chapters together, as key references often overlap between them.

Chapter 1 **A Question of Questions**
Chapter 2 **Of Candelabras and Noah's Arks**
Chapter 3 **The Genetic Detectives**

There are, to my knowledge, no works for a more general audience that treat the wide subject matter

of this book, with the possible exception of John Pfeiffer's *The Emergence of Man* (Harper and Row, New York, 1983). At a more technical level, early prehistory is well summarized by the essays in Eric Delson (ed.) *Ancestors: The Hard Evidence* (Alan R. Liss, New York, 1985). Roger Lewin's short college textbook *Human Evolution* (Blackwell Scientific Publications, Oxford, and Cambridge, Mass., 2nd ed. 1989) is an admirably clear discourse on the basic issues of paleoanthropology, especially when combined with his eloquent *Bones of Contention* (Simon and Schuster, New York, 1987, Penguin Books, Harmondsworth, 1989) which deals with the controversies and personalities. Robert Foley's edited *Human Evolution and Community Ecology* (Academic Press, London, 1984) is fundamental reading for this, and any other, book on early prehistory.

Fred H. Smith and Frank Spencer's massive edited tome, *The Origins of Modern Humans* (Alan R. Liss, New York, 1984) is an essential starting point for anyone entering the academic minefields of modern human ancestry. I cite individual papers from this book in later chapters below. Paul Mellars and Christopher Stringer (eds.) 2-volume *The Human Revolution* (Edinburgh University Press, Edinburgh, 1989 and 1990) is another massive series of essays

on the origins of modern humans. Only Volume 1 was available at press time.

Other References

Cann, Rebecca, and others. "Mitochondrial DNA and human evolution," *Nature*, vol. 325 (1987), 31–36.

Cavalli-Sforza, L.L. and others. "Reconstruction of human evolution: bringing together genetic, archaeological, and linguistic data," *Proceedings of the National Academy of Sciences*, vol. 85 (1988), 6002–6008.

Gould, S.J. "Grimm's Greatest Tale," *Natural History*, vol. 2 (1989), 20–28.

Nei, Masatoshi, and Roychoudhury, A.K. "Genetic Relationship and Evolution of Human Races," *Evolutionary Biology*, vol. 14 (1982), 1–59.

Rightmire, G.P. "The Tempo of Change in the Evolution of Mid-Pleistocene *Homo*," in Eric Delson (ed.) *Ancestors: The Hard Evidence*, Alan R. Liss, New York, 1985, pp. 255–264.

Rouhani, Shahin. "Molecular Genetics and the Pattern of Human Evolution," in Paul Mellars and Christopher Stringer (eds.) *The Human Revolution*, Edinburgh University Press, Edinburgh, 1989, pp. 47–61.

Stoneking, Mark, and Cann, Rebecca. "African Origin of Human Mitochondrial DNA," *in* Paul Mellars and Christopher Stringer (eds.) *The Human Revolution*, Edinburgh University Press, Edinburgh, 1989, pp. 17–30.

Stringer, C.B. "Middle Pleistocene Hominid Variability and the Origin of Late Pleistocene Humans," *in* Eric Delson (ed.) *Ancestors: The Hard Evidence*, Alan R. Liss, New York, 1985, pp. 289–295.

——and Andrews, P. "The origin of modern humans," *Science*, vol. 239 (1988), 1263–1268.

Wolpoff, Milford. "Stasis in the interpretation of evolution in *Homo erectus*," *Paleobiology*, vol. 12 (1986), 325–328.

——"Multiregional Evolution: The Fossil Alternative to Eden," *in* Paul Mellars and Christopher Stringer (eds.) *The Human Revolution*, Edinburgh University Press, Edinburgh, 1989, pp. 62–108.

——and others. "Modern *Homo sapiens* Origins: A General Theory of Hominid Evolution Involving the Fossil Evidence from East Asia," *in* F. Smith and F. Spencer (eds.) *The Origins of Modern Humans*, Alan R. Liss, New York, 1984, pp. 411–486.

——and others. "Reply to Stringer and Andrews," *Science*, vol. 241 (1988), 772–773.

Chapter 4 **The Savanna Homeland**
Chapter 5 **African Ancestors**
Chapter 6 **The Saharan Pump**

The literature is diffuse. Fundamental is Günter Bräuer, "A Craniological Approach to the Origin of Anatomically Modern *Homo sapiens* in Africa and Implications for the Appearance of Modern Europeans," *in* F. Smith and F. Spencer (eds.) *The Origins of Modern Humans* (Alan R. Liss, New York, 1984), pp. 327–410. Also seminal is the same

author's "The Evolution of Modern Humans: Recent Evidence from Southwest Asia," *in* Paul Mellars and Christopher Stringer (eds.) *The Human Revolution* (Edinburgh University Press, Edinburgh, 1989), pp. 123–154. Ronald Singer and John Wymer, *The Middle Stone Age at Klasies River Mouth in South Africa* (University of Chicago Press, Chicago, 1982) is an important monograph, especially useful if amplified by some of the references listed below. The Sahara is well covered by the essays in M.A.J. Williams and H. Faure (eds.) *The Sahara and the Nile* (Balkema, Rotterdam, 1980). J. Desmond Clark's "The Middle Stone Age of East Africa and the Beginnings of Regional Identity," *Journal of World Prehistory*, vol. 2 (1988), 235–306, is a detailed summary that gives the archaeological context. So do the essays in Richard Klein (ed.) *Southern African Prehistory and Paleoenvironments* (Balkema, Rotterdam, 1984).

Other References

Beaumont, Peter, and others. "Modern man in sub-Saharan Africa prior to 49,000 years BP: a review and evaluation with particular reference to Border Cave," *South African Journal of Science*, vol. 74 (1978), 409–419.

Butzer, K.W. and others. "Lithostratigraphy of Border Cave, Kwazulu, South Africa," *Journal of Archaeological Science*, vol. 5 (1978), 317–341.

Clark, J.D. *The Prehistory of Africa*. Thames and Hudson, London, 1970.

——"The Origins and Spread of Modern Humans: a Broad Perspective on the African Evidence," *in* Paul Mellars and Christopher Stringer (eds.) *The Human Revolution*, Edinburgh University Press, Edinburgh, 1989, pp. 565–588.

Deacon, Hilary. "Late Pleistocene Palaeoecology and Archaeology in the Southern Cape, South Africa," *in* Paul Mellars and

Christopher Stringer (eds.) *The Human Revolution*, Edinburgh University Press, Edinburgh, 1989, pp. 547–564.

——and Geleijinse, V.B. "The stratigraphy and sedimentology of the main site sequence, Klasies River, South Africa," *South African Archaeological Bulletin*, vol. 43 (1988), 5–14.

Foley, Robert. "The Ecological Conditions of Speciation: a Comparative Approach to the Origins of Anatomically-Modern Humans," *in* Paul Mellars and Christopher Stringer (eds.) *The Human Revolution*, Edinburgh University Press, Edinburgh, 1989, pp. 298–319.

Klein, Richard. "Environment and subsistence of prehistoric man in the southern Cape Province, South Africa," *World Archaeology*, vol. 5 (1974), 249–284.

——"Middle Stone Age man-animal relationships in southern Africa: evidence from Die Kelders and Klasies River Mouth," *Science*, vol. 190 (1975), 265–267.

——"Stone Age exploitation of animals in southern Africa," *American Scientist*, vol. 67 (1981), 151–160.

——"Biological and Behavioural Perspectives on Modern Human Origins in Southern Africa," *in* Paul Mellars and Christopher Stringer (eds.) *The Human Revolution*, Edinburgh University Press, Edinburgh, 1989, pp. 529–546.

Rightmire, G.P. "Later Pleistocene hominids of eastern and southern Africa," *Anthropologie* (Brno) vol. 19 (1981), 15–26.

——"Middle Stone Age Humans from Eastern and Southern Africa," *in* Paul Mellars and Christopher Stringer (eds.) *The Human Revolution*, Edinburgh University Press, Edinburgh, 1989, pp. 109–122.

Stringer, C.B. "Population relationships of later Pleistocene hominids: a multivariate study of available crania," *Journal of Archaeological Science*, vol. 1 (1974), 317–342.

Thackeray, Anne I. and Kelly, Alison J. "A technological and typological analysis of Middle Stone Age assemblages antecedent to the Howiesons Poort at Klasies River main site," *South African Archaeological Bulletin*, vol. 43 (1988), 15–26.

Wendorf, Fred, Close, A. and Schild, R. "Recent work on the Middle Palaeolithic of the eastern Sahara," *African Archaeological Review*, vol. 5 (1987), 49–64.

Wendorf, Fred, and Schild, Romauld (eds.) *Prehistory of the Eastern Sahara*, Academic Press, New York, 1980.

Chapter 7 **The European Neanderthals**

The Neanderthals have generated more scientific literature than almost any fossil form. A series of useful essays that deal with both the origins and the ultimate fate of these people appear in Eric Delson (ed.), *Ancestors: the Hard Evidence* (Alas R. Liss, New York, 1985). Erik Trinkaus (ed.) *The Mousterian Legacy* (British Archaeological reports, International Series, Oxford, 1983) contains survey articles, while Clive Gamble, *The Palaeolithic Settlement of Europe* (Cambridge University Press, Cambridge and New York, 1986) is a seminal work. Erik Trinkaus, *The Shanidar Neanderthals* (Academic Press, New York, 1983) is an important monograph, and the article by the same author and W.W. Howells "The Neanderthals," *Scientific American*, vol. 241 December (1979), 118–133 is a useful introductory summary. François Bordes' elementary textbook *The Old Stone Age* (McGraw Hill, New York, Weidenfeld, London, 1968) covers the cultural basics for beginners.

Other References

Binford, L.R. "Interassemblage variability – The Mousterian and the Functional Argument," *in* Colin Renfrew (ed.) *The Explanation of Culture Change*, Duckworth, London , 1973, pp. 227–254.

Bordes, F. *Typologie du Paléolithique Ancien et Moyen.* Publications de l'Institut de Préhistoire de l'Université de Bordeaux, Mémoire 1, 1961.

——"Mousterian Cultures in France," *Science*, vol. 134 (1961), 803–810.

——*A Tale of Two Caves.* Harper and Row, New York, 1972.

——and de Sonnerville-Bordes, M."The significance of Variability in Paleolithic Assemblages," *World Archaeology*, vol. 2 (1970), 61–73.

Dibble, H.L. "Reduction Sequences in the Manufacture of Mousterian Implements of France," *in* Olga Soffer (ed.) *The Pleistocene Old World*, Plenum Press, New York, 1987, pp. 33–46.

Gabori, M. *Les civilizations du Paléolithique moyen entre les Alpes et l'Oural.* Academy Press, Budapest, 1976.

Jelinek, A.J. "Form, Function, and Style in Lithic Analysis," *in* C.B. Cleland (ed.) *Cultural Change and Continuity*, Academic Press, New York, 1976, pp. 19–33.

Lieberman, Philip. "The Origins of Some Aspects of Human Language and Cognition," *in* Paul Mellars and Christopher Stringer (eds.) *The Human Revolution*, Edinburgh University Press, Edinburgh, 1989, pp. 391–414.

Mellars, P.A. "The Chronology of Mousterian Industries in the Périgord Region," *Proceedings of the Prehistoric Society*, vol. 35 (1969), 134–171.

Otto M. (ed.) *L'Homme de Neanderthal*, University of Liège, Liège, 1989.

Smith, F. "The Neanderthals and their Evolutionary Significance:

A Brief Historical Survey," *in* F. Smith and F. Spencer (eds.) *The Origins of Modern Humans*, Alan R. Liss, New York, 1984, pp. 1–50.

Chapter 8 **Qafzeh and Skhūl**

The starting point for the Near East must be D.A.E. Garrod and D. Bate, *The Stone Age of Mount Carmel* (Clarendon Press, Oxford, 1937), and Garrod's arguments for the origins of the Upper Paleolithic are well laid out in her "The relations between south-west Asia and Europe in the later palaeolithic age," *Journal of World History*, vol. 1 (1953), 13–38. O. Bar-Yosef, "The Prehistory of the Levant," *Annual Review of Anthropology*, vol. 9 (1980), 101–133, is an overall view. Anthony Marks' "The Middle to Upper Palaeolithic Transition in the Levant," *Advances in World Archaeology*, vol. 2 (1983), 51–98, is a fundamental statement of the complexities of arguing from stone technologies, and should be compared to Arthur Jelinek's "The Middle Palaeolithic of the Levant: Synthesis," *in* J. Cauvin and P. Sanlaville, *Préhistoire du Levant* (CNRS, Paris, 1981). The fossil evidence is well summarized in Erik Trinkaus' "Western Asia," in the Smith and Spencer volume, pp. 251–294.

Other References

Azoury, J. and Hodson, F.R. "Ksar Akil: A Case Study," *World Archaeology*, vol. 4 (1973), 292–306.

Bar-Yosef, O. "Geochronology of the Levantine Middle Palaeolithic," *in* Paul Mellars and Christopher Stringer (eds.) *The Human Revolution*, Edinburgh University Press, Edinburgh, 1989, pp. 589–610.

Clark, G.A. and Lindly, J.M. "The Case of Continuity: Observations on the Biocultural Transition in Europe and Western Asia," *in* Paul Mellars and Christopher Stringer (eds.) *The Human Revolution*, Edinburgh University Press, Edinburgh, 1989, pp. 626–676.

Copeland, L. "The Middle and Upper Palaeolithic of Lebanon and Syria in the light of recent research," *in* Fred Wendorf and A.E. Marks (eds.) *Problems in Prehistory: North Africa and the Levant*, Southern Methodist University Press, Dallas, 1975, pp. 317–350.

Garrod, D.A.E. "A transitional industry at the base of the Upper Palaeolithic in Palestine and Syria," *Journal of the Royal Anthropological Institute*, vol. 81, 121-129.

McBurney, C.B.M. *The Haua Fteah (Cyrenaica) and the Stone Age of the southeast Mediterranean*. Cambridge University Press, Cambridge, 1967.

Ronen, A. and Vandermeersch, B. "The Upper Palaeolithic sequence in the Cave of Qafza (Israel)," *Quaternaria*, vol. 16 (1972), 189–202.

Shea, John J. "A Functional Study of the Lithic Industries Associated with Hominid Fossils in the Kebara and Qafzeh Caves, Israel," *in* Paul Mellars and Christopher Stringer (eds.) *The Human Revolution*, Edinburgh University Press, Edinburgh, 1989, pp. 611–625.

Stringer, C.B. "Human Evolution and Biological Adaptation in the Pleistocene," *in* Robert Foley (ed.) *Human Evolution and Community Ecology*, Academic Press, London, 1984, pp. 55–84.

Trinkaus, Eric, and Smith, Fred H. "The Fate of the Neanderthals," *in* Delson (ed.) *Ancestors: The Hard Evidence*, Alan R. Liss, New York, 1985, pp. 325–333.

Vandermeersch, Bernard. "The Origin of the Neanderthals," *in* Eric Delson (ed.) *Ancestors: The Hard Evidence*, Alan R. Liss, New York, 1985, pp. 306–309.

Vandermeersch, Bernard, "The Evolution of Modern Humans:

Recent Evidence from Southwest Asia," *in* Paul Mellars and Christopher Stringer (eds.) *The Human Revolution*, Edinburgh University Press, Edinburgh, 1989, pp. 155–164.

Chapter 9 **The Primeval Asians**
Chapter 10 **The First Seafarers**

The basic, pioneer work that defines the chopper-chopping tool complex is Hallam Movius, *Early Man and Pleistocene Stratigraphy in South and East Asia* (Peabody Museum, Harvard University, 1944). Peter Bellwood, *The Prehistory of the Indo-Malaysian Archipelago* (Academic Press, Sydney, Australia, 1985) brings the record up to date, as does his article "The Prehistory of Island Southeast Asia: A Multidisciplinary Review of Recent Research," *Journal of World Prehistory*, vol. 1 (2) (1987), 171–224. Kwang-Chih Chang, *The Archaeology of Ancient China* (Yale University Press, New Haven, 4th ed. 1986) has long been the definitive work in English on this subject. J. Peter White and James O'Connell, *A Prehistory of Australia, New Guinea, and Sahul* (Academic Press, Sydney, 1982) is a provocative and sophisticated view of Sahulian prehistory.

Other References

Allen J. and others (eds.) *Sunda and Sahul*. Academic Press, London, 1977.

Bayard, D. (ed.) *Southeast Asian Archaeology*. Proceedings of the XV Pacific Science Congress. University of Dunedin, Otago, New Zealand, 1984.

Bowdler, Sandra. "The Coastal Colonization of Australia," *in* J. Allen and others (eds.) *Sunda and Sahul*, Academic Press, London, 1977, pp. 248–258.

Bowler, J.M. and others. "Pleistocene Human Remains

from Australia: A Living Site and Human Cremation from Lake Mungo, Western New South Wales," *World Archaeology*, vol. 1 (1970), 39–60.

Brooks, S.T. and others. "Radiocarbon dating and palaeoserology of a selected burial series from Niah Caves, Sarawak," *Asian Perspectives*, vol. 20 (1977), 21–31.

Fox, R.B. *The Tabon Caves*. National Museum, Manila, Phillipines, 1970.

Glover, I.C. "The Late Stone Age in eastern Indonesia," *World Archaeology*, vol. 9 (1977), 42–61.

Groves, Colin P. "A Regional Approach to the Problem of Modern Humans in Australasia," *in* Paul Mellars and Christopher Stringer (eds.) *The Human Revolution*, Edinburgh University Press, Edinburgh, 1989, pp. 274–285.

Hapgood, Phillip J. "The Origin of Anatomically Modern Humans in Australasia," *in* Paul Mellars and Christopher Stringer (eds.) *The Human Revolution*, Edinburgh University Press, Edinburgh, 1989, pp. 245–273.

Harrisson, B. "A Classification of Stone Age burials from Niah Great Cave," *Sarawak Museum Journal*, vol. 15, 126-200.

Ha Van Tan. "The Hoabinhian in the context of Vietnam," *Vietnam Studies*, vol. 46 (1978), 127–197.

Howells, W.W. "Physical variation and history in Melanesia and Australia," *American Journal of Physical Anthropology*, vol. 45 (1976), 641–650.

Hutterer, Karl. "An evolutionary approach to the Southeast Asian cultural sequence," *Current Anthropology*, vol. 17 (1976), 221–242.

——"Reinterpreting the Southeast Asian Palaeolithic," *in* J. Allen and others (eds.) *Sunda and Sahul*, Academic Press, London, 1977, pp. 31–71.

Jones, Rhys. "East of Wallace's

Line: Issues and Problems in the Colonization of the Australian Continent," *in* Paul Mellars and Christopher Stringer (eds.) *The Human Revolution*, Edinburgh University Press, Edinburgh, 1989, pp. 743–782.

Kennedy, K.A.R. and Possehl, G.L. (eds.) *Studies in the Archaeology and Palaeoanthropology of South India*. American Institute of Indian Studies and Oxford and IBH Press, New Delhi, 1984.

Kirk, R.L. and Thorne, A.G. (eds.) *Origin of the Australians*. Australian Institute of Aboriginal Studies, Canberra, 1976.

Lourandos, Henry. "Pleistocene Australia: Peopling a Continent," *in* Olga Soffer (ed.) *The Pleistocene Old World*, Plenum Press, New York, 1987, pp. 147–166.

Manabe, S. and Hahn, D. "Simulation of the tropical climate of an Ice Age," *Journal of Geophysical Research*, vol. 82 (1977), 3889–3911.

Misra, V.N. and Bellwood, P. (eds.) *Recent Advances in Indo-Pacific Prehistory*. IBH, New Delhi, 1985.

Mulvaney, D.J. *The Prehistory of Australia*. Penguin Books Australia, rev. ed. 1975.

Pearce, R.H. and Barbetti, M. "A 38,000-Year-Old Archaeological Site at Upper Swan, Western Australia," *Archaeology in Oceania*, vol. 15 (1981), 173–178.

Peterson, G.M. and others. "The continental record of environmental conditions at 18,000 BP: an initial evaluation," *Quaternary Research*, vol. 12 (1979), 47–82.

Thorne, A .G. and Wolpoff, Milford. "Regional Continuity in Pleistocene hominid evolution," *American Journal of Physical Anthropology*, vol. 55 (1982), 337–350.

Wolpoff, Milford. *Palaeoanthropology*. Knopf, New York, 1980.

——and others. "Modern *Homo sapiens sapiens* origins: A general theory of hominid evolution involving the fossil evidence from East Asia," *in* F. Smith and F. Spencer (eds.) *The Origins of Modern Humans*, Alan R. Liss, New York, 1984, pp. 411–483.

Wright, R.V.S. (ed.) *Stone Tools as Cultural Markers*. Australian Institute of Aboriginal Studies, Canberra, 1977.

Chapter 11 **The Rise of the Cro-Magnons**
Chapter 12 **A Cultural Apogee**

Mastering the complex and multilingual literature behind these chapters taxes the expertise of even the most ardent specialist. Clive Gamble's *The Palaeolithic Settlement of Europe* (Cambridge University Press, Cambridge and New York, 1986) is, to my mind, the most important summary of the subject in a generation. Although aimed at a specialist audience, it has much to offer the more general reader. C.B. Stringer and others, "The Origin of Anatomically Modern Humans in Western Europe," *in* F. Smith and F. Spencer (eds.) *The Origins of Modern Humans* (Alan R. Liss, New York, 1984), pp. 51–136, covers the fundamental issues surrounding the arrival of the Cro-Magnons, while Fred Smith, "Fossil Hominids from the Upper Pleistocene of Central Europe and the Origin of Modern Europeans," in the same book, pp. 137–310, makes the case for local replacement. For the archaeology of the early Upper Paleolithic in Europe, see Peter Allsworth-Jones, *The Szeletian* (Clarendon Press, Oxford, 1986) and Jiri Svoboda and Katalin Siman, "The Middle-Upper Paleolithic Transition in Southeastern Central Europe (Czechoslovakia and Hungary)," *World Archaeology*, vol. 3 (3) (1989), 283–322. J.J. Hoffecker and C.A. Wolf (eds.)

The Early Upper Paleolithic (British Archaeological Reports International Series 437, 1988) contains useful summaries of evidence from different European areas and the Near East. Randall White's beautifully illustrated *Dark Caves, Bright Visions* (American Museum of Natural History, New York, 1984) is an elegant and intelligent summary of the Upper Paleolithic, while John Pfeiffer, *The Creative Explosion* (Harper and Row, New York, 1983) deals with the intellectual issues of Upper Paleolithic art. Paul Bahn and Jean Vertut, *Images of the Ice Age* (Windward, London, 1988) is a wonderful synthesis of the same subject, with magnificent illustrations.

Other References

Alexander, Richard D. "Evolution of the Human Psyche," *in* Paul Mellars and Christopher Stringer (eds.) *The Human Revolution*, Edinburgh University Press, Edinburgh, 1989, pp. 455–513.

Bader, Otto. "The Boys of Sungir," *Illustrated London News*, March 7 (1970), 24–26.

Bordes, François. *The Old Stone Age*. McGraw Hill, New York, Weidenfeld, London, 1968.

Breuil, Henri. "Les subdivisions du paléolithique supérieur et leur signification," *Comptes Rendu du 14ᵉ Congrès International d'Anthropologie et d'Archéologie Préhistorique*, Genève (1912), 165–238.

——*Four Hundred Centuries of Cave Art*. Centre d'Etudes et de Documentation Préhistoriques, Montignac, 1952.

Burch, Ernest S. "The Caribou/Wild Reindeer as a Human Resource," *American Antiquity*, vol. 37 (3) (1972), 339–368.

Captain, Louis, and Peyrony, Denis. *La Madeleine: son gisement, son industrie, ses oeuvres d'art*. Nourry, Paris, 1928.

Dennell, Robin. "Needles and Spear-throwers," *Natural History*, vol. 10 (1986), 70–77.

Dibble, Harold L. "The Implications of Stone Tool Types for the Presence of Language During the Lower and Middle Palaeolithic," *in* Paul Mellars and Christopher Stringer (eds.) *The Human Revolution*, Edinburgh University Press, Edinburgh, 1989, pp. 415–432.

Gordon, Bryan C. *Of Men and Reindeer Herds in French Magdalenian Prehistory*. British Archaeological Reports International Series 390, 1988.

Hadingham, Evan. *Secrets of the Ice Age*. Heinemann, London, Walker, New York, 1980.

Harrold, Francis B. "Mousterian, Châtelperronian and Early Aurignacian in Western Europe: Continuity or Discontinuity?" *in* Paul Mellars and Christopher Stringer (eds.) *The Human Revolution*, Edinburgh University Press, Edinburgh, 1989, pp. 677–713.

Kozlowski, Janusz K. "The Gravettian in Central and Eastern Europe," *Advances in World Archaeology*, vol. 5 (1986), 131–200.

Laville, Henri, and others. *Rock Shelters of the Périgord*. Academic Press, New York, 1980.

Leroi-Gourhan, André. *Treasures of Prehistoric Art*. Abrams, New York, 1967.

Lévêque, François, and Vandermeersch, Bernard. "Les découvertes de restes humains dans un horizon châtelperronien de Saint-Césaire (Charente-Maritime)," *Bulletin de la Societé Préhistorique Française*, vol. 77 (1980), 35.

Mellars, Paul. "Technological Changes at the Middle-Upper Palaeolithic Transition: Economic, Social, and Cognitive Perspectives," *in* Paul Mellars and Christopher Stringer (eds.) *The Human Revolution*, Edinburgh University Press, Edinburgh, 1989, pp. 338–365.

Movius, H.L. "The Châtelperronian in French Archaeology: the evidence of Arcy-sur-Cure," *Antiquity*, vol. 43 (1969), 111–123.

——(ed.) *Excavation of the Abri Pataud, Les Eyzies (Dordogne)*. American School of Prehistoric Research, Cambridge, Mass., Bulletins 30 and 31, 1975, 1977.

Smith, Fred, and others. "Geographic Variation in Supraorbital Torus Reduction during the Later Pleistocene (*c.* 80,000 to 15,000 BP)," *in* Paul Mellars and Christopher Stringer (eds.) *The Human Revolution*, Edinburgh University Press, Edinburgh, 1989, pp. 172–193.

Speiss, A.E. *Reindeer and Caribou Hunters: An Archaeological Study*. Academic Press. New York, 1979.

Stringer, C.B. "The Origin of Early Modern Humans: a Comparison of the European and non-European Evidence," *in* Paul Mellars and Christopher Stringer (eds.) *The Human Revolution*, Edinburgh University Press, Edinburgh, 1989, pp. 232–244.

Whallon, Robert. "Elements of Cultural Change in the Later Palaeolithic," *in* Paul Mellars and Christopher Stringer (eds.) *The Human Revolution*, Edinburgh University Press, Edinburgh, 1989, pp. 433–454.

White, Randall. "Rethinking the Middle/Upper Palaeolithic Transition," *Current Anthropology*, vol. 23 (1982), 169–192.

——*Upper Paleolithic Land Use in the Perigord: A Topographic Approach to Subsistence and Settlement*. British Archaeological Reports International Series, Oxford, 1985.

——"Visual Thinking in the Ice Age," *Scientific American*, vol. 261, July 1989, 92–99.

Chapter 13 **The Plains Dwellers**

Chapter 14 **Northeast Asians**

English-speaking readers look, inevitably, at the literature for the USSR and China from the outside. To write these chapters, I relied mainly on English references, most of them summaries of complex specialist literatures. The archaeology of the West Russian plains is the subject of three important books. Richard Klein, *Man and Culture in the Late Pleistocene* (Chandler, San Francisco, 1969) and the same author's *Ice Age Hunters of the Ukraine* (University of Chicago Press, Chicago, 1973) are excellent summaries, while Olga Soffer, *The Upper Palaeolithic of the Central Russian Plain* (Academic Press, New York, 1985), is a highly sophisticated analysis of Mezhirich and other settlements, and the culture associated with them.

For northern Asia and Siberia, Kwang-Chih Chang, *The Archaeology of Ancient China* (Yale University Press, New Haven, 4th ed. 1986) provides a summary, while two articles by Soviet archaeologist Vitaliy Larichev and others provide a synthesis of recent Russian perceptions: "Lower and Middle Paleolithic of Northern Asia: Achievements, Problems, and Perspectives," *Journal of World Prehistory*, vol. 1 (4) (1987), 415–464, and "The Upper Palaeolithic of Northern Asia: Achievements, Problems, and Perspectives. I: Western Siberia," *Journal of World Prehistory*, vol. 2 (1988), 359–396. Microblades receive evaluation by Tang Chung and Gai Pei, "Upper Paleolithic Cultural Traditions in North China," *Journal of World Prehistory*, vol. 5 (1986), 339–364. See also, John Olsen, "Recent Developments in the Upper Pleistocene Prehistory of China," *in* Olga Soffer (ed.), *The Pleistocene Old World* (Plenum Press, New York, 1987), pp. 135–146.

Other References

(These references contain comprehensive listings in Chinese, Russian, and other languages, not cited here.)

Aigner, Jean. "Archaeological Remains in Pleistocene China," *Forschungen Zur Allgemeinen und Vergleichenden Archäologie*, C.H. Beck, Munich, 1981, Band 1.

Aikens, C. Melvin, and Higuchi, Takayasu. *Prehistory of Japan.* Academic Press, New York, 1982.

Chard, Chester S. *Northeast Asia in Prehistory.* University of Wisconsin Press, Madison, 1978.

Coon, C.S. and Ralph, E.K. "Radiocarbon Dates for Kara Kamar, Afghanistan," *Science*, vol. 122 (1955), 921–922.

Davis, Richard S. "Regional Perspectives on the Soviet Central Asian Paleolithic," *in* Olga Soffer (ed.) *The Pleistocene Old World*, Plenum Press, New York, 1987, pp. 121–134.

Dikov, N.N. "Ancestors of Paleo-Indians and Proto-Eskimo-Aleuts in the Paleolithic of Kamchatka," *in* Alan L. Bryan (ed.) *Early Man in America from a Circum-Pacific Perspective*, Archaeological Researches International, Edmonton, 1978, pp. 68–71.

Hahn, J. "Aurignacian and Gravettian settlement patterns in central Europe," *in* Olga Soffer (ed.) *The Pleistocene Old World*, Plenum Press, New York, 1987, pp. 251–262.

Ikawa-Smith, Fumiko. "Late Pleistocene and Early Holocene technologies," *in* Richard J. Pearson (ed.) *Windows on the Japanese Past: Studies in Archaeology and Prehistory*, Center for Japanese Studies, University of Michigan, Ann Arbor, 1986.

Klima, B. *Dolní Věstonice.* Academia, Prague, 1983.

Jia Lanpo and Huang Weiwen. "The Late Palaeolithic of China," *in* Wu Rukang and J.W. Olsen (eds.) *Palaeoanthropology and Palaeolithic Archaeology in the People's Republic of China*, Academic Press, Orlando, 1985, pp. 211–223.

Mochanov, Yuri. "Stratigraphy and Absolute Chronology of the Paleolithic of Northeast Asia according to the work of 1963–1973", *in* Alan L. Bryan (ed.) *Early Man in America from a Circum-Pacific Perspective*, Archaeological Researches International, Edmonton, 1978, pp. 54–66.

——"Stratigraphy and Absolute Chronology of the Paleolithic of Northeast Asia," *in* Alan L. Bryan (ed.) *Early Man in America from a Circum-Pacific Perspective*, Archaeological Researches International, Edmonton, 1978, p. 67.

Praslov, N.D. and others. "The steppes in the Late Palaeolithic," *Antiquity*, vol. 63 (1989), 784–792.

Ranov, V.A. and Davis, R.S. "Toward a New Outline of the Soviet Central Asian Paleolithic," *Current Anthropology*, vol. 20 (1979), 249–270.

Reynolds, T.E.G. and Barnes, G.L. "The Japanese Palaeolithic: A Review," *Proceedings of the Prehistoric Society*, vol. 50 (1984),. 49–62.

Soffer, Olga. "Upper Palaeolithic Connubia, Refugia, and the Archaeological Record from Eastern Europe," *in* Olga Soffer (ed.) *The Pleistocene Old World*, Plenum Press, New York, 1987, pp,. 333–348.

——"The Middle to Upper Palaeolithic Transition on the Russian Plain," *in* Paul Mellars and Christopher Stringer (eds.) *The Human Revolution*, Edinburgh University Press, Edinburgh, 1989, pp. 714–742.

——"Storage, Sedentism, and the Eurasian Palaeolithic record," *Antiquity*, vol. 63 (1989), 719–732.

Wu Rukang and Olsen, J.W. (eds.) *Palaeoanthropology and Palaeolithic Archaeology in the People's Republic of China.* Academic Press, Orlando, 1985.

Wu Xinzhi and Wu Maolin. "Early *Homo sapiens* in China," *in* Wu Rukang and J.W. Olsen (eds.) *Palaeoanthropology and Palaeolithic Archaeology in the People's Republic of China*, Academic Press, Orlando, 1985, pp. 91–106.

Chapter 15 The Settlement of the Americas

The literature on this thorny topic is voluminous, polemical, and confusing. I attempted a summary in *The Great Journey* (Thames and Hudson, London and New York, 1987), which has provoked much discussion, and the general reader could do worse than start there. For a series of summary essays, see R. Carlisle (ed.) *Americans before Columbus: Ice Age Origins* (University of Pittsburgh Ethnology Monographs 12, Pittsburgh, 1988). Some other useful edited volumes include Richard Shutler (ed.) *Early Man in the New World* (Sage Publications, Beverly Hills, 1983), R. Kirk and E. Szathmary (eds.) *Out of Asia: Peopling the Americas and the Pacific* (Journal of Pacific Studies, Canberra, 1985), and Alan L. Bryan (ed.) *New Evidence for the Pleistocene Peopling of the Americas* (Center for the Study of Early Man, University of Maine, Orono, 1986). David Hopkins and others (eds.) *The Paleoecology of Beringia* (Academic Press, New York, 1982) is an authoritative synthesis of the subject. Two articles provide critical overviews: Dena Dincauze, "An Archaeo-Logical Evaluation of the Case for Pre-Clovis Occupations," *Advances in World Archaeology*, vol. 3 (1984), 275–324, and David J. Meltzer, "Why don't we know when the first people came to North America?" *American Antiquity*, vol. 54 (3) (1989), 471–490. Both contain comprehensive bibliographies.

Other References

Andel, Tjeerd H. van. "Late Quaternary sea-level changes and archaeology," *Antiquity*, vol. 63 (1989), 733–745.

Bednarik, R.G. "On the Pleistocene settlement of South America," *Antiquity*, vol. 63 (1989), 101–111.

Brown, James A. "The Case for the Regional Perspective: A New World View," *in* Olga Soffer (ed.) *The Pleistocene Old World*, Plenum Press, New York, 1987, pp. 365–376.

Bryan, Alan. "Paleoamerican Prehistory as Seen from South America," *in* A. L. Bryan (ed.) *New Evidence for the Pleistocene Peopling of the Americas*, Center for the Study of Early Man, University of Maine, Orono, 1986, pp. 1–14.

Dillehay, T. and Collins, M. "Early Cultural Evidence from Monte Verde in Chile," *Nature*, vol. 332 (1988), 150–152.

Dumond, D. "The Archaeology of Alaska and the Peopling of America," *Science*, vol. 209 (1980), 984–991.

Greenberg, J.H. *Language in the Americas*. Stanford University Press, Stanford, 1986.

Greenberg, J.L. and others. "The Settlement of the Americas: A Comparison of the Linguistic, Dental, and Genetic Evidence," *Current Anthropology*, vol. 27, 477–497.

Gruhn, R. "Linguistic Evidence in Support of the Coastal Route of Earliest Entry into the New World," *Man*, vol. 23 (1988), 77–100.

Guidon, N. and Delibrias, G. "Carbon 14 dates point to Man in the Americas 32,000 years ago," *Nature*, vol. 321, 769–771.

Haynes, C.V. "The Earliest Americans," *Science*, vol. 166 (1969), 256–258.

Meltzer, David. "Late Pleistocene Human Adaptations in Eastern North America," *Journal of World Prehistory*, vol. 2 (1988), 1–52.

Powers, William R. and Hoffecker, John F. "Late Pleistocene Settlement in the Nenana Valley, Central Alaska," *American Antiquity*, vol. 54 (2) (1989), 263–287.

Suarez, B.K.J. and others. "Genetic Variation in North Amerindian Populations: The Geography of Gene Frequencies," *American Journal of Physical Anthropology*, vol. 67 (1985), 217–232.

Turner, Christy. "Advances in the Dental Search for Native American Origins," *Acta Anthrogenetica*, vol. 8 (1&2) (1984), 23–78.

——"The Native Americans: The Dental Evidence," *National Geographic Research*, vol. 2 (1986), 37–46.

West, F.H. *The Archaeology of Beringia*. Columbia University Press, New York, 1981.

Chapter 16 **After the Ice Age**
Chapter 17 **The Journey from Eden**

Our summary of the Holocene is at best superficial, and the reader is referred to major regional syntheses of the literature for more information. For Africa, see J. Desmond Clark, *The Prehistory of Africa* (Thames and Hudson, London, 1970), and David Phillipson, *African Archaeology* (Cambridge University Press, Cambridge and New York, 1985). Also, John Parkington's seminal "Prehistory and Paleoenvironments at the Pleistocene-Holocene Boundary in the Western Cape," *in* Olga Soffer (ed.) *The Pleistocene Old World* (Plenum Press, New York, 1987), pp. 349–364. Richard Klein (ed.) *Southern African Prehistory and Palaeoenvironments* (A.A. Balkema, Rotterdam, 1984) contains invaluable perspectives. Clive Gamble, *The Palaeolithic Settlement of Europe* (Cambridge University Press, Cambridge, 1986) is fundamental, and Douglas T. Price, "The Mesolithic of Western Europe," *Journal of World Prehistory*, vol. 1 (3) (1987), 225–305, is an excellent summary of the Mesolithic. See also, Grahame Clark, *The Earlier Stone Age Settlement of Scandinavia* (Cambridge University Press, Cambridge, 1975) and *Mesolithic Prelude* (Edinburgh University Press, Edinburgh, 1979). Ofer Bar-Yosef, "Late Pleistocene adaptations in the Levant," in Olga Soffer (ed.) *The Pleistocene Old World* (Plenum Press, New York, 1987), pp. 219–236, and Donald O. Henry, "Adaptive Evolution within the Epipaleolithic of the Near East," *Advances in World Archaeology*, vol. 2 (1983), 99–160, both cover the Near East. India and south Asia are discussed in Bridget and Raymond Allchin, *The Rise of Civilization in India and Pakistan* (Cambridge University Press, Cambridge and New York, 1982), while Kwang-Chih Chang's *The Archaeology of Ancient China* (Yale University Press, New Haven, 4th ed. 1986) provides an excellent summary of later Chinese prehistory. Australia is well covered by John Mulvaney, *The Prehistory of Australia* (Penguin Books Australia, rev. ed. 1975) and by Peter White and James O'Connell (eds.) *A Prehistory of Australia, New Guinea, and Sahul* (Academic Press, Sydney, 1982). Peter Bellwood, *The Polynesians* (2nd ed., Thames and Hudson, London and New York, 1987) and *Man's Conquest of the Pacific* (Oxford University Press, Oxford, 1979) both cover the last colonization by *Homo sapiens*, while the same author's *The Prehistory of the Indo-Malaysian Archipelago* (Academic Press, Sydney, Australia, 1985) deals with the southeast Asian mainland during the Holocene. Soviet archaeology has an enormous literature, but English summaries or monographs are rare. V.P. Lubine and N.D. Praslov, *Le Paléolithique en URSS: découvertes recent* (Academy of Sciences, Leningrad, 1987) is useful, and there is an excellent summary of later archaeology on the steppes in V. Dergachev's "Neolithic and Bronze Age cultural communities of the steppe zone of the USSR," *Antiquity*, vol. 63 (1989), 793–802. For North America, see my

Ancient North America (Thames and Hudson, London and New York, 1991), and Jesse D. Jennings, *Prehistory of North America* (Mayfield, Palo Alto, rev. ed. 1987). For the Americas generally, the reader is referred to

Stuart Fiedel, *Prehistory of the Americas* (Cambridge University Press, Cambridge, 1987).

Other References

Consult the comprehensive bibliographies in the books cited above.

Index

Page numbers in *italics* refer to maps and drawings; numerals in **bold** refer to numbered plates and their captions.